For Jim and Alice,
Two wonderful friends and
supporters. We have enjoyed
many priceless moments together —
I hope your enjoyment of "Billy Davis"
will contribute to our bonding.

Dick [signature]
9/29/89

THE CIVIL WAR JOURNAL OF BILLY DAVIS

"The beautiful flag" — made by the young ladies of Hopewell in July 1861 at the residence of Reverend John F. Smith. Presented to Company F, 7th Indiana Volunteer Infantry Regiment, August 28, 1861. (Photograph provided courtesy Hopewell Presbyterian Church.)

THE CIVIL WAR JOURNAL OF BILLY DAVIS

From Hopewell, Indiana to Port Republic, Virginia

Edited by

Richard S. Skidmore

The Nugget Publishers

Greencastle, Indiana

Front and back covers:

Men of Company F, 7th Indiana Volunteer Infantry Regiment.
See Appendix A for a complete roster and Appendix B
for an identification of the pictured soldiers.

ISBN: 0-9623292-0-7

Library of Congress Number: 89-090126

Greencastle Offset Printing

For *Wilda*

CONTENTS

PREFACE

Billy Davis referred to his Civil War journal as a "record of my diary," and it is, of course, personal. There is reason to believe, however, that Billy hoped others would read his record.

Billy Davis wrote with an unassuming pride. On a day which concluded with "No news of importance today," he had met with the Chief of Artillery who "commended our courage and perseverance." He had written a letter to the home folks. He had gone to several hospitals to visit sick and wounded comrades. And he had voluntarily helped sweep a hospital. Such was nothing of importance. Billy was adept at understating his character.

Without the journal little would be known of Billy Davis — only a few vital facts found in public documents. Born on a farm near Hopewell, Indiana, he grew to 5' 6" and was of light complexion with brown hair and blue eyes. He enlisted as a 23-year-old Private in the 7th Indiana Volunteer Infantry Regiment for three months on April 22, 1861. After service in western Virginia, he mustered out in August. He re-enlisted in the same regiment for three years on Friday the 13th, September 1861. After a bitter winter, he fought in the Shenandoah Valley Campaign in 1862, taking part in the battles of Kernstown and Port Republic.

Certainly of note, he is mentioned in the official military history of the Civil War, *War of the Rebellion: A Compilation of the Official Records of the Union and Confederate Armies*. Billy volunteered for a dangerous assignment at Port Republic, Virginia in June 1862 and was commended for his personal valor. As he grew older, this event probably became his richest memory of the Civil War.

His obituary affirmed the heroics at Port Republic and told how he had picked up the fallen colors on two battlefields. His surviving comrades thought of Billy Davis as a Civil War hero.

The obituary writer also praised his service to God. William, as he was called in later life, helped organize the Presbyterian Church at Iola, Kansas. He served as an elder for the next 52 years. He had been a church missionary in the Indian Territory where he established 147 Sunday Schools. His neighbors knew William Davis as a man of God.

The Civil War Journal of Billy Davis is presented as it was written with no intrusions. Each chapter of journal entries is followed with a background section to provide a wider perspective for the journal. This two-part method of presentation was chosen, primarily, so the integrity of the journal could be retained. The Appendices provide biographical notes and pictures of Billy's comrades. The obituary is included as Appendix C.

The original handwritten journal is actually three 8" x 11" leatherbound volumes which span the period April 1861 to May 1863. Billy's Civil War service (and probably his diaries) went on for another 16 months. The final months were never transcribed into journal form. Time ran out for 84-year-old Billy Davis when he died in Muskogee, Oklahoma. The never-to-be-completed journals then passed to his wife, Candace, and later to an only daughter. The daughter, Grace, lived until 1970 when she died without heirs. There were no photographs of her father, no mementos. All that remained was a journal of his thoughts and words.

CHAPTER 1

IT IS NO TRIVIAL AFFAIR

Friday April 12, 1861. News reached us that General Beauregard had fired upon Fort Sumter. This news, though not entirely unexpected, was the occasion of great excitement and seemed almost to stop business, nothing else was talked of during the day.

Saturday April 13, 1861. The early news confirms that of yesterday. The bombardment still continued. The excitement was increasing, citizens were on the street before daylight, and farmers living miles in the country, hearing yesterday's news were in town before sunup. An excited crowd gathered in and about the telegraph office at the Depot, and groups gathered about stores and corners with frequent runners for the very latest news. Old gray haired men were as much wrought up over the news as the younger men. As the crowd increased, the excitement grew greater and it was with difficulty that some few were restrained from attempting violence upon some who showed a disposition to excuse the Secessionists or palliate their crime of treason. Mechanics quit their shops and with men from the country, spent the day on the street. There was no business.

We knew somewhat of the preparations of the Secessionists about Charleston, of the unfinished condition of Sumter, and the scarcity of provisions in the Fort and that its reduction was a matter of only a short time. Men from the country forgot what they came to town for and returned home at a late hour without making a purchase. The latest news of the day was that the firing still continued. I remained on the street until a late hour. Between ten and Eleven o'clock p.m., news came that Major Anderson had surrendered, and that the Star Spangled Banner, the beautiful flag of our proud young Republic, had been humbled by a few of the States acting in organized secession. The news was terrible to think of. Men of the stoutest hearts felt that all was gone, some who had been more conservative and hopeful of a peaceful settlement of the troubles now agreed with those holding more extreme or coertion views. I retired and tried to sleep. My rest was very broken. I think I must have felt like one without a country.

The Confederacy's Stars and Bars flying over Fort Sumter.

The Hopewell Presbyterian Church as Billy Davis would have remembered it. This brick building was completed in 1853.

Sunday morning I went early to the telegraph office and found the news of last night confirmed. After breakfast I went again to the office and found the news of the same tenor. A large and greatly excited crowd stood around. Many thought war was inevitable and there was talk of raising a company of volunteers at once. News from all over the north indicates great feeling, a great awakening and uprising. I had promised my Father and some friends to go to Hopewell to church and take the latest news. I walked, and got in after services had commenced. Some of the younger men and older ones too could scarcely wait for the benediction to ask the latest from Sumter. A crowd soon gathered and a feeling of sad disappointment seemed to pervade all. Some turned away with eyes dimmed with tears. Father and the family were there in the carriage. As soon as I had answered a few of the many questions asked by the anxious and bewildered friends and had refused several invitations to dinner, we started for home three miles to the northeast.

On the way and at home, but little was talked of but the fall of Sumter. Father wondered if President Lincoln would call for troops. If he did I thought I would enlist. Some of the family objected. Early in the afternoon I began to talk of going to town. Father said he would take me. When we started, sisters said don't you enlist.

On our way, Father said he had been a Democrat but had always thought slavery wrong, and didn't think it best to molest it where it was nor let it extend farther; and didn't blame the slaves for running away from their masters. Said he had voted for S. A. Douglas for President but would now leave the old party and so far as able sustain Lincoln and the Union. Arriving at Franklin we drove directly to the Depot where we found an excited crowd including many farmers. It looked as though the people in their anxiety had forgotten that it was the Sabbath day. The news of the morning was confirmed with telegrams from many places north and west indicating the feeling of the loyal people. The all-absorbing question is shall this union, this government of the people, live or perish.

Monday April 15th 1861. During the day there has been very little business. In the morning the crowds speculated as to what the administration would do. Mr. Lincoln has said very little indicating the course to be pursued. Will he consider the bombardment of Sumter a sufficient cause to warrant him in calling for troops, or will further peace measures be attempted. There are very few who advocate peace conventions or conciliatory measures. The strongly prevailing sentiment is that matters have passed far beyond any chance of or reason for compromise. 'Coercion' has not so many terrors now as it had a few days ago.

Several leading men of Franklin went to Indianapolis this forenoon. About noon a telegram passed over the wires to the effect that the President had called for 75,000 troops for three months. This caused a thrill of new excitement in which some shouted and hurrahed for the Union, others spoke of it with quivering lips and moistened eyes and grasped each others hands and felt that the Union would yet live. This news gave rise to more hopeful speculations, and when S. P. Oyler and others returned from Indianapolis, and confirmed the news from Washington, and said too, that Governor Morton would issue a call for Indiana's quota, the measure of joy and hope was more than full, many seemed almost wild with excitement. The talk of raising a company here became more urgent and definite.

Tuesday April 16th, 1861. Excitement still continues. Governor O. P. Morton has issued a call for six thousand troops. Early in the day, posters were circulated calling for a meeting of citizens at the Court House tonight. At an early hour the Court room was filled largely by the younger men. Stirring music was furnished by the Martial Band and a quartette sang 'The Star Spangled Banner' and 'My Country Tis of Thee' and long and loud cheering followed the unfurling of the stars and stripes. Speeches were made by Messrs. Overstreet, Hunter, Oyler and others. Among the younger men were T. A. Jeffery, George F. Herriott, Daniel Howe, Ed Meyers and T. J. Morgan and one or two others from the College. Every mention of the stars and stripes brought out hearty applause. It was decided Johnson County should furnish at least one Company. A paper was drawn up and forty or fifty names enrolled. The meeting closed with a rousing cheer for the Union, and for President Lincoln and Governor O. P. Morton. Old party lines seem almost lost sight of except by a few of the more radical Democrats.

Wednesday April 17, 1861. About the first thing heard this morning was the fife and drum. There is much enthusiasm. Many of the young men are enrolling their names. I want to go yet do not know what to do. Had a long talk with Mr J L Jones, Senior, who was a volunteer in the War of 1812, his incidents of camp and campaign are quite interesting. The way the people all over the north and west are enlisting and otherwise responding to the President's call, the war, as W. H. Seward says, will not last over three months.

I know my grandfather was a soldier in the War of 1812. I have heard him speak of different things, especially of being up in or near Canada, on the noted "cold Friday" and I heard father say that my great-grandfather was a

President-elect Abraham Lincoln, February 9, 1861.

President Abraham Lincoln, February 5, 1865.

Revolutionary soldier, and that he (Father) enlisted for the Blackhawk War, but was rejected. I feel that if I do not go that I will be disgraced, and by staying at home will bring reproach upon the family name. When I saw father he suggested that if I enlisted to be careful about my companions. Choose good ones and brave kind officers. I was not in the store much today. In the afternoon, John Hutchison and James Alexander, next door clerks, and I agreed to volunteer and go as chums or comrades. As we went together to enroll our names, I realized a relief from my feeling of doubt and suspense, and yet I know that I felt a trembling sensation when writing my name. Don't believe I ever felt so attached to the old flag as I do today. After volunteering I went to the store and we settled, then I walked out home.

Thursday, April 18, 1861. I reached home before sundown yesterday and found the family more reconciled to my going now that it is decided. Father, who from the first would not say for me not to go, seems glad that I am going. He speaks with much feeling against the southern leaders and says that he had heard several soldiers of the Mexican War say that the report that one of the Indiana Regiments ran at Buena Vista was a falsehood, started by Jeff Davis; says he hopes we will remember Buena Vista and not turn our backs to the enemy but prove ourselves worthy of our citizenship in the great State of Indiana.

On arriving at town I found the Company about full, I believe another company could be raised. Mr and Mrs Jacob Aton on the road to Hopewell have arranged for a party tonight, and invited a number of the volunteers and others with their lady friends. We are going in wagons and anticipate a very enjoyable evening.

Papers state that business is almost suspended over the county. People are occupied with the preparations for war. The President has asked the Governor of Massachusetts who has a large militia force, to send some to Washington at once.

Friday, April 19th, 1861. Our party at Mr Atons last night was a very pleasant affair. Much of the evening was passed in conversation about the prospective war. All wonder when we are to start and where we will go. We who had volunteered were the favorites, usually the center of interested groups or leaders in games or charades. We are already heroes. We are invited to Mr Lists near Hopewell church tonight where we are to meet in a social for the young people of the neighborhood.

An untouched signature.

I went home after the party and did not go to town until afternoon. The Company organized this p.m. by electing Samuel P. Oyler, Captain, Joseph P. Gill, 1st Lieutenant, and William B. Ellis, 2nd Lieutenant. It was decided to go as an Infantry Regiment. They say there will be ten companies together. The Captain sent a telegram to Governor Morton that we are ready for orders.

Late this evening the telegraph brought news that a Massachusetts Regiment was attacked by a mob while passing through Baltimore. The mob attacked with clubs and stones and killed four and wounded thirty-six soldiers. The troops fire in to the mob and fight their way through the city. Several of the mob were killed and many wounded, the streets were crimson with Patriot blood. The secessionists of Baltimore swear that no more troops shall pass through their city. There is great excitement here.

Saturday, April 20th, 1861. We had a very pleasant party at Mr Lists. The evening was spent very much as at Mr Atons with the addition of vocal music. Many patriotic songs were sung. However, the news from Baltimore had a depressing effect, as it showed some of the realities of war. Our fair friends effect to believe that we will all be killed in the first battle. I came home again last night. This morning all the family went to town. Streets were crowded all day. About noon Captain Crittenden and his company from Madison passed here on way to Indianapolis. We met them at the Depot. The Band serenaded them.

Captain Oyler received word today to go to Indianapolis Monday. Orders were given that we rendezvous at McClellans Hall at 8 a.m. Monday. There is to be a great social gathering at the hall tonight in honor of the volunteers. The excitement of the week and parties have about worn me out. I thought best to come out home and rest.

Thomas J. Crittenden passed through Franklin as a Captain on April 20, 1861. He would serve as Colonel of the 6th Indiana Volunteer Infantry Regiment.

Sunday, April 21, 1861. We all went to Hopewell to church. I am the only one of the church who has enlisted and many were the hearty grasp of hand "God bless you" today, especially earnest were words of my Pastor, John F. Smith. All the family were at home for dinner and with us were Uncle Isaac M. McGee and wife.

Monday, April 22, 1861. We were up early and as most of the house folk were loth to have me volunteer, now that the time for starting is so near, were tender on the subject, said but little and went quietly about the preparations. Mother provided shirts, collars, drawers, three pair home knit wool socks, several pocket handkerchiefs, and two quilts; sisters had provided an arrangement (a housewife), containing buttons, needles, pins, threads, yarns, a steel thimble, etc. and a place for my pocket scissors. I had provided myself with a large pocket knife, two combs, towels and toilet soap, and a pocket diary for recording incidents of note, and the Messers. Jones had presented me with a pocket revolver of six chambers, saying that I might get into close quarters and need it. This was my outfit. As an indication of the prevailing idea of "going to war," I might have mentioned in last Friday's note that James T. Alexander and myself had an ambrotype taken in which we each held in one hand a Bible, and in the other a Revolver, or Bowie Knife.

We had previously decided to make the leave taking a home affair, except for Father. When all was ready, the farewell words were spoken and we started. As we drove out around the old meadow in front of the house neither of us spoke. We drove for a half mile along the farm. There was much to call my mind from the recent partings and the prospective war. And yet I could not help feeling that the nation was on the eve of a great conflict, perhaps on the very threshold of a crisis. The result which might change the character of all our institutions and may be the face of the pleasant picture before me and wondered if I should live to return. On the way the neighbors waved handkerchiefs, some were on the way to town to see the soldiers off. Reaching town we found the streets crowded and the excitement rather high over the burning of railroad bridges near Baltimore by Maryland secessionists.

The volunteers were anxious to be off. The Hall soon became the center toward which the soldiers and their friends moved. At half past nine a.m. we formed in the Hall — the tall ones on the right and we short fellows on the left — and marched out on to the street, where we lined up. Our friends came to bid us goodbye, many of the partings were touching. Those who remained generally showed more feeling than the soldiers. We were urged by many to stand by our colors, and parents and Christian friends urged the maintenance of our Christian characters, while mothers and sisters, with more heart and spirit, said "Recollect that while you bear the exposure, hardships, and dangers of camp march and battle, we will pray for your health, success and safe return."

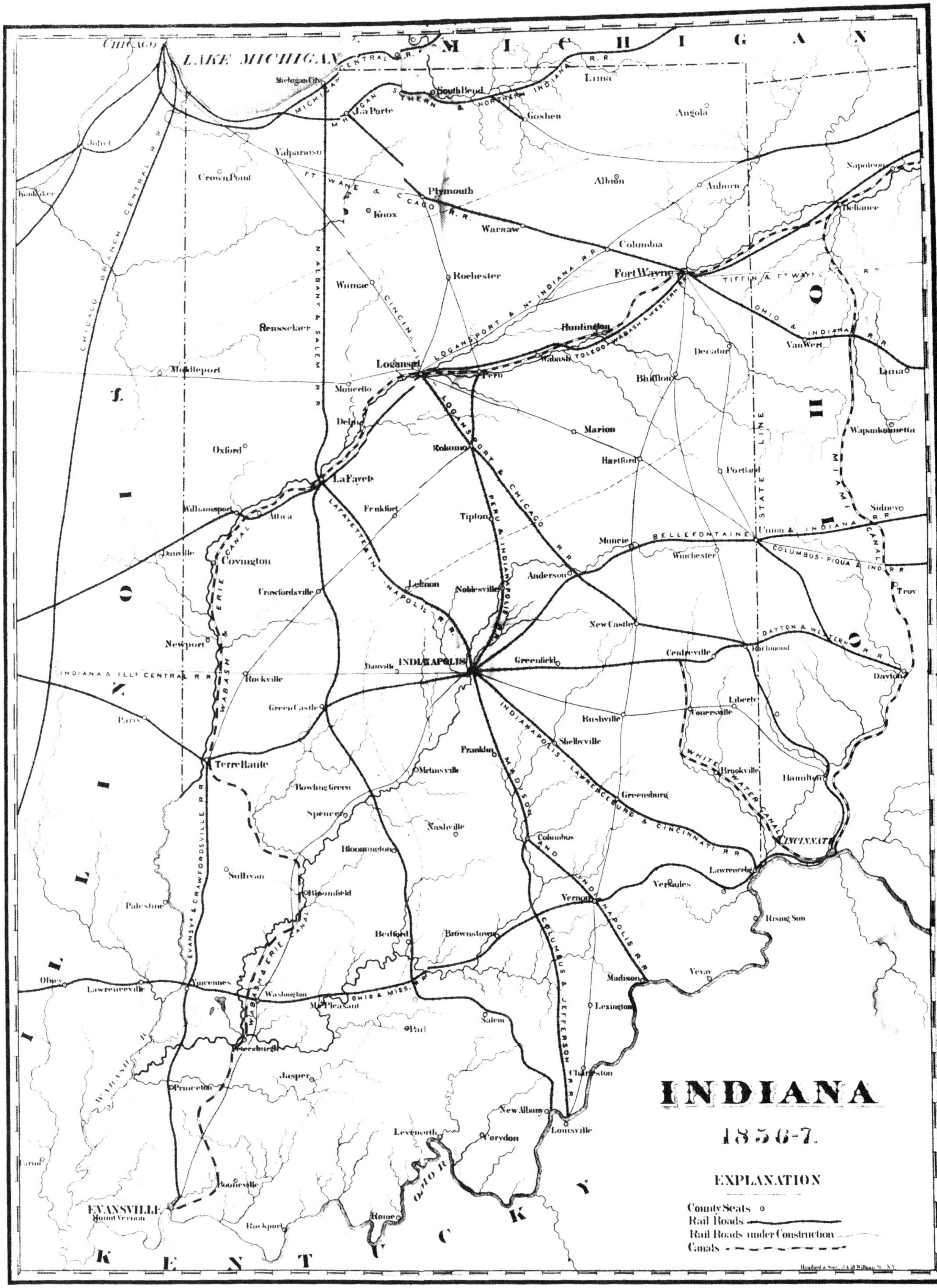

An 1856-7 map of Indiana, highlighting the rail system. Franklin is approximately 20 miles south of Indianapolis.

The Indiana Statehouse was completed in 1835. During the Civil War, the grounds were used for large rallies and a weapons arsenal.

We remained in front of the hall for half an hour, and then marched to the music of fife and drum with flag flying down Jefferson Street to the depot. The greater part of our friends followed. The train did not come and we were called into line again and marched around two blocks and back. No soldier seems to be so much a stranger as to be for a minute without some one to speak to them words of cheer and commendation. It seems the desire of every one who showed any interest in the matter to manifest their great concern for the perpetuity of the Union and the welfare of the soldiers. Many were the assurances given that the families of those who enlisted would be cared for, that if we were sick or wounded and, whether in the field or hospital or at home, every want would be supplied. It is proper however to note that there were some who did not feel so much interest in either the soldier or the country, such usually stood in the back ground apparently making disparaging remarks.

The Democratic Paper here in its last issue, called the volunteers whose fathers had been Democrats, 'degenerate sons of noble sires,' and in other ways offered insult to us young patriots.

When the train whistled below town, there was a stir and bustle, more hurried than before. I know I felt a flutter about my heart as we fell into line and the friends gathered closer to speak the final admonition and good-bye. The train stopped. Father silently grasped my hand and I stepped aboard. The train moved off amid the waving of hats and handkerchiefs, and huzzahs for Lincoln, the Union, Morton and the soldiers. At the little stations and other points along the road were gathered crowds who cheered, and in the fields and houses the people waved handkerchiefs, though it was noticed that some made no demonstration at all.

Arriving at Indianapolis we formed line, led by our Martial Band, marched amid cheers and marked demonstrations, to the State House where we were sworn into the service of the State and after partaking of some refreshments, we marched to 'Camp Morton' north of the city where we arrived about four o'clock, very much fatigued with our march of two or three miles, having been on our feet all day. We are assigned quarters on the East Side of the encampment and near the northeast corner. Captain Crittenden's and some other companies are already here, and some were drilling. They haven't received uniforms nor guns yet. Berths or Bunks have been arranged, one near the ground, the other above it, and large enough for eight or ten persons. Acquaintances group themselves together as messes. The mess to which I belong occupies an upper berth, numbered nine.

Soon after reaching camp a detail went for rations, and we sat down or stood up as we liked to our first meal in camp. About sundown our baggage came, and relieved our anxiety for it had already become a serious question as to how we were to sleep. We are furnished straw to sleep on and there is no lack of blankets and quilts. In our company are a number of professing Christians. Much has been said by our friends about us trying to maintain our Christian integrity. We have talked the matter over and most of us are in one mess and have agreed to make the effort to maintain, when convenient, an evening and Sabbath service.

After our arrival, before bedtime, the boys wandered about the encampment in groups, watching the soldiers drill or seeing how others were situated or formed groups about our quarters to read or hear the news or discuss the probabilities of the war, wondering when we would be sent forward, and where to, and who the commanders would be, and guessing about a thousand other things. One thing very noticeable and also encouraging in the papers is the great uprising of the people in all the Northern States. Volunteers are flocking by thousands to every state rendesvous. Another matter not so encouraging is the reported energy of the rabid secessionists of Maryland. Citizens of Baltimore have telegraphed the Governor of Virginia to reinforce Baltimore. Virginia has seceded. There is much cause for fear. Washington City appears now to be the objective point. Nine o'clock p.m. most of the boys are about quarters and things are more quiet. We of bunk nine gathered within; hung a quilt over the front. Then Thomas A. Jeffrey handed a Bible to me and asked that I lead in the evening devotions. This was my first effort in public. I was much embarrassed.

Tuesday, April 23, 1861. After breakfast we formed line and went out to drill. There were other squads and

A "bird's-eye" view of Indianapolis. The Statehouse is in cenier background.

The Camp Morton landscape. An 1863 photograph after the training camp was converted to a Civil War prison.

companies out drilling. It was very awkward for us. Our officers do not know much about it either. We marched and tried to keep step. After trying a while we rested and watched another company. They got mixed up several times. After about an hour we returned to quarters and there formed line — one rank front — where the officers informed us that there were thirty-five or six more men than could be mustered in the company, that they would be obliged to set out all but sixty-four. Then they went along the line and asked those whom they did not want to step two paces to the front. My place was near the left of the line. Near thirty were asked forward before they reached me. I hoped I might be allowed to remain, but being small and perhaps bleached, I was asked to step out too. I was very much mortified and very greatly disappointed at this, what should I do. I did not want to go home. I could not get into another company. They were all full. This would be the only chance. I felt like I was disgraced. It would be hard to find a more disappointed lot of men than we were. Some were swearing, all were complaining, and some almost crying. To my right was James Herriott, a tall finely proportioned young man from the farm; rejected because he had lost a front tooth. Others were rejected for just as trivial causes. Just to my left was Joseph E. Boswell, a short heavy set little man, a student of Franklin College, set aside, as I was for light weight. I only learned his name yesterday, but our misfortunes being mutual, we were acquainted at once.

We who had been favored (?) with a position two paces to the front, were dismissed with many regrets, and the more fortunate sixty-four were told that they should remain near quarters, as the company would be examined and mustered soon after dinner. As soon as we broke ranks, Boswell and I went to ourselves and conferred as to what we would do. First we decided not to go home if we could avoid it. Second, to stay together if possible. We knew it would be almost impossible to get into another company as all were more than full on their arrival. We decided to remain at quarters and watch for an opportunity to get in if any were rejected in the examination.

Just before dinner, Boswell's Father and Mother and sister came in with a large basket of provisions. I found them very pleasant people. When the basket was opened, J. E. said I should eat with them, that I must not mention that we had been rejected as he feared they would insist that he should go back to school. The dinner was an excellent one, though we were not in a humor to do it full justice. I learned that Mr Boswell lived on his farm a mile or two north east of our camp. After dinner companies were being inspected so that Mr and Mrs and Miss Boswell left camp without learning of our situation. When the company formed, two of the sixty-four were absent without leave. This let Boswell and I in, and we marched with the company to the inspectors office where we passed examination and were received before the missing ones came. This was unspeakable joy to us.

The examination was very rigid. We were stripped and put through all manner of exercises, the various maneuvers tried every limb, joint and muscle. Our lungs were sounded and our bodies thumped and pounded, very much after the horse Jockey Style. The examining Surgeon did not discover that I had one false tooth, though I very much feared he would.

When the examination was over we were marched to the mustering officers office, and after he had taken our descriptions and names, we were sworn into the service of the United States for three months. Some appeared to think lightly of the matter, but for my part, I feel that it is no trivial affair, though I am proud of my position as a volunteer soldier of my country.

The News

The bombardment of Fort Sumter began at 4:30 a.m., Friday, April 12, 1861. The news was relayed, tap-by-tap, through every telegraph office in the country. After word finally reached Franklin, it spread by way of galloping horses. However it came, Americans never forgot the circumstances of hearing the news about Fort Sumter.

The scene Billy Davis described in Franklin is but a small sample of the great excitement taking place in each of Indiana's 92 county seats. People all over the sparcely populated state of 1,350,000 huddled together as never before. Many shouted and waved their hats — probably they would be the first ones called upon to die. Others, perhaps too old to fight and die, quietly uncovered their heads and prayerfully held their hats with both hands at their waist.[(1)]

A celebration at Tammany Hall in New York City, April 24, 1861.

Twenty-three-year-old Billy Davis wrote that he was not one of the "many (who) seemed wild with excitement." Nor was he completely calm. He chose to circle about seeking more information and listening to the latest street-corner analysis.

At 1:30 p.m., April 13 the banner of the 34 states was removed from the flagpole at Fort Sumter.[(2)] Billy was still on the streets between 10 and 11 that night when this news hit. "Terrible to think of" was how he recorded his reaction, then, just as millions of others that night, he went to bed and "tried to sleep."

Billy's Heritage

William, Billy Davis' grandfather, and John, Billy's father, had moved northward from Kentucky in 1822 and settled on the Ohio River in Switzerland County, Indiana. In 1824, William moved farther north to Johnson County where he became one of the early settlers. The William Davises acquired a farm in 1831 — that same year, some three miles to the southwest, a 20' x 30' log meeting house was designated the "Hopewell Church." Neither William nor young John Davis were among the church's first communicants although there is reason to believe they were of the same faith. John married Mary F. "Polly" McGee on September 1, 1836. She was said to be of Dutch and Irish mixture and, like John, had been born in Mercer County, Kentucky. The first born of that marriage was Billy (legally, William with no middle initial), born January 12, 1838 in Hopewell, Indiana.[(3)]

The Hopewell Community

Hopewell was a Dutch Reform Church settlement. The first settlers in 1825 may have brought the name of Hopewell with them from Kentucky or perhaps New Jersey. These proud and energetic religious pioneers could trace their roots to the French Huguenots. When persecuted in France, they fled to Holland and in time were thought of as "lop-eared" Dutch. Venturing into the new world through New Amsterdam (New York) some settled near Hackensack, New Jersey. Others probably settled in Mercer County, New Jersey — the Trenton-Princeton-Hopewell area. Billy Davis' grandfather was born in this area. Moving on with each generation, as seemed the custom of these "Reformed Dutch," the Conowego Settlement was organized near Gettysburg, Pennsylvania in 1765. The next major move was to Harrodsburg, Mercer County, Kentucky. And then in the 1820s, there began a migration to an old Indian campsite near Young's Creek in Johnson County, Indiana. The area, known at the time as Pleasant Hill or Big Springs, was in central Indiana some 20 miles south of Indianapolis.[(4)]

Billy's Immediate Family

Family for Billy Davis included "Father" or John, Billy's closest confidant. "Mother" was actually a stepmother, only 15 years older than Billy. Nevertheless, Billy always referred to this relatively young woman as "Mother." Martha Ann Vanarsdale was a native Kentuckian in her early 30s when she had married John Davis. John was a 41-year-old widower with five young children — the oldest being Billy. (Billy's birth mother, Polly Davis, had died in 1852 at the age of 38.) When Billy wrote of his family in 1861, he referred to: Father, 48; "Mother," 38; Martha Jane, 20; Mary Ellen, 19; Daniel, 16; Rachael, 10; and two half-brothers, five-year-old Abraham and two-year-old John. Billy also had two brothers-in-law; Elisha T. Vanarsdall who wed Martha Jane and John W. Davis who married Mary Ellen.[(5)]

Early Life

Billy grew up on a 57-acre farm 2½ miles northwest of Franklin, Indiana in the Hopewell area. Little is known of Billy's childhood experiences, although being the first son, he would have performed farm chores at an early age.

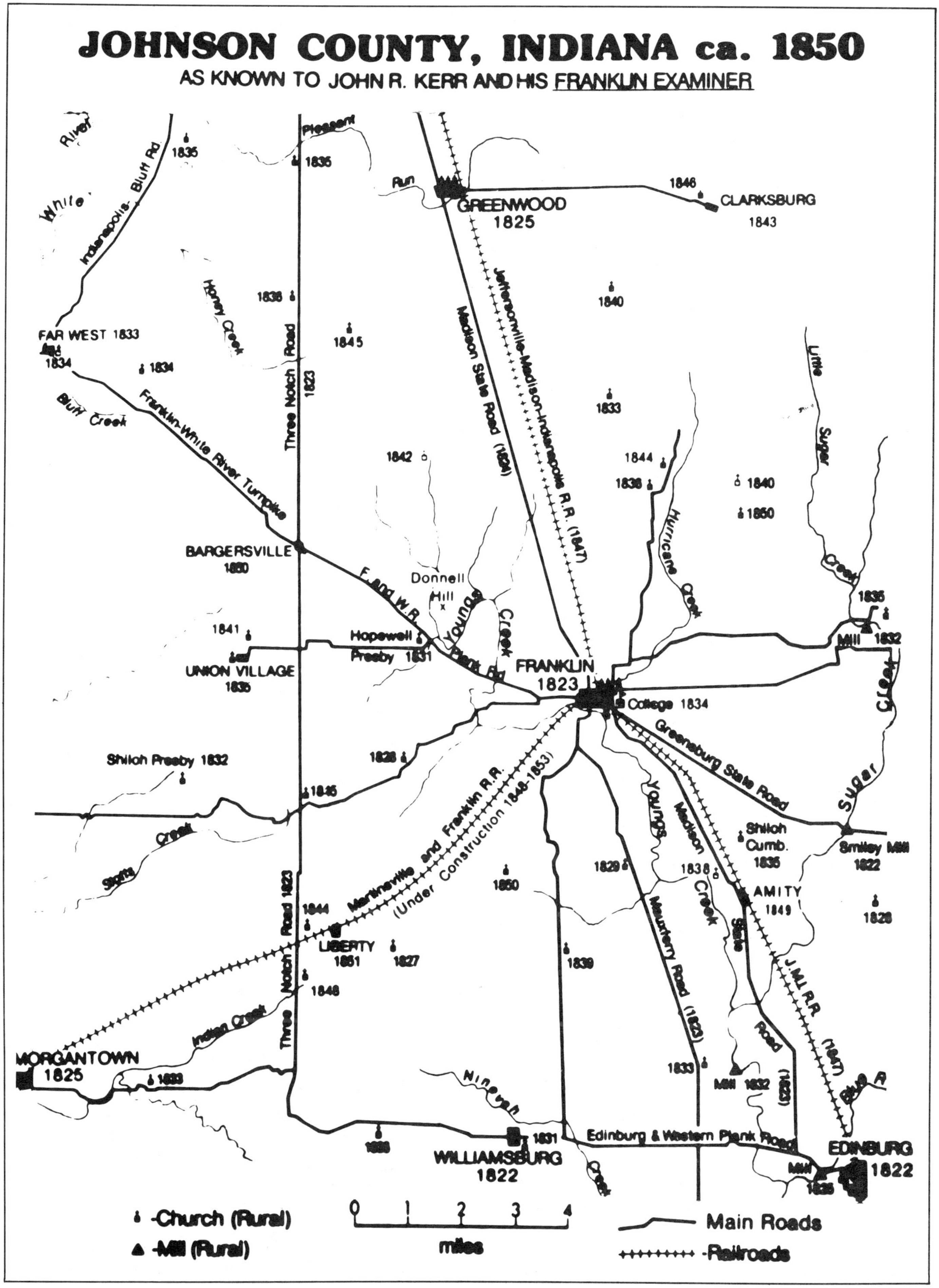

Johnson County, Indiana, circa 1850. Billy Davis' home was approximately 2½ miles northwest of Franklin near a branch of Young's Creek.

In later life, Billy was quoted as stating he was "educated in the better schools of the time."[6] One such school would have been the 1831 "Meeting House" operated by the Hopewell Presbyterian Church. The Johnson County pioneers were said to have been as zealous in the cause of education as they were in the matters of religion, so schools began to dot the farmland in the 1830s. These small schools were privately donated log buildings and were attended only on subscription basis. Usually the cabin-like structures were 16' x 18' with a huge fireplace at one end. Split logs served as seats and hewn boards as desk tops. A log was removed from one wall to make an opening. Covered with oil paper the opening became a "window."[7]

The quality of teaching in those early days is questionable. Some educators were fondly remembered for their scholarship and discipline. Others however, were remembered for quite different reasons. One early local historian recalled: "There was a one-eyed teacher; the single-handed teacher; the lame teacher; the teacher who had fits; the teacher who had been educated for the ministry, but owing to his habits of hard drink had turned pedagogue; the teacher who got drunk on Saturday and whipped the entire school on Monday."[8] Billy's reference to the "better schools" may refer only to the reading, writing and arithmetic provided by his church.

The years 1854 through 1859 were years of great revivals at the Hopewell Church — 109 people professed their faith in those five years. On April 24, 1858 during one of those revivals, Billy took his vows of God and became a member. His father had professed earlier in 1837 and "Mother" in 1855.[9]

In 1859, at the age of 21, Billy left the family homestead and tried to make his way in the world as a farm hand. He earned only $15 that first summer. Discouraged with farming and its rewards, he enrolled at the Hopewell Academy in September. The Academy had been built by the church in 1856 for the purpose of "establishing a school of higher order." The new Kentucky-plantation style building was adjacent to the three-year-old all-brick Hopewell Presbyterian Church. Six rooms, three up and three down, provided for the teaching of philosophy, American history, botany, algebra, geometry, Latin and Greek. A student completing a full year would be acceptable as a sophomore at Hanover College, a Presbyterian-sponsored school near Madison, Indiana. To have enrolled at the Academy, Billy would have had to demonstrate a solid educational and moral background.[10]

Evidently Billy's $15 ran out after one term. He dropped out of school in December and found a $10-a-month job as a clerk in a Franklin store. Or perhaps vice-versa.

Billy was employed by the firm of J. L. Jones and Sons — dry goods, groceries, etc. The store was located at Main and Jefferson, across from the courthouse. The elder J. L. Jones was a minister, while apparently one son, John, managed the store. John Jones, 35, provided Billy with living quarters in his two-story brick home on Main Street behind the store. Here Billy lived with John, his wife, Eliza, and their three small daughters.[11]

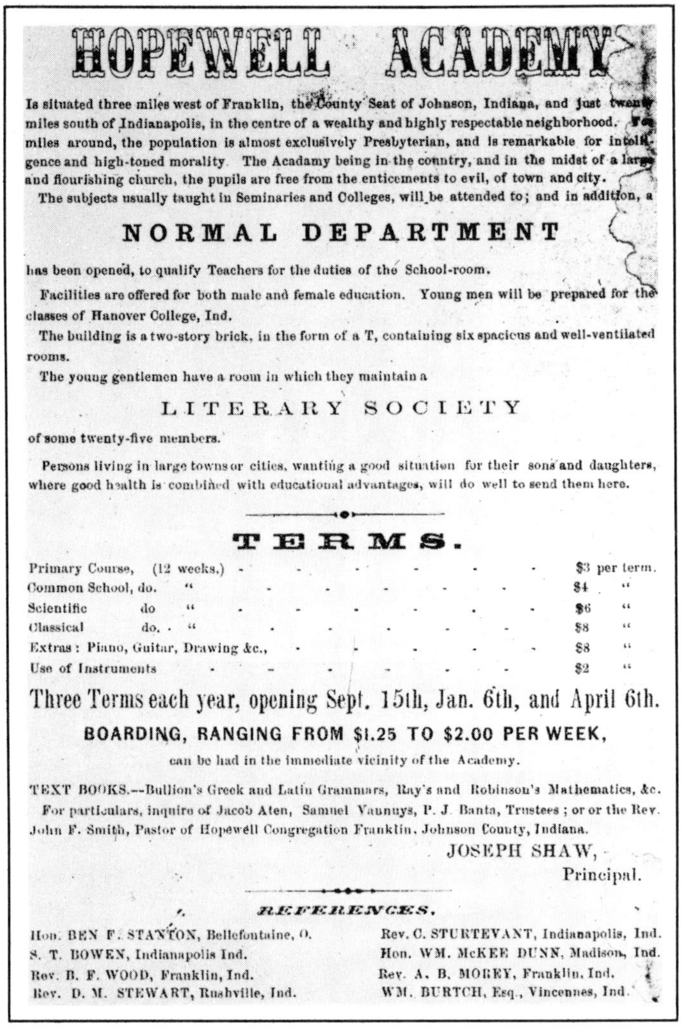

HOPEWELL ACADEMY

Is situated three miles west of Franklin, the County Seat of Johnson, Indiana, and just twenty miles south of Indianapolis, in the centre of a wealthy and highly respectable neighborhood. For miles around, the population is almost exclusively Presbyterian, and is remarkable for intelli-gence and high-toned morality. The Acadamy being in the country, and in the midst of a large and flourishing church, the pupils are free from the enticements to evil, of town and city.

The subjects usually taught in Seminaries and Colleges, will be attended to; and in addition, a

NORMAL DEPARTMENT

has been opened, to qualify Teachers for the duties of the School-room.

Facilities are offered for both male and female education. Young men will be prepared for the classes of Hanover College, Ind.

The building is a two-story brick, in the form of a T, containing six spacicus and well-ventilated rooms.

The young gentlemen have a room in which they maintain a

LITERARY SOCIETY

of some twenty-five members.

Persons living in large towns or cities, wanting a good situation for their sons and daughters, where good health is combined with educational advantages, will do well to send them here.

TERMS.

Primary Course, (12 weeks.)		$3 per term.
Common School, do.	"	$4 "
Scientific do	"	$6 "
Classical do.	"	$8 "
Extras: Piano, Guitar, Drawing &c.,		$8 "
Use of Instruments		$2 "

Three Terms each year, opening Sept. 15th, Jan. 6th, and April 6th.

BOARDING, RANGING FROM $1.25 TO $2.00 PER WEEK,

can be had in the immediate vicinity of the Academy.

TEXT BOOKS.--Bullion's Greek and Latin Grammars, Ray's and Robinson's Mathematics, &c.

For particulars, inquire of Jacob Aten, Samuel Vaunuys, P. J. Banta, Trustees; or or the Rev. John F. Smith, Pastor of Hopewell Congregation Franklin, Johnson County, Indiana.

JOSEPH SHAW,
Principal.

REFERENCES.

Hon. BEN F. STANTON, Bellefontaine, O.
S. T. BOWEN, Indianapolis Ind.
Rev. B. F. WOOD, Franklin, Ind.
Rev. D. M. STEWART, Rushville, Ind.
Rev. C. STURTEVANT, Indianapolis, Ind.
Hon. WM. McKEE DUNN, Madison, Ind.
Rev. A. B. MOREY, Franklin, Ind.
WM. BURTCH, Esq., Vincennes, Ind.

An 1863 advertisement for the Hopewell Academy.

By September 1860, Billy's financial problems were somewhat alleviated so he enrolled in another school of advanced study. Working mornings, evenings and Saturdays for his board, he probably attended classes at the Franklin Academy.[12]

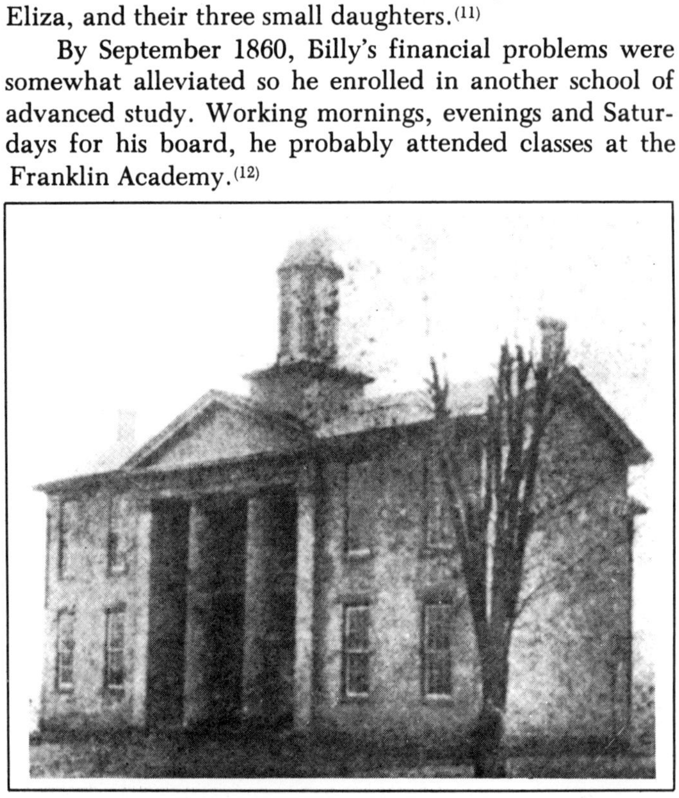

The Hopewell Academy, completed in 1856 — "a school of higher order."

Now old enough to vote, he took the time on Tuesday, November 6, to cast his first ballot for Abraham Lincoln.[13] Billy became absorbed in what he called "the disturbed condition of the public mind" and sought answers in *Harper's Weekly* and the *Indianapolis Journal.* The *Journal*, the daily Republican banner for the Indianapolis area, "scoffed that the threats of secession in the southern press were mere election-year bluffs." The *Journal* further denounced a state's right to secede but hesitated to encourage coercion.[14]

Billy wrote that he became distracted by the national issues and terminated his formal education in March 1861. Distracted or not, he continued clerking full time for Mr. Jones.

Franklin

Ordinarily Franklin was a serene little country town; the 1860 population was 1,724. There was the county courthouse, a public market, two newspapers (one Republican, one Democrat), seven churches, nine attorneys, nine physicians and no undertakers. There was a brewery and a jail. Two railroads intersected the town and a major north-south state road ran through the downtown area. Grocery and dry goods comprised the greatest number of businesses in Franklin; there were at least 11 such stores. In the same block where Billy worked as a grocery and dry goods clerk, there were eight businesses — four were selling "Groceries and Dry Goods," including the one next door.[15]

Three blocks to the east of the Jones' grocery stood the depot. This structure was the emotional center of gravitation in Johnson County in mid-April 1861. It was here that the "news reached us," it was here that the crowds gathered, and it was here that Billy read the latest war dispatches.

On Sunday morning, this time a carrier of news, Billy walked the four miles northwestward from Franklin to the Hopewell Church. Along the way Billy would pass 10 or so houses, mostly farmhouses, mostly Presbyterian. This was Billy's old neighborhood — hard-working, church-going, farm people.

The Church

Church was special for Billy Davis, the spiritual and social hub of his life. The building was of classic red-brick construction, rectangular, just 70' x 45', all under a trussed roof which leaked. Inside, it was plain with a 20-foot-high ceiling, walnut pews in two sections separated by the main aisles and a small balcony in the back. The preacher stood behind a modest pulpit which sat on a riser only two steps up from the congregation.[16]

A relatively new pastor would have been in the pulpit that April Sunday in 1861. Reverend John Smith was a Princeton man, but he was "at home" in Hopewell. The Presbytery thought Pastor Smith was destined for a bigger city church, but as the father of six children he had chosen

Men gathered in front of the J. L. Jones & Co. store. Billy Davis marched on this street to the trains which took him to the American Civil War.

the calm educational setting provided in Hopewell. Likewise, the congregation appreciated John Smith.[17]

When Billy announced the latest Fort Sumter news to the Sunday morning assembly, he noted the sad disappointment. He remembered, "Some turned away with eyes dimmed with tears." In the days ahead Pastor Smith would be called upon to resolve some "violent political issues in the congregation varying from consecrated zeal for the cause of the Union to avowed sympathy for the rebellion."[18] A war was coming to a peaceful little country church.

The interior of the 1853 Hopewell Presbyterian Church.

Indiana's war governor, Oliver P. Morton.

A Big Decision

The next big news was Lincoln's call for 75,000 volunteers. Indiana was expected to furnish 4,683. In Franklin 40 or 50 signed up immediately — young William Davis was not one of them. He attended a big rally and heard "stirring music," "hearty applause," and a "rousing cheer for the Union." The same proceedings were reported somewhat differently by the local Democratic newspaper. Under the heading of "Volunteers," the *Herald* informed its readers, "They are having quite a lively time in town beating up volunteers to fill the requisitions of the Government." The *Herald*'s editorial struck a softer chord: "From every part of the country we have news of the thorough preparation for war. In every little village throughout the North the ranks are fast filling up. The call for 75,000 troops will be more than doubled; but advisors say that all will be accepted. In the South the people seem to be equally bent on resistance. The telegraph informs us this morning that Kentucky and Tennessee alone will send 50,000 troops to assist the Southern confederacy. God forbid that such contending forces shall ever come in contact upon American soil."[19]

Whether Billy ever read this editorial is unknown, but he was fully aware of the "contending forces." On Wednesday, April 17, Billy made his decision. He signed up. It came down to pride in himself and his family. He would not be the first to disgrace the Davis name. Another influencing element was two friends who were signing up and all three could go as "chums or comrades." And maybe he was influenced by the popular belief that, "the war. . . will not last over three months." Supposedly nobody would get hurt.

Billy did not fail to grasp the fact he was going to be part of history. Hopefully, he could document that fact in a photograph to be taken with James Alexander — posing together with Bibles in one hand and weapons in the other.[20]

For a few days Billy would be loved and venerated as never before, and probably, as never again. He attended two parties which were hosted by two pillars of the Hopewell church. Billy called them "pleasant affairs." The *Herald* reported on another party where the women of Franklin presented a splendid flag to a fine body of young men.[21] Billy missed this one, choosing to spend Saturday evening at home with his family.

The following day was Billy's last Sunday at home and, of course, church. Again Billy was the center of attention as he was the first church member about to leave.

Off To A War

The festive spirit was apparent as Billy and his father made their way over the country roads toward the Franklin depot. They passed the Ransdell farm, the Freeman place, and the Terrill's, while heading southeastward for Franklin. There was moral support expressed with a husky shout and blessings provided with a wave of a lady's dainty handkerchief.

A Franklin College student, about to depart in the same group with Billy, wrote that "thousands gathered" and "thronged the sidewalks," "tender-hearted women. . . wept, but most of the spectators and volunteers wore smiling faces." He concluded that, "It was a great day for the staid old town."[22]

The *Herald* observed that the streets of Franklin were filled with the parading of newly-formed companies and sounds of martial music. The only reference to Billy and his group was the article reporting that 105 men left on the 22nd — they were to be called the Johnson County Riflemen, "a fine body of young men, and will do credit to our country."[23]

The train Billy boarded for the war was on the Madison and Indianapolis line, completed in 1847. In 1860 there were 2,200 miles of iron rails in Indiana.[24] Billy would need only 20 miles of those rails to pass through Whiteland, Greenwood, Southport and on into Indianapolis.

The old railroad depot in Franklin, circa 1910.

The Indianapolis Union Station, completed in 1853 — a single terminal for all railroads — the first of its kind.

Indianapolis

In 1820, Indianapolis had been selected as a potential steamboat landing site on the White River. Although never a port of note, the area was so promising it quickly became the state capital. During the 1840s and '50s, Indianapolis began to emerge as a major rail center. By the '60s, the Madison and Indianapolis Railroad and five other major systems formed an iron web stretching out in every direction from a base in Indianapolis. There, a Union Station, the first of its kind, had been completed in 1853.[25]

Indianapolis by 1861 was a bustling community of 19,000 people. The city had been laid out much like the District of Columbia: a mile square with right-angled streets and wide avenues intersecting at a center point. In Washington the mid-point was the Capitol; in Indianapolis, it was intended to be the Governor's house. By 1861 the Governor's place had been torn down and the prominent feature of the area was five mainline churches.[26]

Even with all the sophisticated transportation arteries, Indianapolis was not ready for the 12,000 recruits that were to swarm about the city. There were no existing camps for shelter, no uniforms for warmth, no military stores for supplies — not even weapons to fire. However, there were a lot of young men with flags and horns and drums and enthusiasm. One author reported, "The streets were alive with them."[27]

When Billy Davis and 104 other Johnson County Riflemen arrived at Union Station (without rifles), they were just five blocks from the new Statehouse. There, they were sworn in for state service — not yet ready for United States service.

From the downtown Statehouse it was approximately 1½ miles north to the new military quarters at the State Fairgrounds. Indianapolis had one main street — the east-west National Road. There were brick sidewalks and some four-story buildings in the downtown district. Where Billy was headed there was not much "city," only a few houses, mostly farms and an occasional orchard.[28]

Indianapolis in 1854. North side of Washington Street, between Meridian and Pennsylvania streets.

North side of Washington Street, between Illinois and Meridian streets.

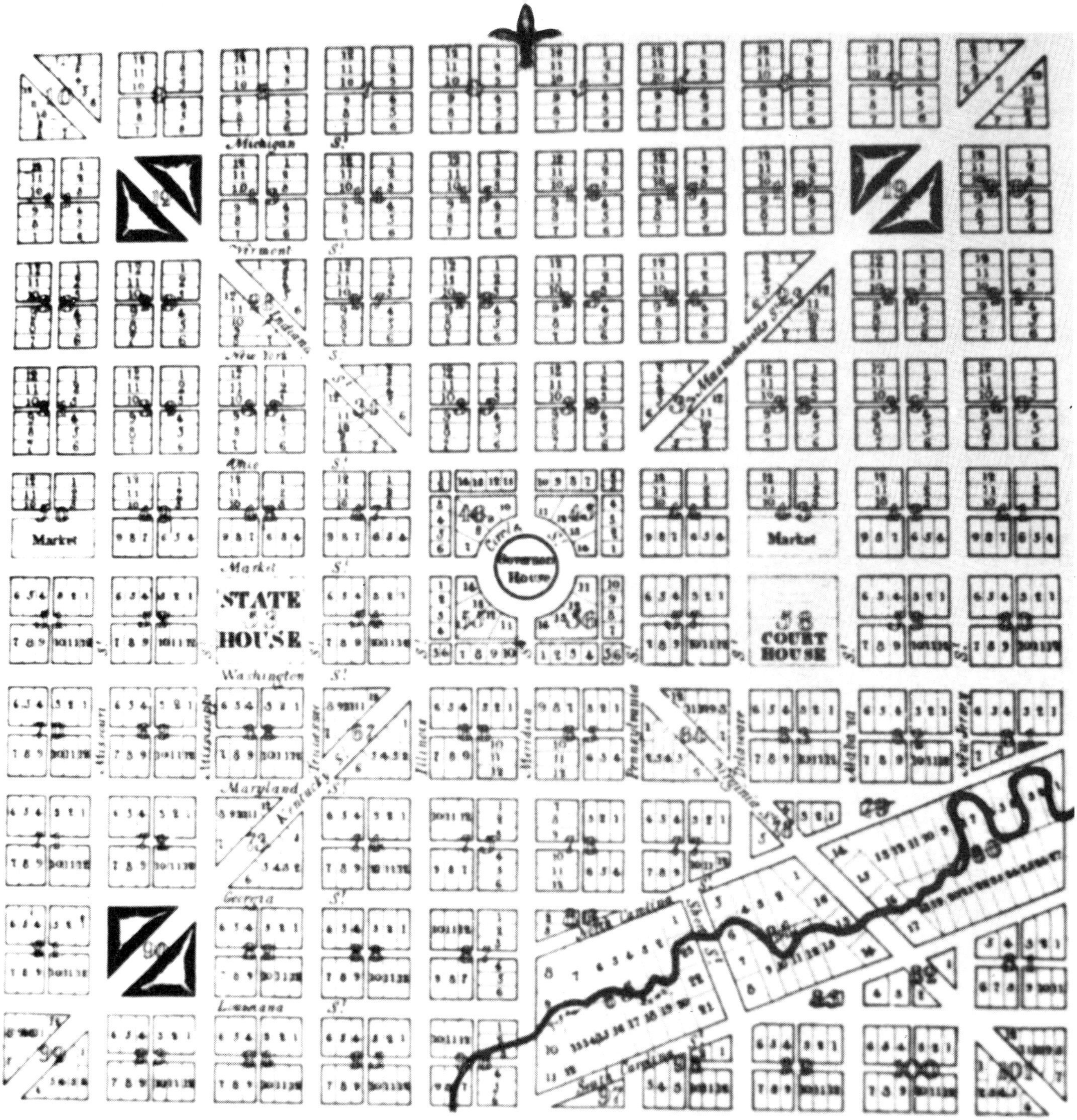

An 1821 plat map of Indianapolis. Note the Governor's House in the geometric center (an area now referred to as the Circle). The Union Station was four blocks south of the Circle. In April 1861, Camp Morton was the equivalent of 19 blocks north of the Circle (and off this map).

Camp Morton

The 36 acre State Fairgrounds — an area approximately 400 yards by 450 yards — was to be camp for the new Indiana Civil War soldiers. Along the northern edge was a shed once thought inadequate for the stabling of horses. There were stalls for cattle and pens for pigs at the western border. A large exhibition hall and dining room had been constructed to accommodate fair goers. There was even a two-story office building for the administrators. In mid-April, Indiana's foremost patriot, Governor Morton, and his newly-named adjutant, Lew Wallace, named this site Camp Morton.

Additional sheds had to be built quickly; there would be six to seven thousand men in need of shelter. Two more rows of sheds were thrown up along the eastern and southern edge of the fairgrounds. Like the existing "housing," they had one side exposed to the weather.(29) New perhaps, but more befitting show cattle than humans.

Billy Davis and his company were assigned to the new barracks on the east side. As in the other sheds, there were at least two tiers of bunks placed within each stall. Billy said there was enough room on his upper tier for eight to 10 men and referred to their new community as "mess number nine." Straw was provided for bedding and a quilt was hung over the opening to keep out the elements. Such was the life of a soldier. Billy Davis did not record any complaints.

Another 1863 view of Camp Morton. (Note the sheds.)

Acceptance

It is generally thought that the Civil War pre-muster physical examination was superficial at best. One medical science historian referred to the process as "abominable," "a sham" and cites an example of one doctor who bragged he could examine 100 men an hour.[30] Even a few women slipped through the "examinations." For those early Indiana volunteers, the routine was not so haphazard. The regimental historian of Billy's unit wrote, "At that time men were striving to get in, and Uncle Sam did not accept everyone who presented himself."[31] Indeed, the ranks of the Johnson County Riflemen were reduced by about a third. And Billy Davis was one of those rejected because he was judged to be too short.

A man's height was important in the military culture of 1861. The 6th Indiana, a unit going through muster at the same time as Billy boasted of 83 men over six feet. "They were giants in those days," recorded the regimental historian with pride.[32] Daniel Howe from Billy's own company also felt the torment of being too short. He and the other "smallest" man in the company were banished to the rear.[33]

No doubt some of the enrollees in April of 1861 were chosen solely on the basis of their height. By war's end, however, loftiness was of little consequence. Of 118,254 Indiana enlistments sampled after the war, 28 percent were 5'6" tall (Billy's height) or less.[34]

It is curious that the examiner did not detect Billy's false tooth. Teeth were an important consideration in the examining process, since soldiers used their teeth to tear open the small paper cartridge bags prior to loading a musket. Dentures were becoming common in 1861. In fact, there were two dentists doing business in Franklin in 1860. The most popular replacement tooth of the times would have been a manufactured porcelain crown on a wooden base. The wooden anchor was jammed into the root canal, then the moisture in the mouth would cause the wood to swell. It is likely an anesthesia was administered.[35] However miserable the process, an artificial tooth could go unnoticed.

Given a second chance, Billy passed muster. Relieved and proud, he had been accepted as a volunteer soldier.

The tallest man to serve in the Union Army, 6' 10½" David Van Buskirk, Company F, 27th Indiana Infantry.

END NOTES

(1) Merrill and Company, Editors. *The Soldier of Indiana* (Indianapolis, 1866); pp. 11-12. Maybe one is never "too old to fight." A gray-haired Hoosier was reported to have shouted, "Ninety is not too old for such a cause; and the young people know nothing of war." For further, but brief, discussions of Indiana's response to the Fort Sumter news: David Stevenson, *Indiana's Roll of Honor* (2 Volumes, Indianapolis, 1864), v. I, pp. 13-32. Also, Emma Lou Thornbrough, *Indiana in the Civil War Era* (Indianapolis, 1965) v. III, pp. 103-106. Also, W. H. H. Terrill, *Report of the Adjutant General of the State of Indiana* (8 Volumes, Indianapolis, 1866) v. I, p. 5.

(2) W. A. Swanberg, *First Blood: The Story of Fort Sumter* (New York, 1957), p. 320.

(3) Genealogical information concerning Billy's early life is found in L. Wallace Duncan and Charles F. Scott, editors and compilers, *History of Allen and Woodson Counties, Kansas* (Iola, Kansas, 1901; reproduced by the Allen County Historical Society, Dudley Henderson, President, 1976); pp. 528-530.

(4) George Curry, Editor, *History of the Hopewell Presbyterian Church* (Franklin, Indiana, 1981). This is primarily a church history preserved through newspaper articles written by Robert Allen Brown who lived 1858-1922. George Curry edited the articles for the church's sesquicentennial celebration in 1981. Various articles provide an early history of both the community and the church. The history of Hopewell and Johnson County can also be found in D. D. Banta, *A Historical Sketch of Johnson County, Indiana* (Chicago, 1881), reproduced by the Johnson County Historical Society in 1976. Also, Elba L. Branigan, *History of Johnson County, Indiana* (Indianapolis, 1888 and 1913).

(5) Duncan and Scott, *History of Allen and Woodson Counties, Kansas;* p. 528. Note that a genealogical curiosity (or nightmare) occurred when Billy's sister, Mary Ellen, married a man named John Davis. Mary Ellen's father was named John Davis, a brother was named John Davis, and her husband was named John Davis. "Vanarsdall" is spelled variously as Vannarsdoll and Vanarsdale. Even Billy is not consistent.

(6) *Ibid*, P. 529. The phrase was used also in Billy Davis' obituary, the Iola, Kansas *Register*, November 24, 1922.

(7) Banta, *A Historical Sketch of Johnson County, Indiana;* p. 67.

(8) Livvy A. Young, *A Backward Glance at Old Union* (Reprinted Franklin, 1940); p. 57. Also printed as "Early Union Township Schools" in the *Nostalgia News*, a publication of the Johnson County Historical Society, Rachel Henry, Editor, (Spring 1984) Issue Number 17, p. 20.

(9) Curry, *History of the Hopewell Presbyterian Church;* Appendix section, "Chronological Roll of Communicants."

(10) "The Hopewell Academy, 1855-1888," written by Ruth Mathena Baughman, Historian, Hopewell Presbyterian Church; *Nostalgia News*, (Spring, 1984); Issue Number 17, p. 24.

(11) Billy refers to this living arrangement in the introductory remarks to his April 13, 1861 entry. *Census Records, 1860* provide information on the Jones family.

(12) The only clue as to the school Billy attended in Franklin is found in his journal. He simply states that before the war, he had started to the "Franklin school" which could mean either an Academy or the College. The Franklin College records, although not complete, do not list Billy as a student and the Franklin Academy records are not extant.

(13) Another journal reference. Lincoln carried Indiana with 139,033 or 51 percent of the total; Douglas, 115,509; Breckinridge, 12,294; Bell, 5,306. Historian Branigan, *History of Johnson County, Indiana*, recorded that Douglas carried Johnson County with 1,392 votes or 46 percent, Lincoln tallied 1,303 or 43 percent of the vote, 336 for Breckinridge and 60 votes for Bell. (Four years later McClellan, the so-called peace candidate, carried the county, 1,713 to Lincoln's 1,532.) For more background, see G. R. Tredway, *Democratic Opposition to the Lincoln Administration* (Indianapolis, 1973).

(14) Thornbrough, *Indiana in the Civil War Era;* pp. 96, 98.

(15) *Johnson County Atlas* (Reprinted by the Johnson County Historical Society, 1983-1984); pp. 157 (map), 294-295.

(16) Curry, *History of the Hopewell Presbyterian Church;* p. 31.

(17) *Ibid.*, p. 41.

(18) *Ibid.*, p. 42.

(19) Franklin, Indiana *Democratic Herald*, April 18, 1861.

(20) This ambrotype has not been located. From the military records, it is known James T. Alexander was 20 years old, 5'9" tall, brown eyes and dark hair, of fair complexion.

(21) *Democratic Herald*, April 25, 1861. This issue reflected all the excitement. Of particular interest to the publishers was the fact that the editor of their rival paper, the *Jeffersonian*, had been elected Captain of the Johnson County Minutemen. The event was reported on the front page of the *Herald:* "We congratulate him [George Allison, editor of the *Jeffersonian*] upon his appointment, but trust if he crosses the tented field, that his onslaught upon the enemy may prove more disastrous than his attacks upon the *Herald.*" Although Allison served for only about a year, the unit became a company in the 17th Indiana Infantry Regiment which was a part of the famed Lightning Brigade.

(22) Daniel Wait Howe, *Civil War Times* (Indianapolis, 1902); p. 9.

(23) *Democratic Herald*, April 25, 1861.

(24) Edward A. Leary, *The Nineteenth State: Indiana* (Indianapolis, 1966 and 1967); p. 31.

(25) *Ibid.*, pp. 29, 32. Also see James H. Madison, *The Indiana Way* (Indianapolis, 1986), for the history of Indiana. Also, John Hampden Holliday's *Indianapolis and the Civil War* (published by The Society of Indiana Pioneers, 1972).

(26) *Ibid.*, p. 26. Also, Arville Funk, *The Marion County Civil War Commission (1960-65)* (Indianapolis, 1965); p. 2. The Indiana Soldiers' and Sailors' Monument now stands at the geographical center of "1861 Indianapolis."

(27) Holliday, *Indianapolis and the Civil War;* p. 25.

(28) Hattie Lou Winslow and Joseph R.H. Moore, *Camp Morton 1861-1865: Indianapolis Prison Camp* (Indianapolis, 1940); p. 237. Also, Funk, *The Marion County Civil War Commission (1960-65);* p. 2.

(29) *Ibid.*, pp. 240-241.

(30) Stewart Brooks, *Civil War Medicine* (Springfield, 1966); p. 8.

(31) Orville Thomson, *Seventh Indiana Infantry in the War for the Union* (Published by the author, 190?); p. 7.

(32) A. J. Grayson, *History of the Sixth Indiana Regiment* (Madison, 1875?); p. 16.

(33) Howe, *Civil War Times;* p. 9.

(34) David I. McCormick, *Indiana Battle Flag Commission: Battle Flags and Organizations* (Indianapolis, 1929); p. 662.

(35) Arthur Ward Lufkin, D.D.S., *A History of Dentistry* (Philadelphia, 1938); pp. 209, 210, 227.

PICTURE CREDITS

— 1— Courtesy, United States Army Military Historical Institute, Carlisle, Pennsylvania. Hereafter referred to as USAMHI.

— 2— Courtesy, Hopewell Presbyterian Church, Mrs. Ruth Baughman, Historian.

— 3— The Lloyd Ostendorf Collection.

— 3— Same.

— 4— *History of the Sixth Regiment* by C. C. Briant.

— 5— Map. Indiana State Historical Society.

— 6— Courtesy, Indiana State Library.

— 6— Same.

— 7— *The Photographic History of the Civil War* by Frances Trevelyan Miller, Editor. Hereafter referred to as Miller's *Photographic History*.

— 8— *The Soldier in Our Civil War* by Paul Fleury Mottelay.

— 9— Map. Reprint of *Johnson County Atlas*, Courtesy, Johnson County Historical Society; Mrs. Rachel Henry and Mrs. Mary Ann Plummer.

—10— Courtesy, Hopewell Presbyterian Church.

—10— Same.

—11— *Johnson County Atlas.*

—11— Courtesy, Hopewell Presbyterian Church.

—12— Courtesy, The Louis A. Warren Lincoln Library and Museum, Fort Wayne, Indiana, Mark E. Neely, Director. (Lincoln National Life Insurance Company.)

—13— Courtesy, Johnson County Historical Society.

—14— Courtesy, Indiana State Library.

—14— Same.

—14— Same.

—15— Map. Same.

—16— Courtesy, University of Georgia Library.

—17— *The Twenty-Seventh Indiana Volunteer Infantry* by E. R Brown.

CHAPTER 2 THIS WOULD HAVE BEEN AMUSING

The gates of Camp Morton, circa 1863.

Wednesday, April 24, 1861. After breakfast we went out and drilled, or tried to, and then went to camp after resting. The Sargeants took out squads and drilled, while the officers studied. They do almost as well as the officers, we are all as awkward as can be. After dinner we were drilled for a time by an officer of the United States Army, he had a sword on, and spoke very quick and sharp. He said "Attention" so sharply that it made many of us jump; then "right dress," "front," before we had time to think; we didn't do it right, and he made us try it several times, he then marched us by the left front — I think he called it — and had us keep in line and right dress, while we were marching he kept saying "left," "left," "left," all the time and when we were thinking of that and trying to put the left foot down as he said left, he suddenly said "right about face march," we didn't get this near right. Then he showed us just how it was done, my how easy it was for him. We tried it several times while standing, and I guess did it real well, for he started us off again by the left front, saying "left," "left," and just when we were thinking of that or

William Pearson James Landon Joseph Homan

Some boys from Company A, 7th Indiana Infantry, three months service.

something else, he said "right about face, march," some turned to the right and some to the left, and many only half way to the right or left, and most of us started off, some marched in the right direction and some marched into others, and others away from some, this broke the line all up, and we were so terribly scattered and mixed that he halted us, and made us get our places facing him. Then we marked time. All lifted the left foot at the same time, moving it forward a little and back, sat it down in the same place, and then the same with the right foot, this would have been amusing, if we had not all been in such earnest. The officer had us try many movements, in all of which we were equally awkward.

When marching it was amusing to see our efforts to keep step. The officer would say "left," "left" and we tried to put the left foot down at the word, it generally went down with an emphatic stamp, and on slow time, soon the right foot would go down on the time of the left. Then would come a sudden half step and a short quick step of the right foot, and a sort of hop on the left foot, in an effort to bring it down on time. This was really two steps in less than one time and amounted to a very awkward movement, and kept us constantly stumbling on the next mans heels. Part of the time our officers looked on and part of the time they were in the ranks.

When the officer left, he said we did very well, may be we did, but it didn't appear so to us. We thought he was too strict and cross. We can't see what it all has to do with our duty as soldiers. We didn't have much leisure around camp to day, and the soldiers in camp were as busy as we were drilling. Some new Companies came in, and one company seemed busy most of the forenoon with wheelbarrows and rakes and shovels cleaning camp. It rained some to day. I wrote a letter home, and one to Miss T.

Orders were issued to day that all lights must be put out at nine o'clock.

Thursday, April 25, 1861. This morning early we heard a Fife and Drum playing at Head Quarters, building, and our orderly Sergeant came along to every bunk and said "get up to roll call." We were soon out and in line as our names were called we had to answer "here." Then we dressed up on the right, and the Sergeant saluted the Captain, and said, "All present or accounted for." Captain said this would be done every morning, as the orderly had to report to Head Quarters, the number present, etc.

After breakfast I went with others to provision quarters for rations for to day. Then we drilled for two hours. There were other companies and squads out drilling also, sometimes only two or three at a place, and from sun up to dark, the various commands can be heard all over camp. Frequently a number of officers can be seen out being drilled by a "Regular." While we were out several of our Gentlemen and Lady friends from Franklin came to our quarters. When dinner was ready we asked them to dine with us. They had brought baskets of provisions with them which they then spread on our table, and invited us. Then the Captain called us into line and ordered us to "charge," which we did in fine style. We thought the dinner an extra good one as our friends brought Butter, Pickels, Pies, Cakes, Jellies and the like, things that have not been issued to us yet. We drilled for two hours after dinner. I went on guard duty from four till six, but didn't have any gun, they gave us a stick. After supper we drilled again till nearly dark. At half past eight o'clock, a number, as usual, gathered in bunk Nine and held a short prayer meeting.

Friday, April 26, 1861. The Drums awoke us again at five o'clock. We drilled from six till nine o'clock. Then our officers went to Head Quarters for officers drill. While we were drilling Wm O. Tricket got sick and fell in ranks. While at dinner, Rev. John L. Jones, and his son John L. Jones, jr. of Franklin came. They brought some Towells and other things as presents for some of the boys. Rev. Mr Jones related several interesting incidents of his life as a soldier in the war of 1812.

This afternoon Captain Oyler went to Head Quarters to assist in the formation of another Regiment. Report says one has been formed and called the Sixth. Dont know why they began with six, some think it was to save confusion with the five Regiments in the Mexican war.

Virgil Lyons

John King

Aquilla McCormick

All six were from Hendricks County.

Lieutenant Gill drilled the Co. while the Captain was gone. It is rumored that Capt. Oyler is to be made major. This p.m. we received a barrell of green apples. After supper we drilled an hour, then Captain called me to open the barrell, and we feasted on apples. The boys declared that apples never tasted so good before.

Our friends are certainly very thoughtful and kind, and the boys are equally thankfull.

Saturday April 27, 1861. At four o'clock this morning I was called to go on guard till six. The company were out drilling before breakfast. After breakfast I went again to the Commissary Department for rations. All the Co. except those on guard last night went to Head Quarters for directions, about working in camp. Companies take turns, one each day cleaning camp. It rained and they returned to quarters. After dinner we went with Wheelbarrows & shovels. The Companies clean up their own quarters; this we wheeled away. It rained near all afternoon. I received a letter from home.

Papers stated a day or two ago, that volunteer troops of Illinois took possession of Cairo at the junction of the Ohio and Mississippi Rivers and now they state preparations for defense are being made at Cairo.

Sunday April 28th, 1861. The rain was over this morning and the sun shining brightly. Camp Morton is a beautiful open Grove only the larger trees standing, here and there, and the ground mostly covered with a green sword of Blue Grass. Soldiers loiter in groups or singly about, or lounge in the shade reading books or papers, conversing quietly here and there squads drilling.

I went to hear a Mr J. L. Boyd, a volunteer preacher. Most of the Boys sat about quarters or strolled leisurely about camp. Drilled in the afternoon and again after supper for a short time, but very much against the will of many. Several of us went this evening to hear a sermon by a Minister here in camp.

For the most part, this our first Sabbath in camp has been pleasant enough, but strangely different from what we are accustomed to.

Monday April 29, 1861. Another clear bright morning. Drilled early, when we returned to quarters Captain Samuel P. Oyler resigned his captaincy, thanking the Company for the favors shown him. Said he had been chosen Major of the Seventh Regiment, and had accepted, but that he would still feel an interest in the Company, that he had no doubt but that we would be brave and good soldiers, and do our part in maintaining the good name of the State, the authority of the Government, and the Honor of the Flag. And then we gave three hearty cheers for our Major, not forgetting Morton, Lincoln, the Union and the Stars and Stripes.

Major Oyler says our is to be Company "H" in the 7th Regiment. An election was then held, and 1st Lieutenant Joseph P. Gill was elected Captain and 2nd Lieutenant Wm B. Ellis was selected 1st Lieutenant and Wm McLaughlin, a private, was elected 2nd Lieutenant or Ensign. This occupied the forenoon. Drilled some during the afternoon. There is great activity in organizing and drilling in camp, and the news from all the North and West shows the great uprising of the people and the wonderful energy in preparing for war.

Tuesday April 30, 1861. We were drilled this forenoon by the "Zouave" Wheat, like the U.S. Army officer who drilled us last week he is very quick spoken, but I expect knows all about tactics. We have learned some of the movements, but are very awkward in most of them. There are several drill masters busy with squads and companies all the time. Many of our friends Ladies and Gentlemen from Franklin visited us to day. My Cousin David G. McGee, from near Greenwood, spent an hour or two in camp. Captain Gill and orderly sergeant Branham went home this afternoon.

We understand that Ebenezer Dumont is Colonel and Benj. Spooner, Lieutenant Colonel and James Gavin Adjutant of the 7th Regt.

Wednesday May 1, 1861. Drilled before breakfast. Then orders came for us to move to the West side of the encampment. They say this is to get all the Regt. together. Our quarters are near the north west corner of the camp. There is an old canal a few rods in front of us. After dinner we were marched with all the Companies of the Regt. to the Quarter Master Generals Head Quarters, where we

A newly formed Union regiment at drill near Washington D. C. There are 10 companies at "shoulder arms," the band is out front, and the officers are observing from horseback.

received our fire arms (muskets) and accouterments (a heavy leather box for ammunition and a cap box and, a leather scabbard for the Bayonet, and two belts, one around the waist and the other over the shoulder.) These are going to be heavy to carry.

Thursday May 2nd, 1861. New Companies are constantly arriving, and the encampment is now about full. We went at eight o'clock A.M. out into the Northern part of the city and drilled till near noon. Several friends from Franklin and vicinity came in again to day on a visit, and brought with them some refreshments. Every day there are dozens of such parties about the various Company quarters in camp. There is certainly great interest shown in the soldier by most of the citizens. At two o'clock we marched to the Lafayette Depot where we had a Regimental drill of two and a half hours. We were favored with a sight of our Regimental Officers. Col. Dumont is a small man perhaps fifty years old, and has a very peculiar speaking voice, not very strong. He looks like he was not in good health. Lieut. Col. Spooner is a larger man quite fleshy, and not so old as the Col., has a pleasant face and a good voice. Major Oyler is not as fleshy as Spooner, has a Roman nose, and a strong voice, except that he speaks through his nose somewhat. Adjutant Gavin is the youngest, perhaps thirty or thirty five years old is light complected, very quick and active, has a clear strong voice, and like the others doesn't sit well in the saddle. Neither of them are good riders. I understand all of them are Lawyers. The Colonel didn't seem to be in a very good humor to day. Some one said that when Sumter was fired on, a large meeting was held in which certain men offered Gov. Morton certain sums of money to help get equipment etc, and that Col. Dumont said he "would give a horse with a man on his back." That the peculiarity of his voice and the novelty of his gift caused quite a hearty laugh. I understand that he was a soldier in the Mexican War. We marched to camp in great haste, though almost tired out. Now that we have our guns and are organized, it is thought we will be sent to the front in a few days, some say to Washington City, others think we will go down the Mississippi River. James T. Alexander went home this afternoon. I received two letters to day one from Miss Maggie Terrill, the other from James M. Bone.

Friday May 3rd, 1861. I was on guard from four to six o'clock this morning. Just as day light began to appear, I saw two or three men climb hurriedly over the high fence at the "beat" south of me and run rapidly to their quarters. The guard nearest that point may have seen them, but likely not as he was walking a way at the time. It rained all night and while I was on guard. Went out for Company drill at eight, but rain drove us in and rained so at noon that we ate our dinner in quarters. Drilled some in a drizzling rain, and were to have had Regimental drill at five, but rain prevented. This p.m. I ate a piece of Cocoanut which made me quite sick for an hour or two.

Saturday May 4, 1861. Company drill from eight to ten o'clock. While preparing dinner, several friends from Franklin and Vicinity came to camp. Among them was my Father and Robert E. Henderson. Father brought with him six lbs of Butter and some sweet cake, both are relished by us now, as the Commissary Department does not furnish either. We some times buy Butter, but can't get a good article like this from home. Mr Henderson is an old schoolmate, he owns a farm cornering with father's, and, being a single man, makes his home at father's. Regimental drill from one to four. Father and Mr H. went with us to the drill ground, and watched us in the different maneuvers. When we were resting father said it reminded him of the "Muster days" when he was a young man. He said that if he could leave the family and the farm he would enlist, though he is now past forty eight.

Sabbath May 5, 1861. It was almost clear at day light but soon clouded up. I was on guard from ten o'clock till noon, rained near all day did not get to church at all. Wrote a letter to Miss ______ and one to Samuel V. List, a schoolmate of Hopewell.

Monday May 6, 1861. Still raining. At eight o'clock Company "H" reported at Head Quarters for Wheel barrow duty. Our work was done by eleven. About that time some friends from Franklin and Hopewell came in, among them Rev. J. F. Smith, Pastor of Hopewell church, and Miss Maggie Terrill and her brother Peterson, of our neighborhood, and Miss Julia Sneathen, a School Teacher. Mr Smith and the Young Ladies took dinner with my mess. The Butter Mother sent me, added considerably to our bill of fare, though I felt that it was too bad that for dishes had only tin pans and cups, and no knives and forks. We are getting used to these, and to taking the victuals in our fingers, we made the usual table apologies, but the ladies declared that every thing was nice as could be, that they could manage; that they had heard it said that "fingers were made before forks." It rained all afternoon so had opportunity to see and entertain our friends.

Tuesday May 7, 1861. A bright beautiful morning and a very pleasant day. At 8 o'clock Company "H" went into a pasture just west of Camp, and were drilled for three hours by Captain Wheat, we were trying to learn the manual of arms, we can't see why we should be required to learn more than how to load and fire, but we haven't any ammunition yet. Captain Wheat has us perform many movements with our muskets. Shoulder Arms, Right Shoulder Shift Arms, Support Arms, Carry Arms, Order Arms, and Present Arms, are some of the maneuvers. We can't understand so many times and motions as he talks about. After dinner were drilled by Captain Wheat and then by a Stranger and on Regimental drill at half past two.

Company "H" were favored again to day with visitors from Franklin.

Wednesday May 8, 1861. At Seven this morning my brother Daniel C. and brother in law Elisha Vannarsdoll came in to camp had some delicacies from home for us. Went on Co. Drill at 8. Capt Gill drilled the Co. for a time then gave place to the stranger who drilled us yesterday. I understand to day that he is to drill the Regt. Mr W.W.

Another view of Camp Morton in 1863 when it was a prison camp.

Jones and Wife, of firm of J.L. Jones and Co. of Franklin, came to visit us. They brought Cakes, Pies and Pickles, said they had heard we were not furnished such things, and thought they would taste good to us. They are certainly very thoughtful, and it seems to me such things do taste better now.

Regimental drill at three p.m. after which we were formed in closed columns, and the Regiment received a beautiful Flag from the Ladies of Dearborn Co. The presentation Speech was made by our Congressman Hon. A.G. Porter, in a very patriotic and eloquent speech, our Col. E. Dumont responded in a very appropriate speech.

Thursday May 9, 1861. We were called early, after breakfast we drilled, for some time, when orders came for us to pack up and move with the rest of the Regt. to Wallace Barracks. By 11 were on the move. Wallace Barracks is the old Bellefontaine Rail Road Depot in eastern portion of the city. Upon our arrival each Co. was assigned a certain portion, with orders to clean up our part. When about done, it was discovered that several companies were in the wrong place, we had to move. At 5 p.m. the Regt. formed for a short drill. Lights are ordered out at the tap of the drum at 9 p.m. After all had retired several companies got to cheering and yelling. The Captain of the guard ordered them to keep quiet.

The Marion County Courthouse in Indianapolis.

Friday May 10, 1861. At four o'clock I was called to go on camp guard. At six the Co. went out and drilled an hour. At eight a large detail reported at Head Quarters for Wheel barrow duty and the rest of the Co. went out for drill. Regimental drill in p.m. and Dressparade at five o'clock. In Dressparade, all the companies form in one line and then to the rear open march and line up, then the 1st Sergeants are ordered to the front and center of the Regt. then they turn to the front and face the Col. and march out a few paces and halt, then each in his turn beginning on the right holds the gun at a shoulder and with the right salutes the Col. and says all present and accounted for; they then about face and march back to the Regt. and turn to the right and left and then to their places. Then the Captains all march to the front and center to a point near the Colonel where they halt, salute and orders are given them. The Adjutant who stands near the Col. commands "about face to your rear march." When this is done the Col. puts the Regt. through the manual of arms.

I found leisure to day to write letter to D.G. McGee.

Saturday May 11, 1861. Cloudy and threatening rain this morning. At the morning roll call, one from each mess was detailed to cook. It fell to my lot to prepare rations for mess #9. The rest of the Co. went on drill. After Breakfast I was detailed to report at guard house at 8 a.m. when there, was put on picket guard till ten, was then released for four hours.

This mornings papers contain an account of an affair at St. Louis, Mo. Captain Nathaniel Lyon in command of Regulars, and Frank P. Blair, commanding Missouri Home Guards, attacked camp of Rebel-Troops near St. Louis and captured over eight hundred prisoners and all their preparations for war.

An engraving of the Governor's Mansion in 1861.

Camp Dumont, May 12, 1861. Commenced raining at four o'clock this morning, and continued all day. Nothing of note, until at three p.m. when were called to church service here in camp. Sermon was excellent. Text 1st Tim 2:4.

Invitations to attend Young Mens Prayer Meeting at Roberts Chapel at Six p.m. Through the kindness of Col. Dumont, twenty of our Co. were permitted to go in charge of an officer. Meeting was largely attended and led by soldiers.

At close of services we repaired to audience room and listened to excellent sermon by the Minister who addressed us in Camp from 8th V. 2 Ch 1st Tim.

Indianapolis, May 13, 1861. When Reveille sounds we are obliged to get up to roll call. About 9 a.m. when on drill some of my relatives from near Greenwood came to camp. I was not permitted to leave ranks to see them after waiting a time they went down town.

When we quit drilling I obtained my first pass and went down town where I found them and spent an hour very pleasantly. Also met J.L. Jones jr and son.

On my return to camp found Mr Jacob Aton and wife and Miss Mattie Hathaway, and several other friends from Hopewell. Company drill at 2 p.m. and Regimental drill at 4 p.m. and Parade at 5 p.m.

Evening devotional services in Mess No. 9.

Camp Dumont, May 14, 1861. A beautiful morning found Company "H" in line early. After marching half mile and back, had breakfast. Then the regiment formed to go to the Arsenal, but were dismissed till ten a.m. Just as we broke ranks several friends from Franklin came in, among them Miss Mary C. Vannuys, Miss Mollie Read, Miss Rose Adams, and the two Missess McColloughs. There being no drill, time passed pleasantly with our Lady friends. All are schoolmates of mine, getting hold of my pocket Bible, Miss Adams wrote "We'll meet above," "Rose." Miss Read wrote, "Friend Billy, When this you see remember our school-days, Mollie." And Miss Vannuys wrote, "Friend Billy; You go to fight for us, we will pray for you, may you fight bravely, and should you fall may you die happy, Kate."

An Indianapolis foundry.

Promptly at ten o'clock the regiment formed and marched to the State House yard, while resting here I met Mr R.T. Overstreet and Lady, and other friends with well filled baskets of delicacies from Home; these were opened and a few friends invited to help discuss the contents; this gave an opportunity to introduce my friend J.E. Boswell, thus squared accounts with him for the excellent dinner from his fathers and mothers baskets, on the day when we were rejected. These visits from friends form pleasant oasis in our soldier life, and the good things they bring are an agreeable change from Beans, Potatoes, Bacon etc., and highly appreciated.

Soon the regiment were furnished with a heavy leather box with tin box apartments for forty rounds of ammunition, a leather box for Caps and leather Scabbard for the Bayonet, and two leather belts; one for the waist, fastened with a brass buckle marked US, the other to go over the shoulder. Were not given any Cartridges or Caps. When all were supplied with accouterments we marched back to camp where we rested till 2 p.m., regimental Drill at 4, and Parade at 5 p.m.

May 15, 1861. Another bright morning. Father came this morning, bringing with him Butter, Cake and other delicacies. A friend of Mess No. 6 brought Pie and Stewed Peaches. These are kept for supper. There have been very few days in which some friend of some one of the Company did not come with baskets well filled, and sometimes there are twenty or thirty such visitors in Company quarters, and the same is true of all the Companies though some of them are from Counties on the Ohio River.

Company drill at 2 p.m. and Regt. Drill at 4, after many manueuvers, regiment formed in close column by companies and Adjutant Gavin on behalf of the officer of the regiment, in a brief speech presents Col. E. Dumont with an elegant sword. The Col. in accepting, made an appropriate and very patriotic speech.

Camp Dumont, May 16, 1861. We learn from this mornings "Journal" that our officers have orders to march.

Little's Hotel in Indianapolis.

We do not know when or where to, but we suppose to St. Louis, Mo. Papers state that Gen. Beauregard has died from wounds received at Sumter and that John C. Breckinridge is to take command under Col. Anderson.

Among the friends from Franklin to day was Mr Wm McCaslin, and Mr Hampton Terrill and his sons Peterson and John, and Mr Isaac Voorhies and Wife. They brought provisions for Dinner and Supper.

Usual Drills and Parades.

May 17, 1861. Usual routine; i.e. Roll call, Drill, Breakfast, Drill, Drill. Friends from Franklin with a good bill of fare. Captain Geo. W. Allison's Company from Johnson County arrived at Camp Morton to-day. After Dinner Lieut. Ellis was kind enough to take Co. "H" to the River bathing. On our return we called to see Captain Allison's Co. found the boys in fine spirits, perhaps more so than they will be when they have soldiered as long as we

Pierre Gustave Toutant Beauregard — rumored as dead.

have. Quite an excitement in our camp over the removal of some provisions from the Commissary department, prevailing opinion is that we will move soon, but the arrival of a much larger amount this p.m. brought a change over our dreams.

May 18, 1861. Am on guard. Very strange, there are no friends from Franklin to day. Have employed Thomas Hill to do cooking for our two messes, this will give us more time for our duties and more leisure, and will relieve us of a vexacious matter for we frequently have too little or too much, never well and neatly done, which always reminds us by contrast of our good Mothers and Sisters. Perhaps there will be less complaint about what we have to eat. Received our Blankets and Straps for carrying them. Regiment were furnished with blank Cartridges. After Parade each Company were permitted to fire twice. There was much excitement over the matter, as the guns seemed disposed to kick back. We salute the Col. as he passed. Those off duty, formed line and as the Col. passed the gun was brought to a "present," a perpendicular position in front of the body. The right arm almost straight holding the stock just below the hammer, the left hand holding the gun barrell loosely, with the fore arm almost square across the body; the Col. would bring his right hand to his hat rim, the gun was then brought to a shoulder. We were exceedingly awkward. There is one Captain detailed each day and called "officer of the day." He is saluted in the same manner, when he comes around. And when on guard, we are required to salute all officers who pass. Have a guard around camp, at Quartermasters and other places.

Sabbath May 19, 1861. Being relieved from guard duty at 4 a.m. I went to quarters and slept. This forenoon we received our clothing. The color is gray, and quite neat when a fellow gets a fit, but such fortunate ones are few. My friend Boswell was given a pair of pants long enough for "Dad Billingsly," who stands at the head of the Company. And I received a coat large enough for George W. Whitlock, our Two hundred and forty Pound Veteran of the Mexican War. The shirts were no better, but by Swapping we arranged tolerable fits.

At 3 p.m. a Presbyterian Minister favored us with an excellent Sermon. After Dress Parade private T.J. Morgan obtained pass and twelve of us went to Masonic Hall and listened to a good Sermon.

Monday May 20, 1861. Rained all day, no drill except Manual of Arms in quarters. Several of Captain Allison's company came to camp, among them several old friends one a cousin — Brenton, of Acton. Several of Co. "H" went down town. Some returned drunk, others are out.

May 21, 1861. A beautiful morning. At breakfast time the missing boys returned, and report having been to Franklin. They are still drunk. While on Co. drill this morning I was permitted to load and fire my gun for the first time.

After dinner Co. boxed up surplus Blankets and Clothing to send some; this started a report that two companies had orders to march, that three days rations had been boxed for them. The opinion prevails that all will go soon, we are anxious to be off to the front and can't understand why there is such delay.

Wednesday May 22, 1861. Considerable excitement last night over our prospect of moving soon, many believed it would be our last night at this place. Among the friends from Franklin was Messrs Overstreet and Hunter and their wives, and Rev's A.B. Money and Jno H. Martin.

May 23, 1861. Were each furnished a pair of Socks and Haversack and a Rubber Blanket, to shelter us from the rain. Have orders to clean up our muskets.

Camp Dumont, May 24, 1861. Immediately after morning roll call Company went out for an hours drill, and returned with sharpened appetites. Here is the Bill of fare. Dry Bakers Bread, Salt Side Meat. Two Pots of Coffee, and a little Sugar. The bread and sugar soon gave out, we then finished on meat without bread and Coffee without Sugar. Having given us a light breakfast, they furnished the Regt. the Picks, Spades and grubbing hoes. At two p.m. the Regt. formed and marched to an open space west of the Old Fair Grounds where we met four other Regts. and formed line for Review.

Soon Major General George B. McClellan of Ohio with his staff, accompanied by Gov. Dennison of Ohio, Gov. Yates of Illinois, Hon. Lyman Trumball of Ills, Gov. Morton of Indiana, and other officers and citizens of note passed in front and rear, then to the front and center. As the reviewing party passed, each Regiment presented arms, this was recognized and responded to by the General and others. When the General and party halted in the center, the Regiment formed columns by companies and passed in front of the Reviewing party at present arms; then wheeled into line and marched to our respective camps. The Review was witnessed by a large concourse of citizens from Indianapolis and other places over the State. Col. Dumont brought us back along Washington Street, putting us through several manueuvers on the way. We reached camp very fatigued.

*Nothing of note for Saturday.

Major General George McClellan.

Governor Richard Yates of Illinois.

Senator Lyman Trumbull of Illinois.

Governor William Dennison of Ohio.

Sabbath, May 26, 1861. While on guard last night, some soldiers came in past one of the guards and several noisy chickens.

A very warm day. Preaching at 3 p.m. and 8 p.m. Quarters were comparatively quiet all day, a good percent of the men have books and papers to read, and many have their Bibles which are not neglected.

May 27, 1861. When I awoke about four this morning I found my bed fellow had rolled himself in the Blankets and me out. Weather is cooler, with a strong wind from the west blowing Camp Kettles, buckets and tin plates about camp promiscuously. While on Drill this morning Capt. Gill informed me that I could have a pass home at any time. Canteens were furnished to day, are of tin covered with a coarse cloth, with a muslin string to go over the shoulder. Are for water on long marches and in battle, will hold near a quart. Some of the boys think them good for Buttermilk, Cider or something stronger.

Received our tents to day, and commenced to put them up. Most of us are very awkward. Boys from Franklin College marked their tent, "AJAX." Received furlough and started for home at five p.m. Met many friends on my arrival at Franklin. On my way down street stopped in Barber Shop, soon W.W. Jones came in and said I must go to the store; through the kindness of Messrs J.L. Jones and Sons was furnished horse to go out home. On the way, fell in with friend James M. Bone who is full of enthusiasm and like so many others talks of little else than the war, and soldiering. Believes that with the great rush to arms all over the north, the war will not last long. Bone went with me near to the house, then turned for home. Arriving at home at 8 p.m. found only mother at the house, Father and Brother were at work burning logs in a clearing, went to them and remained until ten o'clock helping to put the burning logs together.

Tuesday May 28, 1861. After breakfast visited Sister Martha Jane, saw several of the neighbors, then returned home, and bidding family good bye, started for town. Stopped at Mr Chas. Freemans and Mr H. Terrills and saw some other friends on the way. Dined with Mr J.L. Jones and family, then went to Art gallery for two pictures for Sisters Martha and Mary.

Called on several friends and visited the public school. After supper called on W.W. Jones and family on way to Depot.

I find that we soldiers are already heroes. Almost every one manifests a marked interest in any one who has enlisted. The down train brought Lieutenant McLaughlin who says the 7th Regt. will leave camp tomorrow.

Wednesday May 29, 1861. Lay with my head on a gum blanket last night and found my face almost blistered this morning. Camp filled with rumors as to where we are going. Orders came early to pack up. Drew provisions with orders to cook it all at once. Had orders to strike tents at 11:30 a.m., march at noon, and board cars at one p.m. At noon were told would not take train till 8 p.m. During the afternoon baggage was put aboard the train. Rumor says other Regts. are preparing to move.

After Dress parade, Regiment formed column by Cos. and each soldier not supplied was given a Testament by a Baptist Minister. After singing Star Spangled Banner, line was again formed and the Col. presented the little daughter of Captain Scott of Martinsville, as "The Daughter of the Regiment."

We then marched near the Barracks, which we left when we went into our tents, here we stacked arms and rested. I filled my Canteen for the first time. There is much excitement over our going, and the boys are in high glee over the prospect of getting to the front. No one appears to know where we are going. At eight p.m. we boarded the cars and started east we suppose to Washington City where a large force is gathering. Boys are tired and sleepy, easily put out of humor.

A New York regiment in parade ground formation.

A spirited rally at the Indiana State Capitol for the swearing in of 11th Indiana Infantry Regiment.

CHAPTER TWO BACKGROUND

Friends and Family

During April and May 1861, the dusty, narrow, roads leading to Camp Morton were clogged with "friends" — all bearing gifts. One soldier estimated the ratio of visitors-to-soldiers as two-to-one.(1) It is of significance that Billy did not record the presence of friends or family on Sundays. After the crowds of Sunday April 21st, the authorities quickly established a policy of no more visitations on the Sabbath.(2)

Billy identified 31 friends or family members who visited him in 36 days. There were many visitors he did not record by name, only as "several of our Gentlemen and Lady friends," or "many of our friends," and "friends from Franklin with a good bill of fare."

The historian for Billy's unit had an explanation for the phenomenon at Camp Morton: "Word had gone home, by what means none but the sender knew, doubtless by some one who had never in his life had a full belly, that men were starving. . .This stirred up our home friends to a proper sense of our necessities, and that first Saturday afternoon Co's B and F were surprised by a delegation from home bringing huge boxes, full of home comforts — pies and cakes, fried spring chicken, and our mother's home-made bread. The eating thereof deferred for Sunday dinner, which [when] disposed of, an Irish comrade quaintly remarked, 'If this be war, God grant we may niver have pace."(3)

The School of the Soldier

The military commands the officers were trying to memorize and the recruits were trying to perform were the "general rules" for the School of the Soldier. These instructions were contained in Hardee's *Rifle and Light Infantry Tactics*. The School of the Soldier consisted of three parts. First, "what ought to be taught to recruits without arms;" secondly, "the manual of arms" including loading and firing and lastly there were the "the principles of alignment, the march by the front, the different steps, the march by the flank, the principles of wheeling, and those of change of direction. . .also, long marches in double quick and the run." Fortunately, each of these parts was broken down into smaller lessons.

Billy's first day in the Army, April 24, was spent learning Part III, Lessons 1 and 2. Little wonder that the officers were struggling in preparation for conducting the lessons. Perhaps the simplest of alignments, "Right Dress," was described in the manual as follows:

> "317. At this, the rank, except the two men placed in advance as a basis of alignment, will move up in quick time, and place themselves on the new line, according to the principles prescribed in No. 312."(4)

A 37-word sentence; but more is required:

> "312. Each recruit, as designated by his number, will turn the head and eyes to the right as prescribed in

A New York regiment stands ready for inspection.

the first lesson of the first part, and will march in quick time two paces forward, shortening the last, so as to find himself about six inches behind the new alignment, which he ought never to pass: he will next move up steadily by steps of two or three inches, the hands extended, to the side of the man next to him on the alignment, so that, without deranging the head, the line of the eyes, or that of the shoulders, he may find himself in the exact line of his neighbor, whose elbow he will lightly touch without opening his own."[5]

Indeed, "without deranging the head." There are 122 words in that sentence.

Some officers, finding it difficult to remember the instructions, instinctively reverted to an earlier and simpler life. Newly-learned commands such as "Halt" frequently slipped the officers' memories. For example, one captain, an ex-railroader, was heard to shout, "down brakes," "down brakes." Another recalled "whoa."[6]

"Getting back in step" or, militarily, the command "Change Step" was concisely described by Billy as taking "two steps in less than one time." Hardee, in his *Tactics*, needed 45 words.

Billy and his comrades seemed to have their greatest difficulty with "Right (or Left) About Face - March." This command required individual dexterity and mass coordination. Predictably, Billy observed the troops became "terribly scattered."

The Daily Routine

To help instill discipline where there was none, there were numerous bugle calls to signal the next activity:

Reveille	6 a.m.	Dinner	12:30 p.m.
Police Call	6:15 a.m.	Drill	2 p.m.
Breakfast	7 a.m.	Retreat Parade	5 p.m.
Guard Mounting	8 a.m.	Supper	6 p.m.
Drill	8:30 a.m.	Tattoo	9 p.m.
Drill	11 a.m.	Taps	10 p.m.[7]

Billy wrote of many variations from these regulations. On the morning of April 26, he "drilled from six to nine o'clock," and, evidently, there were special considerations for the visiting with family and friends.

The Organization

Many of the men who crowded into Camp Morton would be formed into six military regiments of 10 companies each. The 10 companies of approximately 100 men and officers were alphabetized A through K — almost. "J" had always been skipped over. It was military tradition. The first six regiments would be indexed as the 6th through the 11th. The numerical designations 1st through the 5th would not be used out of deference for the five Indiana regiments which served in the Mexican War. The Johnson County Riflemen became Company H of the 7th Indiana Volunteer Infantry Regiment (otherwise, "the 7th Indiana").

Colonel Dumont

The commander of the 7th Indiana was Ebenezer Dumont. It was believed that Dumont became Colonel of the 7th quite by chance. Supposedly he and Thomas J. Crittenden were to decide who would command the 6th and who would command the 7th. Dumont spoke out and quoted an old Irish ballad, "there is luck in odd numbers says Rory O'Moore." And that was how Ebenezer Dumont became Colonel of the 7th Indiana.[(8)]

A story of coincidence: Of the first six Indiana Civil War regiments organized, Dumont was to have the 7th and Lew Wallace was to command the 11th. In 1837 Dumont's father had run against Wallace's father in the gubernatorial race in Indiana. (Lew Wallace's father won.)

The 7th Indiana's first commander, Ebenezer Dumont.

Dumont was described by Billy Davis as a "small man about 50 years old, and has a peculiar speaking voice." An 1866 book, which otherwise extolled the countless merits of Indiana's Civil War colonels, appraised Dumont by a different light. Those observers thought he was: "sallow, lean, small, with an irascible, melancholy countenance, lighted up by a keen, deep-set eye, and sometimes additionally illuminated with flashes of dry humor. . .sort of a contrast within himself, and consequently has earned an unenviable reputation for eccentricity."[(9)]

The 46-year-old Dumont had been born in Vevay, Indiana. It was said when Ebenezer reached voting age, he proclaimed to his Whig father that he was a Democrat. With that, the father stomped out of the house. Dumont served honorably in the Mexican War under General Zachary Zaylor. Then, upon the firing on Fort Sumter, Dumont made a moving and patriotic speech "uttered in a voice so peculiar that. . .he [simultaneously] drew tears and laughter. . ."[(10)] It was at this meeting that Dumont made the offer of a horse with a man on his back — the popular story Billy would hear later at Camp Morton.

I Timothy 2:8

For the 20 men permitted to go to the Young Men's Prayer Meeting that Sunday evening at Robert's Chapel, it would have been approximately an eight-block walk. Although the men went as a military contingent they (still) would have been dressed in civilian clothes.

The scripture as quoted from I Timothy:

"I will therefore that men pray everywhere,
lifting up holy hands, without wrath and doubting."

Army Food, Clothing and Shelter

Salty meat, wormy apples and, worst of all, burnt beans in the coffee. Such was the wrath from Camp Morton."[(11)] (Billy was not a chronic complainer although there was a reference to a light breakfast on May 24th: "meat without bread and Coffee without Sugar." Throughout the journal he makes note of "meat without salt." This he believed causes diarrhea.)

The fare was not all that bad; but it was not down-home style. If anything, the recruits had too much food. Food fights were common as loaves of bread, potatoes and chunks of bacon were fired at each other in fun. The politicians heard only the complaints and responded by legislating an increase in the daily supplies by 25 to 150 percent. Also, the politicians proclaimed that there will be fresh bread, pickles and dried fruit. Still not good enough, the local merchant who volunteered as the Commissary General on April 15 was forced out of office by May 30.[(12)]

The daily food ration for each soldier as prescribed by Army Regulations was: 12 ounces of pork or bacon, or, one pound and four ounces of salt or fresh beef; one pound and six ounces of soft bread or flour, or, one pound of hard bread, or, one pound and four ounces of corn meal; and to every one hundred rations, fifteen pounds of beans or peas, and ten pounds of rice or hominy; ten pounds of green coffee, or eight pounds of roasted (or roasted and ground) coffee, or, one pound and eight ounces of tea; fifteen pounds of sugar; four quarts of vinegar;. . .three pounds and twelve ounces of salt; four ounces of pepper; thirty pounds of potatoes, when practicable, and one quart of molasses.[(13)] In Indiana the rations were increased, but the complaining persisted.

Each mess of eight or ten men arranged for their own cooking. The most common procedure was for each messmate to take a turn. In Billy's mess, the men eventually thought they would come out ahead if they paid some soldier to do the cooking.

The 7th Indiana Infantry Regiment received the garments of soldiers on May 19. For four weeks they had trained in the clothes they brought from home. The new

Robert's Chapel.

Another Indianapolis street scene. This merchant had it all — deer, squirrels, ducks, oysters, whatever.

uniforms were gray, possibly satinet (definitely not wool), and either too large or too small. A. J. Grayson, a member of the 6th Indiana, commented on the quality as "an inferior material of grey."[14] The two-piece uniforms cost less than $8; the shirts, $1.40; hats (grayish with a tall crown), $1.25; shoes $1.15.[15]

When Camp Morton became overcrowded, Billy and the 7th Indiana were fortunate enough to be moved to the Bellfontaine Railroad Freight Depot. These new quarters were in the vicinity of Massachusetts Avenue and Bellfontaine Street.[16] The freight depot, or Camp Dumont as it was named, was about a mile from Camp Morton, as the crow flies. Orville Thomson, the regimental historian thought it was "a lovely location, surrounded by a large common, which afforded an excellent drill-ground." No more animal stalls, greater freedom, and nearness to the downtown area. It was a welcome move. However, as Thomson pointed out, "this condition was to last but a brief while."[16]

END NOTES

(1) Winslow and Moore, *Camp Morton;* p. 243.

(2) *Ibid.*, p. 244. The authors cite their sources as the Indianapolis *Sentinel* and the Indianapolis *Journal.*

G. W. H. Kemper served with Company B, 7th Indiana.

(3) Thomson, *Seventh Indiana;* p. 12. For additional information concerning camp life, see G.W.H. Kemper, "The Seventh Regiment," published in *War Papers Read Before the Indiana Commandery Military Order of the Loyal Legion* (Indianapolis, 1898); pp. 117-131. Hereafter cited as *War Papers.*

(4) W.J. Hardee, Brevet Lieutenant-Colonel, U.S. Army, *Rifle and Light Infantry Tactics; for the Exercise and Maneuvers of Troops when Acting as Light Infantry or Riflemen* (Philadelphia, 1861, two volumes); v. I, p. 69.

(5) *Ibid*, p. 68.

(6) Winslow and Moore, *Camp Morton;* p. 243.

(7) *Ibid*, p. 244.

(8) Thomson, *Seventh Indiana;* p. 8.

(9) Merrill and Company, Editors, *The Soldier of Indiana;* p. 25.

(10) *Ibid.*

(11) Terrell, *Indiana Adjutant General's Report;* v. I, p. 451.

(12) Winslow and Moore, *Camp Morton;* pp. 247-249.

(13) Bell I. Wiley, *The Life of Billy Yank* (New York, 1971); p. 224.

(14) Grayson, *History of the Sixth Indiana;* p. 9.

(15) Holliday, *Indianapolis and the Civil War;* p. 32. Also Kemper, *War Papers;* p. 121.

(16) Modern sources such as Funk, *The Marion County Civil War Centennial Commission (1960-65)* describe the location of Camp Dumont as "probably at the Bellfontaine RR shop, Mass. Ave." An 1876 map of Indianapolis depicts railroad-support buildings and rail sidings along the mainline some four blocks to the south of the intersection of Massachusetts and Bellfontaine. The 7th's regimental historian, Orville Thomson, went back to the area of Camp Dumont some 40 years after the war, only to be told by "the oldest inhabitant" that he had never heard of the common or an old freight depot. The location of the camp remains inexact, although it is probably in the vicinity of modern-day Michigan and Davidson streets.

(17) Thomson, *Seventh Indiana;* p. 13.

PICTURE CREDITS

—19— Courtesy, USAMHI.

—20— —21— All six portraits (carte de visites) are courtesy of Craig Dunn.

—22— Miller's *Photographic History.*

—23— Courtesy, USAMHI.

—24— —25— All four engravings are courtesy of the Indiana State Library.

—26— *Generals of the Confederate States Army 1861-1865.*

—27— Top left and right, courtesy USAMHI; bottom left and right, courtesy The Louis A. Warren Lincoln Library and Museum.

—28— Miller's *Photographic History.*

—29— Courtesy, Indiana State Library.

—30— Miller's *Photographic History.*

—31— Courtesy, USAMHI.

—32— Top and bottom, courtesy of the Indiana State Library.

—33— *War Papers.*

CHAPTER 3 OUR FIRST VIEW OF REBELDOM

Thursday May 30, 1861. I slept greater part of the night so did most of the boys, but I am not much rested. About daylight came to a beautiful stream of water, said to be the Little Miami. Passing over some fine country, came to Piqua, some distance beyond the train stopped, no one knew what for but every one asked every one else why and what for, and many other questions. Shortly Captain Rabb, of Rising Sun, came through our car — a Passenger Coach — and reported that the tents of "H," "I," & "K," had been burned by a spark from the Engine catching in a broom. Crossed a beautiful country then passed Urbana, finely situated, train stopped and some of the volunteers got off and I understand demolished a Grocery — Grog Shop —. Over a rough country and then swamps, to a small village, where I tried again to get water in my canteen, but failed. Some of the Boys started again for the grocery, but were ordered back by the Colonel. A baggage car was left upon which was rations for Co. "H.," were to have been put on this train but through carelessness were not. At Columbus at noon, were furnished a dinner by citizens. Col. obtained tents to replace those burned. Left C. at 2 pm, passed Newark at 3:30 p.m. then passed some bridges guarded by soldiers with muskets. Small box houses had been built for them; then came to a large river, passed through a rocky gorge down the river to Newton, where we were informed that when we crossed the river "Muskingum" we would find supper awaiting us. On arriving at Zanesville, we found the vicinity of the Depot and R.R. crowded with citizens, waving handkerchiefs and Hats and hurrahing for Abraham Lincoln and the Union, and cheering the soldiers. Soon the cars were crowded with Ladies and Gentlemen with baskets of Bread and butter, beef, ham, Pies, cakes, Jellies, tarts, milk, coffee, apples, Ice water and almost every thing to eat. Leaving Z., followed down the river several miles when 74 miles from Columbus, came to a grade where two Engines were necessary. At Concord the citizens were out in force with their baskets well filled with such things as our Mothers used to give us at home. Steep grades and short curves, three engines necessary at one place. Passed through a long Tunnell, came to Cambridge, saw several Oil wells. Fine scenery, train creeps slowly around the almost mountains; the tops of which towered far above us, while the hollows are so deep that we look out over tops of large trees. Stopped frequently. Side tracked at Gibson. At Nine p.m. passed through a Tunnell and stopped in a deep cut, could see houses fifty feet above us, part of Barnesville. Leaving Barnesville, I slept to Bellair where we arrived at 11 p.m. From the train went to quarters for the night in a car shop, tired out with 27 hours ride on train.

Friday May 31, 1861. Bellair, is on Ohio River, hemmed in by high hills, timbers and in grass. Don't look as though could ever have been cultivated. Went bathing in river. Saw Steamboat, my first. After breakfast wrote letter to J. L. Jones & Son. Joseph E. Boswell and I obtained permission to pass guards for a ramble over the hills, at foot of first saw Coal Pit, but having no candle or lamp did not venture in. Went up to a lone Maple tree near the summit, where we had a fine view of the village and river, and hills or half mountains on the Virginia side. Our first view of rebeldom. Rested here for near an hour and talked over the prospects of the war, how it would be won, peace declared and the Union saved before our Three months service closed, while sitting here saw two steamboats land at the wharf. Is small village on opposite side of river. Saw a train of cars loaded with soldiers leave the village going down the river. We go next, and have no doubt but that there will be great battle soon, certainly so if Gov. Letcher of Va. undertakes to enforce his late order. He calls all northern troops "Invaders," and orders them to leave within twenty four hours. On our way to quarters found piece of candle at mouth of Coal Pit which we lighted and ventured in several hundred feet where we found large excavations like great rooms and halls. Having but little candle we returned. After dinner were ordered to cross the river. Landed on disputed territory about four o'clock. Is a nail factory in the village — "Benwood." Our mess met in an Iron car for prayers. Arranged for sleeping, but before retiring were ordered to load our muskets with Powder and Ball. This made me nervous, we all feel sure there is danger of an attack and camp was soon very quiet.

An early oil derrick.

Railroad bridge over the Monongahela at Fairmont, (West) Virginia, built in 1852.

A Civil War era railroad engine with blockhouse in right background.

The **Major Anderson** *was built at Jeffersonville, Indiana in 1861. It would run the Cincinnati-Wheeling trade.*

The Grafton station — to the left for Parkersburg and to the right for Bellaire.

The western reaches of the Baltimore and Ohio Railroad in 1861.

Saturday June 1, 1861. My first nights rest in Va. was disturbed by the car moving, we thought it was leaving and gathering up our bedding were out in double quick time. Soon myself and others were detailed to carry our Tents and camp equipment from Boat to car. Left Benwood at 11 o'clock a.m., passed down the river with very high hills on our left. At Moundsville, turned to the left, leaving the river behind us passing up a crooked stream the Ohio hills were soon out of sight. First station out was Eaton, dodging around the hills soon came to one we could neither dodge, go over or around, but we did go through or under it by means of a short Tunnell. Hills are covered more or less with Pine and Cedar. Passed some Oilwell Derricks.

At Cameron 28 miles from Benwood. The Platform doors, yards and street at or near the Depot were crowded with people, who waved handkerchiefs, cheered and hurrahed, and shook hands with every soldier they could get in reach of. And it is said some of the young ladies threw kisses at some of the officers. They want us to drive all the Secessionists out of Virginia and many were the hearty well wishes for our safety and success.

Just after leaving C. passed through a tunnell half mile long. In vicinity of Belton, the hills are covered with a fine growth of Pine and Cedar. As we are following the course of a small stream, we travel at all points of the compass.

Are many wild flowers along the stream and on the sides of the Mountains. Following down the stream the valley widens and we saw now and then a house and small farm. Passed through several tunnells one three fourths of mile long. A recent rain shower has made the stream muddy, but has brightened all nature on the mountain side and in the valley. Ohio troops of Col. Irvins Regt. are guarding bridges. They say there are not many Rebels in this vicinity. At Glovers Gap a narrow pass were more Soldiers, some of them far up the side of the mountain.

Strange and wild scenery every where. After passing Mannington a few miles came to a larger stream where soldiers and workmen were repairing two bridges, burned a few days ago by Rebels. At Farmington some of the citizens failed to respond to our cheers for the Union. Report says a citizen was arrested here for burning the bridges. Apparently more rebels at Barnesville.

At Fairmount crossed the Monongahela River, saw large suspension bridge. Our course was then up the Tygarts Valley River. At Bentons Ferry, learned that Rebels had fled from Grafton, going to Phillippi. The hills are now mountains with grand scenery on every side, new at every turn. Passed Charming View, then Valley Falls; then a beautiful village on the side of hill, and some of the 9th Ind. Regt. at station who said the village was Prunytown. Passing camp of 9th who had their tents up, soon came to Grafton, at the Junction of the Wheeling and Parkersburg branches of the B&O R.R. surrounded on all sides by the rugged Alleghaney Mountains. Here we found part of the ____Ohio camped, much army stores and a great deal of bustle. After a few moments delay, were taken back near the 9th Ind. where we debarked, pitched our tents and lay down to sleep.

Near Grafton, W. Va., Sunday June 2, 1861. I was detailed early for guard. Twenty from Each Co. were detailed to clear off the camp and pitch the tents in order. Are encamped in grove of large Oak, Pine etc. on north side of railroad, less than one mile from Grafton. Before tents were all removed Col. Dumont returned from Grafton, when all the regt. except "D" & "H" were ordered to prepare to March. Rations were drawn and the eight Companies were ready to move at 5 o'clock p.m. Soon the train came and they left as we supposed for Phillippi where the Rebels are reported in force and fortified. Report says that Col. Kelley, of 1st West Va. in command of his own regt., 9th Ind. and other troops, 16th Ohio, started east this forenoon, on cars some say on route for Washington City, but some think for Phillippi.

Reports are out that a battle is expected at Phillippi tomorrow or very soon. Is much disappointment and bitter dissatisfaction in Co.s "D" & "H" on account of being left here as guards. Some think our officers are to blame. To day two slaves came into camp and said their masters had sent them as spies, and want the officers to send out and arrest them.

General Morris of Ind. and his staff arrived at Grafton last night. Commenced raining soon after the troops left. The Sixth Ind. passed after dusk.

Thomas A. Morris — Commander of the "Indiana Brigade."

Monday June 3, 1861. Still raining this morning. I was again detailed for guard for 24 hours. About ten o'clock A.M. report came that the troops under Col.s Kelley and Dumont attacked Rebels at Phillippi at 4 A.M. and had been fighting for an hour and half when the messenger left. The news flew like wild fire over the camp, and caused great excitement, and indignation, that we should have been kept here, and not allowed a share of the honor. Another report said that Col. B. F. Kelley was wounded, and another that he was dead, and that a large number of Rebels had been killed, more wounded and still more taken prisoners. that many cattle and horses had been captured.

There were many other reports flying about camp concerning the affair and there is much anxiety to know the facts. This morning the two slaves and two white men who had been taken were sent to headquarters. This afternoon a train passed on which were several cannon and some soldiers, were from Lafayette, Ind.

About sundown two citizens rode up, and were directed to headquarters; soon they returned and called for Capt. Cheek, of Co. "D," who being in command of our camp ordered Lieut. Wm Ellis to take twelve men from "D" & "H" and go with the two citizens about seven miles and get the County officers, so report said.

Tuesday Morning June 4, 1861. Stood guard three hours last night in the rain. Still raining. Was awakened by Orderly Branham, calling for fifteen men to go on Picket above Grafton. Our blankets and clothing all wet. Cleared off about noon. Scouting party under Ellis returned about Ten a.m., they made no captures, but are tired out. This p.m. several wagons passed camp loaded with Muskets captured at Phillippi. Soon several soldiers came in direct from the Battle fields and confirmed many of the reports.

Wednesday June 5, 1861. Was called at 4 o'clock for guard duty, on being releaved at 6 o'clock learned that two Cos. of the 7th had returned from Phillippi. Near noon fifteen men were detailed to go as guards for tents and provisions to the 7th at Philippi. Soon another detail of twenty from Co. "H" was made for same purpose. On the first detail J. E. Boswell and I were left, as we were too small to endure the march, this time we insisted to be given a chance.

We took cars at Grafton and rode to Webster, where we met Lieut. Ellis and his squad of fifteen. Sixth Ind. was here. A heavy rain shower came up, found shelter in a large frame house. While here, soldiers carried Col. Kelley past on way to G.

Met Captain Rabb, just returning from Phillippi, his Co. reached our camp last night. Capt. was detained on the way by an accident. One of his men fell and discharged his gun, the bullet striking one man in the knee and another in the thigh. Capt. remained with the latter, who died this morning and was buried by the Captain near the road. The wagons were loaded and are started at nine p.m. for Phillippi, twelve miles distant.

Our road was a good Turnpike, leading over hills and across narrow deep valleys. About eleven p.m. we commenced the ascent of a long steep hill or mountain. The heavy rain had made the pike wet and very disagreeable walking, and worse for the teams. We rested frequently. When at the top of the long hill were told we were just halfway to Phillippi. After watering the horses at a Spring we trudged on very much fatigued. When the teams stopped to rest we would sit down and generally went to sleep.

Thursday June 6, 1861. At sunrise we arrived on the hill near town where we found the Artillery in camp. A

From the heights overlooking Phillippi, (West) Virginia. This was the Union artillery position and camp site of the 7th Indiana.

dense fog in the valley below hid the Town, River, Camps etc. Winding down around the hill, were soon on the bank of the river. After following its windings for some distance came to a long covered Bridge over which we crossed, and marched to Head Quarters at the Court House, where we stacked Arms and were dismissed. Jos. E. Boswell and myself asked about the battle whereupon an acquaintance of Co. "G" who had been in the battle, and whom we looked upon as a veteran offered to show us over the field, "The bloody battlefield." The first battlefield of the war; or what would have been the first if the enemy had not run. We accepted his kind offer and though much fatigued with

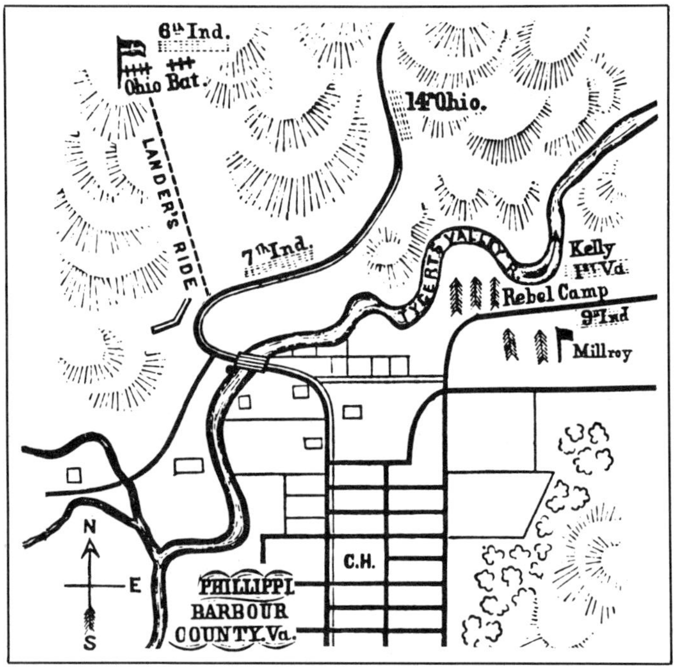

Sketch of Phillippi and Union troop positions.

our all night march in a rain, we started at once, not waiting for our breakfasts. As we walked toward the outskirts of the village, he said, "on that high point to the left of the road over the hill is where Col. Lander placed the Artillery, and when it opened fire and the race began, he rode at full gallop down that steep rocky road to the bridge. The 14th Ohio was on the right of the road and the Sixth Ind. supported the Artillery. The 7th came down the road and were under the hill there when the first shot was fired, which, as it passed directly over us, startled us, and must have caused many of us to dodge and hesitate; for the Col. shouted 'close up boys; close up, if the enemy were to shoot now, they couldn't hit one of you.' This cheered us up and we went at a double quick to and over the bridge, past the baricade and toward the rebel camp. Just at this time Col. Kelley's command appeared on the hill here to our right, coming on the run, but were too late to get in the rear of the enemy and cut off their retreat, for at the first shot they had fled pell-mell helter skelter without boots, hats, coats or pants. A genuine shirt-tail retreat through the town and up the Stanton Pike. Before the ball opened, we were so tired we could scarcely walk, but the excitement gave us new life, and on we rushed after the fleeing foe, until halted two or three miles below town. Some of the Rebels were quartered in houses but most of them were in tents out on that level common."

"The Rebel commander, Col. Porterfield's private Sec'y was secreted in this hay, a soldiers bayonet brought him out in mortal terror, and ready and anxious to take the oath, he said he had been thinking sirously of the matter for some little time. In this stable is where a rebel soldier lost a leg by a solid shot from our artillery, here we found him. See here is the blood. He ran in here to get a horse, he is at the Hotel now. Dr. New assisted to amputate his

limb."*[Then as a later addition to the journal, Billy had penciled in the following: The Rebel soldiers name was Hanger. The Barn belonged to Mr Johnson.]*

There were no Union soldiers killed, and but two wounded, Col. B. F. Kelley of 1st Western Va. Regt. and the commander of the Column of attack on the left; and one private. The enemy were completely routed, with a loss of about forty killed and wounded, and as many taken prisoners, and over twenty-five thousand dollars worth of property including fifteen boxes of old Flint Lock Muskets — just arrived — and a number of fine banners, one on blue silk, presented just two days before, by the ladies of Bath, still fresh with exhortations to bravery and fidelity. We went over the camp, then looked over the village, which is nestled between the right bank of the river on the west, and high hills on the east and south, in fact it appears to be completely hemmed in by the almost mountains. Many of the houses are deserted and the streets dirty and every thing untidy.

After breakfast I went to an old barn loft and slept until dinner. This afternoon the remainder of Co. "H" came. Capt. Gill found quarters for the Co. in a house on east part of town near foot of the hills. The lady said her husband was in the rebel army. Eighteen of us were quartered in one upstairs room.

Friday June 7, 1861. After breakfast Co. "H" was ordered on Picket. Forming in lines we marched north of the town, some distance after crossing river where we found Captain Scott and his Co. of Martinsville. At the Capts. Headquarters, Capt. Gill stopped with twelve men, two stopped on a high hill, and five at the forks of the road. The remainder of the Co. was divided into two equal squads, each went out on one of the roads. Boswell and myself are with the five at the junction of the roads. We were told to keep a constant watch which we did for a time, but as no enemy appeared we grew less vigilant, and in the afternoon we climbed a very high hill near our post, when on top had good view of surrounding hills away to the north could see Mountains. We staid on the hill until one stood watch, an hour at a time while the rest slept.

Phillippi, Va. Saturday June 8, 1861. A beautiful Morning. The timber on the hills and Mts are filled with many birds, some fine singers, when not seen. Almost all of them are very shy. This morning about daybreak heard a number of Whippoorwills, but could not get to see them. Relief came at ten and we returned to town.

Benjamin Franklin Kelley — wounded at Phillippi.

Phillippi, Barbour Co. Va. Sunday June 9, 1861. This has been a beautiful day, had Co. drill at 8 a.m. after dinner J. K. Howard, N. Harris and myself, went upon the hill North East of town, and, lounged under a Sugar Maple tree, and read several chapters in the New Testament. Had Regimental drill at three p.m. and Dress Parade at close. To day a Rebel Captain came in and gave himself up. Said his Co. had deserted him. He was closely questioned and believed to be a good Union man. He was set at liberty on a parole of honor, and started for home, but was brought back.

June 10, 1861. The Captain who came in yesterday was more closely examined to day, and I understand considerable information was obtained from him and others who were questioned. Drill and dressparade same as yesterday. I wrote two letters.

Tuesday June 11, 1861. Another beautiful day. Nothing going on but drilling. It is thought by many that we will march soon. All are anxious to be moving on the rebels. To day two privates of the 9th Ind went foraging, and when after some chickens one shot the other.

Wednesday June 12, 1861. When at the river bathing this morning, I learned that Captain Crawford of Co. "F," 14th Ohio, while officer of the day, and going the grand rounds last night was shot by one of the Pickets. The bullet driving one of the buttons of his coat through his body, he died instantly. The cannon were fired three times in the morning, three times at noon and three times at sundown. Lieut. McLaughlin drilled the Co. by rally by fours. Learned of skirmish near Fort Monroe at Big Bethel Va. at which Union troops were defeated, many killed wounded and prisoners. Cannon were spiked and left. About nine p.m. Capt. Gill came from Headquarters with a batch of mail I received letter from Samuel H. Covert.

Thursday, June 13, 1861. Slept well last night. This morning I straightened up my clothing and rubbed up my gun. Captain Crawford, who was killed by the picket guard was burried to day. The funeral procession was formed as follows. First, was the Captains Co. then the remains, on a Gun carriage then the Martial Band followed by the remainder of the Regt. and other Ohio troops. Also many of the officers and men of Indiana, and Virginia troops, formed in rear. The line moved slowly, stepping to the tap of Muffled Drums, to the Cemetery, where the Co. formed line facing the graves, the remains were lowered. Then three volleys were fired by the Co. "F," and other troops. After the vollies were fired, the Brass Band played the Death Knell. It was a solemn and impressive scene.

This afternoon two Ohio Regts. went to Buckhanan a distance of fifteen miles.

Friday June 14, 1861. I was on guard last night. Ohio Troops did not start to B. until 3 o'clock this morning. A rumor circulated to day to the effect that the Ohio troops on their way to Buckhannan had an engagement with the Rebels, capturing one thousand prisoners, and several hundred horses. Not much credence is placed in the report. Report also says an attack is expected here to night. Many believe the report and quite an excitement prevails.

As most of our mess are on guards, I went with Mess No. 6 for evening devotions.

Phillippi, W.Va. Saturday June 15, 1861. At ten minutes past ten o'clock last night an alarm gun was fired, followed in quick succession by another and one or two small volleys. The long roll was beatten in Camp and we were ordered to get guns and accouterments and load in double quick time. Not many moments elapsed before we were in line and marching for Headquarters. A line was soon formed by Col. Dumont around the Court House. At first Officers and men were very much excited, but soon passed and every thing was as quiet as if on dress parade.

All the troops were in line, with loaded and primed muskets awaiting an attack by the enemy. Were still in line at day break, were then told to rest at will. About sunup Captain Gill, came from Headquarters with our mail. A letter for me from J. L. Jones and Co. Soon Col. came and said there seemed to be no immediate danger of an attack. That we would soon be dismissed· that if there was another alarm for each Co. to form where they were standing. We then went to our quarters. Some were reading letters or papers from home, but generally, the boys were relating how quickly they had got in line and loaded in nine times. Several including myself went to writing letters to inform our friends of the night alarm, and how very bravely we had acted. Nothing more of note transpired until about the time we were ready for Regimental drill. Orders came to pack up, as the regt. would move to the hill north west of town. Our march to our new camp was an irregular affair. Are on a high ridge overlooking the River and town, among large Chestnut Trees, underbrush all cut out and well set in blue grass. The Turnpike to Grafton, just in front of camp. A beautiful place for a camp.

Sabbath, June 16, 1861. This was a beautiful morning. Jos. E. Boswell and myself strayed out of camp, and wandered up and down and over the hills we climbed. When we had climbed a very high hill we saw higher hills, or mountains South East, East and North East of us, which we supposed to be the Laurel Hill range, upon which the rebels are reported to be in large force and strongly fortified, where the Pike to Beverly crosses. In our wanderings we found some fine wild strawberries. It was about two p.m. when we returned to camp, having been far outside our lines and no doubt in great danger of capture. A number of Co. "H" died with measles last night, and was buried late this afternoon with military honors. About sundown I walked down to the bridge to the Breastworks being thrown up to guard against the crossing of the enemy, are not very extensive, but strong.

Monday June 17, 1861. A clear beautiful day. Nothing of note occurred till while on drill, Colonel ordered all Captains to assemble at his headquarters immediately after drill. This, we privates thought indicated a move of some kind. When they returned the orderlies were ordered to get rations for Twenty four hours, which confirmed our guesses. Was soon quite an excitement about camp. All seemed glad of a prospective chance to get at the rebels, and the Boys began with out orders to pack up.

Tuesday June 18, 1861. All last night we momentarily expected to be called upon to march, or for some kind of hard duty. Although anxious to go where ever duty might call yet it was very pleasant to remain in camp and enjoy a

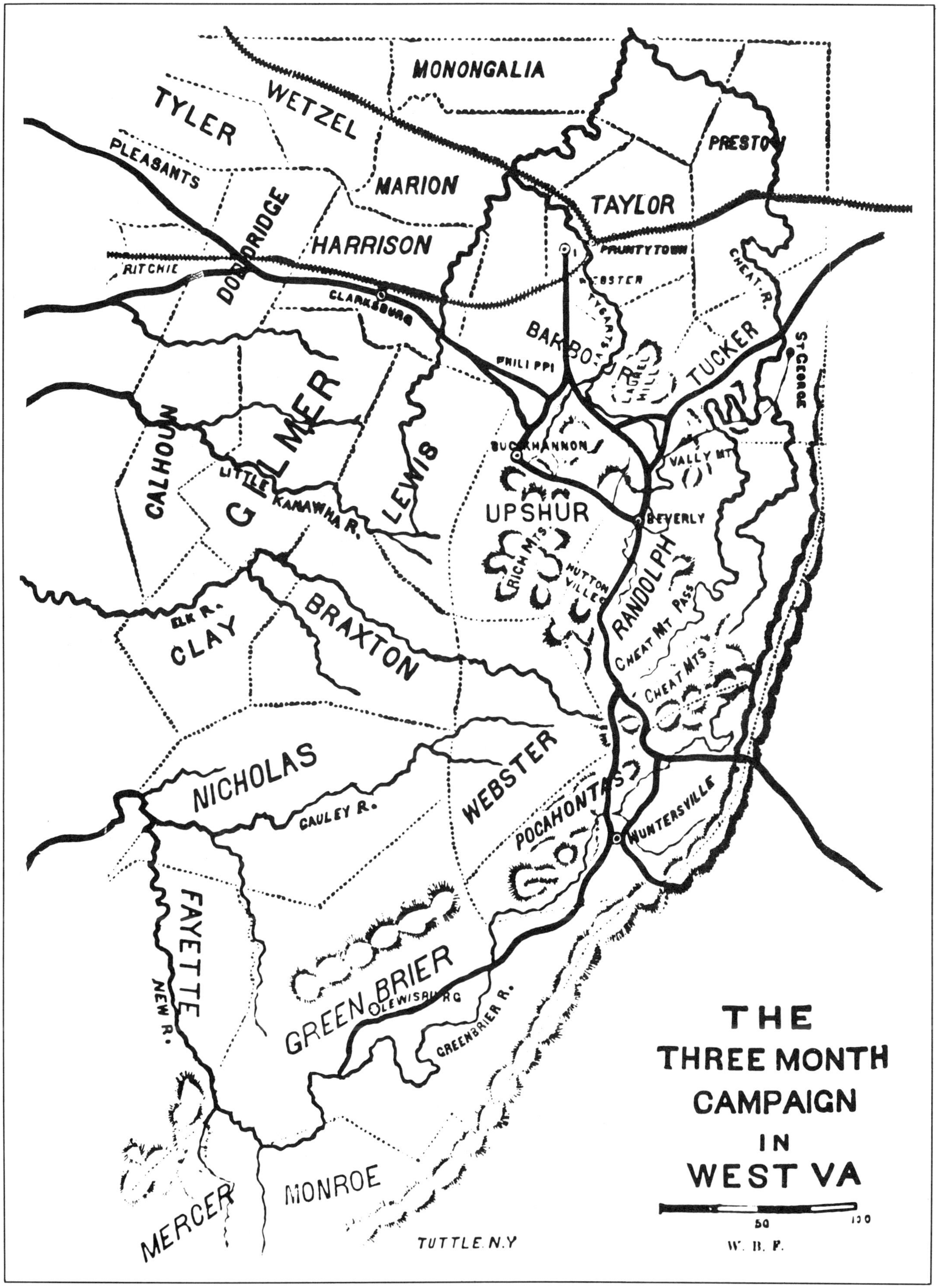

The 1861 (West) Virginia Campaign area.

quiet nights rest. Some did not sleep much. This morning a hundred rumors are about camp as to why we were not called upon to march. Some however begin to doubt whether a march was intended, and some say an attack was expected. That the Col. thought best to remain and receive the comers, and such a reception as it would have been has not been, has not tendered many rebels. This afternoon a report is out that two Ohio boys were shot by Rebel Bushwhackers while out scouting. This p.m. Co. "H" were ordered on Picket. With haversacks our blankets and guns we formed, then marched, a short distance past the bridge on the Buckhanan road where we relieved Lieut Day of Capt. Scotts Co. "K" of 7th Ind. Myself with five others stayed with Lieut McLaughlin in a house.

Our post was in the road not far from the bridge. While I was on guard, between One and Two o'clock, Two horsemen came through town at full speed, but were halted at the bridge. Soon the drums beat the long roll and quite a stir was heard in camp. Lieut McLaughlin went to the bridge and there learned that the Cavalry or mounted scouts had been attacked, routed, and all killed or taken prisoners by two. An hour later a number of the scouts came in and halted near the bridge, formed line, numbered, and called the roll. Thirty three present.

Wednesday June 19, 1861. I understand this morning that one of the horsemen who came in last night in such a hurry, received a shot through the top of his hat. They came here yesterday from Grafton as guards for Capt. Terry, of our regt. who went to G for money to pay us.

We have now been paid Five Dollars in Indiana State Bank money. To day I was taken to Town and placed on guard at Provost Marshal headquarters.

This afternoon four Companies of Infantry and a number of horsemen, started, rumor says to attack some Rebel camp. A report is current that a Federal Lieut was captured yesterday.

Thursday June 20, 1861. A beautiful day. Still on guard. Nothing of note.

Friday June 21, 1861. Report about camp to effect that we are going home soon. It appears that we are not to get in another battle, if not we had as well be at home. Yesterday and to day there have been newspapers in camp for sale. Soldiers were all willing to buy but the newsboys could not change our five dollar bills. Boys are all in fine spirits to night. Some are reading papers, others writing, but most are singing.

Saturday June 22, 1861. Last night was a fearful one. One of the worst wind and rain storms I was ever in passed our camp. It took all of us to keep number 6 tent to the ground. Word came this evening that Gen. George B. McClellan, commander of this department would be here soon. If he comes it is thought there will be some fighting done. We are now on Picket.

Sabbath June 23, 1861. A beautiful morning. A perfect storm of rumors in camp to day. The one most joyfully received says there will be four or five thousand new troops in from Grafton to day. Brigadier Gen. Hill of Ohio will be with Ohio troops. About three o'clock p.m. the 6th Ohio Regt. and 9th Ind. and one Virginia Regt. and the 7th were ordered in line and marched about two miles out on the Webster road where we waited at the side of the road about two hours for Gen. Hill and his troops, but they did not come we then went to our several drill grounds and after parade came to camp. Col. Dumont was out with us to day he looks quite slim having had ague. Report says he was a soldier in the Mexican war, and in several battles. Cos. "C," "D," and "I" were ordered out at ten P.M. no one knows where.

Colonel Dumont — returned after malarial fever.

Near Phillippi June 24, 1861. This morning I learned that an attack was expected, the enemy being within five miles of camp. It is said that the three Cos. ordered out last night were placed on guard a mile or two from town. On going out on regimental drill this afternoon we were rejoiced to find Col. Dumont at the head of the Battalion, after putting us through a number of evolutions, he formed the regt. by divisions and marched us over a steep hill and across a deep hollow, then we formed by Companies and while on the side of the hill we wheeled to the left, and when half way up the hill Col. gave the command "Double Quick," and the Captains ordered arms at a "right shoulder shift," and away we went. Some fell and most of us stumbled about some over others. Bayonetts were fixed. Saw one man going to camp with a bloody face, none were siriously injured.

This evening two of Co. "H" fell to quarrelling, hot words passed knucks, clubs and blows followed, and they were sent to the guard house.

Tuesday June 25, 1861. This morning my friend Thos Williams of Franklin Ind. called and reported that the remaining Six Cos. of his Regt. 6th Ind. had arrived at an early hour this morning. While on Co. Drill Major Oyler ordered the sick to pack up and be ready at noon to go to Grafton. It is said that some with sore feet ran to ask if they were to go too. We suspect that a march is expected. While our mess were at dinner and we had a good one —

The Ohio Zouaves, "German Turners" of Cincinnati, passed our camp. All brave hearty looking fellows. Sick did not start until near night. About sundown orders came for Co. "H" to go on advance Picket, we were soon ready with guns and blankets, and with the Major at the head of the line. Adjutant Gavin soon overtook us. About two and half miles out on the Webster road, we turned to the right and followed a dirt road down a small stream for half mile when we halted. Six trusty men were taken some distance ahead and two left at the forks of the road, and two were farther out on each of the small roads. The remainder of the Co. were placed in ambush on the right of the road above a fence on the side of a steep hill. We were hurried from camp without water, and were not permitted to fill canteens on the way. Orderly Branham being a good natured fellow, said if some would take the Canteens, he would go with them for water. Five of us started for a spring near a mile back, and as it was very dark we concluded that brook water would do. When we have lain in ambush for near a mile back, and many were asleep it was decided that our position was not well taken. A prospecting party were sent out, and soon returned reporting a much better place. The Sleepers were arroused and we groped and stumbled our way along for near one hundred yards and halted. Some selected posts or trees behind which to fight if the enemy came while others prepared for sleeping. Just then it began to rain. I lay down under my gum blanket, but the hill was so steep I could not stay under it.

Wednesday June 26, 1861. We had a fearful time on picket, it rained all night, and we got but little sleep, but a thorough wetting. Started for camp at daybreak and were near headquarters when the morning gun was fired at sun-up. Found a good warm breakfast awaiting us. Rained several hard showers to day. Blankets and clothing all wet, and no sun to dry them.

Friday June 28, 1861. Nothing of note yesterday. Clear weather has enabled us to dry our clothing and blankets. The Virginia troops who have been living in brush tents or booths now have good tents. Captains Lord & Cheek, occupying Grabbers Hill to the right of our position have fortified.

Saturday June 29, 1861. This afternoon when ready for regimental drill, were ordered out along with other troops here to meet Gen. T. A. Morris of Indiana. Upon the Generals arrival the cannon fired a salute and the regiments formed beside the road presented as the General and his escort passed. Several regiments accompanied the Gen. from Grafton & Webster. The Gen. pitched his headquarters tents on our parade ground.

June 30, 1861. We retired early but were called up about Midnight and ordered to prepare to march with one days rations. Report says some rebels were heard of with a wagon forage train out about Nine Miles. Eight Companies, four of the 7th Indiana, including "H" started at half past one. Ohio troops in front. Over hills, rocks and across hollows, we went, the 9th as fast as they could go, and we trying hard to keep up. At day break we were on high ridge from which we could see Laural Hills to our left, where rebels are to be strongly fortified. Sunup found us at Meadowville where we expected to find the Enemy in force. They were not there having passed during the early part of the night. As we neared the village, two or three persons were seen making double quick time across some fields and over the hills.

After resting a few moments, formed line and Col. commanded "about face," and we started on our return. Soon it commenced raining, and continued all day. On the return the four Companies of 7th were in the advance, and having been so sorely pressed to keep up with the 9th now got down to their best marching gait, and it is said kept the 9th on the double quick time much of the time. Many of the boys gave out. We reached camp about ten o'clock, having marched eighteen miles over Mountains in Eight hours and a half.

Monday July 1st, 1861. Was still raining this morning. Orders to clean up guns and arrange for Review and general Inspection at 11 o'clock A.M. The Ohio Regt. and 6th and 9th Ind. were inspected in the A.M. The 7th went to the parade ground about one p.m. When we had made a few maneuvers, a severe wind and rain storm came up. We went to quarters; The Inspection was by Major Love of the Regular Army. Report says rebels are evacuating Laural Hill.

Tuesday July 2, 1861. A report is in circulation that ex. Gov. Wise of Va. had sent word that he would be into this camp for breakfast, July 4th. Many express a desire that he would come. While on regimental drill, the Artillery rgt. came on to our parade ground. Col. Dumont ordered us over the fence into the wagon yard where we formed line then ordered a charge through an Orchard and up "Grabbers Hill," where two Cos. of this regt. have fortified and are supporting the Artillery, forming line we rested at will for a few minutes, then Attention was called and Col. marched us down the North East side of the hill into the road near the river, then to the parade ground, where we found the Artillery executing some maneuvers. After Dress Parade, went to camp. It seemed to please the Col. to see us privates climbing the fences and scampering over the hills. Last night while lying in my tent I accidentally saw a Comet in the north. I was somewhat surprised, as I had not heard that one was visable.

July 3, 1861. Last night eighteen privates of Co. "H" went out the Webster river road on picket. About 11 o'clock A.M. today while at an early dinner an alarm gun was fired, and the Long Roll beaten, we dropped dishes, dinner and every thing and rushed to our tents for our fighting rigs, a hasty line was formed on Co. street and we marched to the place assigned us by the Col. a few days ago in case of an attack. All the Regt. except "D" & "G" (on "Grabbers Hill") are in a line extending from Cols. Headquarters on our left, Southward along the road in front of our Camp. Here we waited in great suspense for some time, Momentarily expecting an attack. Runners were sent to the front. No enemy appeared and could not be found. We were dismissed with instructions to remain in quarters, ready for duty at a moments warning. It was subsequently learned that the 6th Indiana had been out firing by plattoons.

Near Phillippi, Va. Thursday July 4, 1861. This was a beautiful morning, and continued fine all day. Immediately after the morning gun, one was fired for each state of the Union including all the so called Seceded States. The Stars and Stripes proudly floated from each Co. headquarters. About nine o'clock A.M. Maj. Oyler went to Grabbers Hill, where the Grabber Boys raised a very tall pole and ran the grand Old Flag to the top, and the major made a speech. On his return we were told to prepare for review at eleven o'clock. At the appointed hour, all were ready, with clothing and accouterments in order and muskets as bright as if just from the manufactory. All the Brigade formed Column by regiments on our parade ground fronting an improvised stand around which were two Brass Bands, and a large Choir of Singers selected from the Volunteers of the several Regiments, of the number was T. J. Morgan, Thos Tilson, and others of Co. "H" and the several field officers. The Choir sang "Star Spangled Banner" and Band played "My Country tis of Thee." After Prayer by ______ the "Declaration of Independence" was read by a private in an Ohio Battery, followed by Vocal and Instrumental Music. After which we listened to a good Oration by a Lieutenant Colonel. Said he hoped to have been permitted to deliver his Oration to us on Laural Hill. After more excellent music and the Benediction, we repaired to our quarters. This has been a very pleasant 4th differing from a Celebration of the 4th at home only in the better order through Regimental organisations; and the absence of the Ladies, small boys and Gingerbread.

July 5, 1861. The Guthrie Grays, 6th Ohio Regt. arrived late yesterday, the day being exceedingly warm many gave out on the road from Webster and were brought in wagons.

Two Secession officers were taken prisoners and brought into camp. A skirmish took place between Federal pickets, a Confederate is thought to have been killed as a horse was captured. Some arms and two Rebels were taken this evening.

Saturday July 6, 1861. This afternoon a Captain brought in a Rebel with his arms tied with a rope sitting behind him on a horse. Co. "H" went on Picket except a few left here for guard duty tomorrow. I was of the number left in camp and went to bed at ten but was awakened at eleven with orders to prepare for a long march to start at One A.M. Every body flew about in great haste cooking provision, taking down tents, packing etc. etc. Is usual amount of wondering and guessing where we are going to. Though the prevailing opinion is that we are bound for Laural Hill.

It is proper to mention here two incidents that occurred at this camp, not found in my diary, but very vividly recalled. The first occurred in a day or two after we pitched our tents. It grew out of our Co. being left at Grafton as guards at time of fight at Phillippi. Some of the boys believed that Captain Gill had requested that "H" be left. One day Edw. Meyers got drunk enough to be foolish and accused the Capt. to his face of being a coward, whereupon the Captain, being an Englishman and a good Boxer, slapped Meyers over. Meyers, got to his feet and taking a stage position, "By the Eternals I'll avenge this wrong," but he never did.

The second was a day or two before leaving camp, was the visit of Whitelaw Reid, "Agate" of Cincinnati Gazette, *from the Column under Gen. McClellan at Buckhanan, while here he dined with Officers of Co. "H." He sent a glowing account to the* Gazette *describing minutely our several camps, and paying a very high tribute to the soldiers; Materially augmented our numbers and greatly strengthened our positions.*

Colonel George Alexander Porterfield, the Confederate commander at Phillippi. He would be criticized for "want of forethought and vigilance."

Destination: A Foreign Shore

One thousand young men on one train for a total of 27 hours! Billy wrote mostly of the scenery and only once mentioned any orneriness — that was the destruction of the Grog Shop in Urbana, Ohio. Farther east, the folks in Zanesville "touched the hearts" of the 7th Indiana, wrote Orville Thomson. Assistant Surgeon Kemper recorded that anyone who was there, would never forget it. The 9th Indiana had passed through earlier and alerted the town to the 7th's coming. Just as Billy was impressed with the food baskets, Thomson wrote of "bread well buttered" and "meats of many kinds." Adding to this binge, the regimental historian recorded that "great barrels" of Wheeling Stogies were passed out later.[(1)]

Perhaps as time went on, the citizens of those small Ohio railroad towns became exhausted — or smarter. An early 20th century Cambridge, Ohio historian wrote of his boyhood: "During the war days I tried making a little money by selling apples and cakes to the passengers on the trains, down at the station. I bought my cakes [from the baker] for ten cents a dozen, and sold them at the rate of three for five cents [or 100 per cent profit.] Trains loaded with soldiers would pass through Cambridge frequently, and it was then I had the best business. These soldier trains were made up of 10 or 15 boxcars each. The soldiers sat on boards placed crosswise in the cars. Side doors were kept open for ventilation. At the rear was a passenger coach in which the officers would ride."[(2)] When Billy Davis passed through Cambridge for the first time, foodstuffs were lavished freely on the soldiers and even Privates smoked cigars in passenger coaches.

The Railroads of the 1860s

The basic design of railroad cars has not changed much since 1861. Billy would have entered a passenger coach using a platform and door at one end. He would have seen two soft bench seats on each side of a center aisle, overhead there were kerosene lamps for light, and stoves at each end for heat (when needed). Boxcars and flat cars of the Civil War era were small by today's standards but otherwise similar. In the north, the wood-burning locomotives could click along at 60 miles an hour under the best of conditions — a light load and a good road bed. Forty miles an hour on malleable iron tracks was the norm for the day.[(3)]

The scheduling and dispatching of wartime trains was less than efficient, or safe. At best, there would be reliable schedules and confirming telegraph messages. At its worst, as one author wrote, "the trains moved with no orders except those dictated by caution, courage and necessity."[(4)]

With Indianapolis as the western terminus, the Indianapolis and Bellfontaine (Ohio) Railroad, which Billy boarded, ran northeastward to Muncie and then angled directly east and crossed into Ohio at Union (now Union City). The cars left the Bellfontaine road at Union, were switched to the Central Ohio Railroad line, and proceeded eastward through Columbus, Zanesville, and Barnesville, terminating at Bellaire.

Bellaire is four miles south of Wheeling on the west bank of the Ohio River. On the east bank lay Benwood, Virginia. (Forty-eight counties of northwestern Virginia, which encompassed Wheeling and Benwood, became West Virginia upon receiving statehood in 1863. Two more counties joined in later.)

Typical rolling stock of the 1860s.

A recruitment station for Union soldiers in Morgantown, (West) Virginia.

In 1861, Benwood, Virginia was the western terminal for the Baltimore and Ohio main line. The B&O Railroad controlled nearly 3,800 engines and cars for the 513 miles of line.[5] The railroad, with its eastern extremities at Baltimore and Washington D.C., had been stretched westward to Benwood and Wheeling, Virginia in 1853. An auxiliary branch, the Northwestern Virginia Railroad, had been completed from Grafton, Virginia to the Ohio River at Parkersburg, Virginia in 1857. This giant railroad system would be of strategic importance to both the Union and the Confederacy. Whoever commanded the B&O would have easy access to the enemy. In June of 1861, the line was split, held in part by both the Union forces and the Confederate forces — in other words, Yanks and Rebs were both riding the B&O line.[6]

The Military Situation in Western Virginia

To Billy, the trip into "disputed territory" on the B&O mainline was wondrous — but of major military and political significance. The trans-Allegheny Mountain counties of Virginia were predominantly Unionist although caution was the watchword as loyalties were divided. This was an area of brother-against-brother and neighbor-against-neighbor.

Both governments, North and South, were appealing to the men of western Virginia. Union General George B. McClellan, asked on May 26, "Now that we are in your midst, I call upon you to fly to arms and support the general government, sever the connections that bind you to traitors."[7] Likewise, Robert E. Lee, thought by many to be the most astute military mind in the South, was charged with tying western Virginia to the Confederacy.[8]

McClellan, the Department Commander of Ohio at the time, understood that the greatest threat to his military responsibility (Ohio) was along its southeastern boundary. To carry out his mission, McClellan would execute a "good" offense in western Virginia as his best defense of Ohio.

Both sides were taking action to control the B&O. The Confederates had already captured B&O rolling stock and rail yards at Harper's Ferry on April 18 — the day after Virginia seceded. Union forces, under the command of Colonel Benjamin F. Kelley, first entered western Virginia by train on May 27.

The political uncertainty in western Virginia was of vital concern to the Confederacy. To stabilize the area, General Lee intended to establish a military post at Wheeling, across the river and only four miles from the Union camps at Bellaire. Another camp would be set up at Parkersburg, three more at Grafton and one at Harper's Ferry.[9]

To support this plan, Lee ordered Colonel George A. Porterfield and his 750 troops to secure the rail center at Grafton. On June 1, Porterfield was at Phillippi, 15 miles from Grafton. That same day, approximately 4,000 Union soldiers stepped off the trains at Grafton.[10] There would be no Confederate camp at Grafton.

The Battle of Phillippi

Companies D and H of the 7th Indiana were designated for guard duty "near Grafton" when the first land battle of the Civil War was fought at Phillippi. Billy Davis, of Company H, expressed his personal feelings at being left behind as "disappointment and bitter dissatisfaction."

The shelling of Phillippi.

Brigadier General Thomas Morris, from Indianapolis, was the new Union army commander at Grafton. It was he who approved Colonel Kelley's earlier plan for a difficult two-pronged attack. This pincer movement was to be made upon Colonel Porterfield and the Confederates at Phillippi. Kelley took command of one "prong" of 1,600 men with Ebenezer Dumont in charge of the other force of 1,400 men. Dumont's column included the eight companies from the 7th Indiana. The two bands of men would start out nine miles apart but were to converge on Phillippi at four in the morning of June 3. Kelley began his march at noon on June 2 and Dumont left his jumping-off-point at eight that evening.(11)

Rain, thunder and lightning that night added to the difficulty for the Union troops as they made their way over the rugged terrain. Dumont's command reached its destination at precisely four o'clock and immediately started firing upon Phillippi. Unfortunately for the boys in blue, Kelley did not arrive for another 15 minutes — and he approached from the wrong direction. According to the plan, it was Kelley who was to snare the fleeing Confederates. The Confederates fled the streets of Phillippi, as anticipated, but none were captured. The Union forces occupied Phillippi and the "battle" was heralded in Washington as a great Union victory.(12) However, the American Civil War's first land battle had been fought without loss of life — to be recorded in Civil War military history as The Phillippi Races.

END NOTES

(1) Thomson, *Seventh Indiana;* p. 16-17. Also, Kemper, *War Papers;* p. 121.

(2) William G. Wolfe, *Stories of Guernsey County, Ohio* (Cambridge, Ohio, 1943); pp. 290-291. The story was related to Wolfe by William Harris.

(3) George Edgar Turner, *Victory Rode the Rails* (Indianapolis, 1953); p. 40-43.

(4) *Ibid,.* p. 44.

(5) Festus P. Summers, *The Baltimore and Ohio in the Civil War* (New York, 1939); p. 44. The B&O holdings included 236 freight and passenger locomotives; 128 passenger coaches; and 3,451 coal, freight and ballast cars.

(6) *Ibid.*, pp. 15-18. Also, for further discussion and photographs, see Stan Cohen, *The Civil War in West Virginia: A Pictorial History* (Charleston, 1985); p. 16.

(7) George B. McClellan, *McClellan's Own Story* (New York, 1887); p. 51. That same day, McClellan urged his own men to ". . . cross the frontier and enter upon the soil of Virginia. Your mission is to restore peace and confidence, to protect the majesty of the law and rescue your brethren from the grasp of armed traitors."

(8) Boyd B. Stutler, *West Virginia in the Civil War* (Charleston, 1966); p. 24.

(9) *Ibid.*

(10) Ibid., p. 26.

(11) Robert Blair Boem, *The Civil War in Western Virginia: the Decisive Battles of 1861.* (Ohio State University, 1957); p. 35-37. Boem relates a story (and cites a source) of a soldier in the 7th Indiana, Private Charles Denger, who mortally wounded himself while crossing a creek on the march to Phillippi. Private Denger is probably the unidentified man Billy recorded (on June 5) as dying the night of June 4. Captain Rabb evidently told Billy of how two men were injured by the accidental discharge of a gun. One was mortally wounded. It is likely this was the same Private Charles Denger who was buried along the Webster-Phillippi road. Regimental historian Orville Thomson did not mention this incident and Terrell, *Indiana Adjutant Generals Report*, indicates that a Charles Denger, Company I was "[k]illed in West Va. about June 15, '61."

(12) Eva Margaret Carnes, *The Tygart Valley Line: June-July 1861* (Clarksburg, 1961); pp. 44-46. Carnes provides much local history and folklore in addition to the battle description.

James Edward Hanger, first man to be wounded by a cannonball (at Phillippi) and first man to have leg amputated in the Civil War. While convalescing he designed and constructed homemade artificial legs which he made available to other amputees. Today this undertaking continues as the J. E. Hanger Company.

PICTURE CREDITS

—35— (From left to right, top to bottom:) courtesy the Drake Well Museum, Tutusville, Pennsylvania; *The Baltimore and Ohio in the Civil War* by Festus Summers; courtesy USAMHI; the Howard Steamboat Museum, Jeffersonville, Indiana; the B & O Railroad Museum, Baltimore, Maryland.

—36— *The Baltimore and Ohio in the Civil War.*

—37— *The Soldier of Indiana.*

—38— Courtesy, The Barbour County (West Virginia) Historical Society, Hazel Lindsey Wolfe and Patricia McCauley, current President.

—38— *The Soldier of Indiana.*

—39— Courtesy, USAMHI.

—41— *The Soldier of Indiana.*

—42— *The Tygart Valley Line,* courtesy, Barbour County Historical Society.

—44— Courtesy, Barbour County Historical Society.

—45— Courtesy, USAMHI.

—46— Courtesy, West Virginia University, Morgantown.

—47— Courtesy, Library of Congress.

—47— *The Tygart Valley Line.*

CHAPTER 4 WE LEARN THAT WE HAVE SUDDENLY BECOME HEROES

Sunday July 7, 1861. We were ready and started at the appointed hour. Passed through Phillippi following the Staunton Pike. Brigadier Gen. T. A. Morris, of Ind. is in command of this column. The march was uneventful, except frequent stops. At day light were in sight of Laural Hills. When it became light we found that while the road led over very considerable hills that Tygarts Valley River lay near on our right.

About eight o'clock came to a considerable stream where the column was halted, and soon the advanced regiments began forming line on both sides of the road. The position of the 7th was about half way up the hill on the left of the road. After advancing perhaps half mile, skirmishing began, with only an occasional shot. Capt. Moodys Co. of 9th Ind. had been deployed as skirmishers and were advancing. We halted and rested for some time,

Union troops in line of battle at Belington, July 8, 1861.

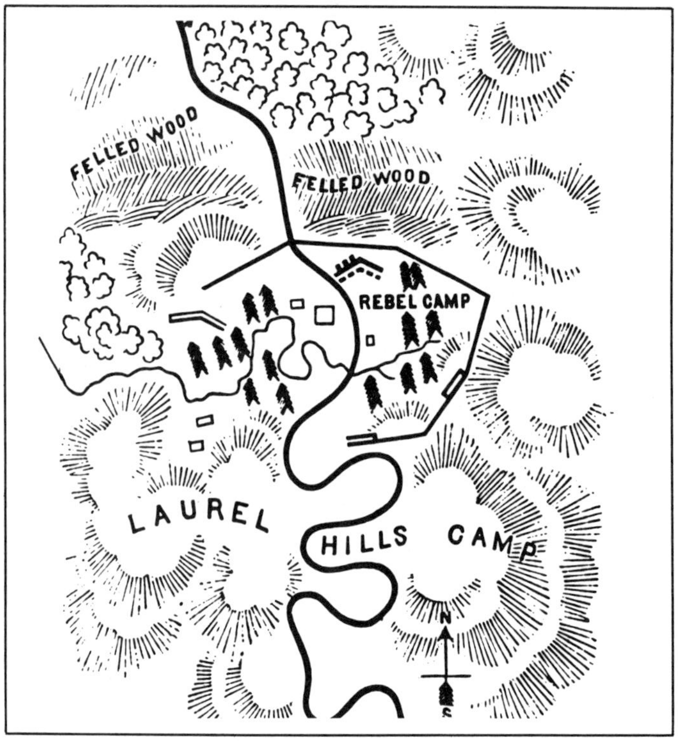

Union camps were west of the north-south road.

a shower of rain came up. I lay down on some brush and put my gum blanket over me. The shower was a short one and the sun came out but I had gone to sleep; and when I awakened, was as hot as if in a Bake oven. Report says Capt. Moody drove the enemy, and had lost one killed and one missing. During the afternoon we moved up to an old orchard, near the village of Belington. Is small place only few houses. Skirmish line has advanced to edge of timber at foot of hill beyond town. Frequent stops are exchanged by the skirmishers.

During a quiet at the front, some of the boys with out officers or orders, went into town, and began foraging, being in long range of Rebel pickets they opened fire and advanced driving our front line back into town. This started the foragers in a hurry, but most of them had secured something. Some had meat, bread, pans of milk, chickens, quilts, blankets, pillows, and one fellow a feather bed. They found the houses deserted. Understand Gen. Morris has ordered everything returned. It is said we have stopped here to await an attack by Gen. McClellan from Buckhanan.

Belington, Va. July 8, 1861. Last night we formed line and slept on our arms, but were aroused several times, by the pickets firing. About 8 o'clock this A.M. while I was writing a letter to J. L. Jones & Co. of Franklin, Ind, were called into line, and now at nine o'clock the left wing of the 7th is at a fence facing to the South East, while the right wing is at a fence behind us facing to the North west. Are all waiting in line. Can hear Bugle calls in Rebel camp and an occasional shot at the front. Belington lies to our right beyond the 9th. on the Pike. In front of Belington is a coneshaped hill on right of road, densely covered with timber. On left of road and more directly in our front is another round hill also timbered. Our picket line is at or near the border of this timber. It was on the hill to right where Captain Moody lost the two men yesterday. The one killed was Wm. T. Girrard, he with others had advanced well into the timber and up the hill when shot in the head. The soldiers have named the hill for the hero. Gen. Morris has established his headquarters at the Elliott farm house where we first formed. The owner is said to be a bitter rebel. We were dismissed and again called into line twice before noon. Were in line several times this afternoon. About five o'clock P.M. rebels came farther down the hill. Federals advanced, but rebels being behind trees our boys could do nothing. A few shots from a Battery dropped into the timber sent the rebels back in a hurry and our boys after them. More immediately in our front is an old field with here and there a clump of bushes, or briars, or a pile of logs. These were held by our skirmishers. John Anton, a private of the 9th Ind. having taken a revolver from the person of a rebel officer killed in a skirmish, advanced to the road and at a favorable opportunity, crossed the road and entered the Laurel, two shots were fired, followed by a shrill scream of agony which still rings in my ears. Our skirmishers dashed into the woods, and there found Anton's bleeding, lifeless body. In one advance our men went far enough it is said to see the rebel camp and breastwork. Beside Anton killed we had two wounded. It is thought several rebels were killed.

Belington, Va. July 9, 1861. I should have mentioned in yesterdays record that Brown a private of the 6th Ind. went in the face of six rebels who were behind a crude earthwork and carried from a tree near by some cooking utensils and blankets; and placing them safely; returned, but on his way back with more blankets, the rebels fired, he turned and replied with a deliberate shot, then walked quietly and firmly to his comrades, and said, "I am shot but the Cowards don't know it."

To day the hill to our right, now known as "Girard Hill" was taken from a Georgia Regt. by fifteen privates without an officer. They took one prisoner and found many articles of contraband. They found the young man Girard, who was killed on Sunday, he had been partially buried, — one hand being left out. Some officer or scout discovered the enemy cutting timber on a hill in front of their camp. A few shells from our Cannon dispersed them. Not so much firing today and we were not called to our place so frequently. Have had summer showers to day.

July 10, 1861. This morning a detail was made from our regt. to cut a road up the side of a hill, where a battery was placed with good range of part of the enemys camp. Early this afternoon two bodies of troops were seen to leave the rebel camp; the 14th Ohio and 9th Ind. prepared to meet them; soon they appeared in the timber in our front; quite an engagement ensued, the enemy gave back; and as our line advanced, the rebel cavalry attempted a flank attack; the Union line fell back and the enemy advanced again. A few shells from our artillery sent them in a hurry to shelter in the timber, when our troops advanced again, the rebels were driven still farther back, but again rallied, and in turn forced our troops to shelter behind their logs & bushes. The Artillery again opened fire. Col. Milroy, on our main line listening, heard the skirmishers shout "farther to the right." A few shots thrown as directed soon dispersed the enemy. John R. Smith a young man

Company C of the 9th Indiana.

who had walked thirty miles to enlist was killed. Have not yet learned the number wounded.

Late this afternoon a scouting party of about five hundred, under command of Col. Dumont went out, they passed through a vacated rebel camp, and some distance beyond, and for fear of an attempt to cut them off, they returned by another route, reaching camp near dark.

July 11, 1861. About dark yesterday Co. "H" was ordered to prepare for picket duty. We went up the valley to the right and not far from the river, and were posted in a "Sugar Camp," our advance near that of the enemy, with very strict orders to watch with the greatest caution. Just as we were stationed a heavy thunder storm came up, rained very hard for some time, and continued a wetting drizzle all night. Had a very exciting alarm last night. Horace Weaver, being of the advanced post, thought he saw an enemy crouched at a tree. He calls his musket "Betsy." He called out "Halt, who comes there," and getting no response, said "Betsy, if you ever did your duty, do it now" and fired, the reserve sprang to their feet and prepared for defense, supposing we had been attacked. The long roll was sounded in both camps, and friend and foe stood in line of battle for several hours, in a rain, each expecting a night attack, all because Betsy was required to do her duty. An examination this morning proved the object fired at to have been a sugar trough. When we returned to camp found our Cook had arrived. I received two letters. Some occasional shots are fired, at which we rally to our place along the fence. Has rained most of the day.

Friday July 12, 1861. A cloudy gloomy morning, but cleared off by ten A.M. Just before noon, orders came to fall in, five minutes after found the 7th and 9th Ind. in the line to go, as we supposed, for the hundredth time to our place in line. Very few took coat, canteen or Haversack and perhaps not one a blanket; but without stopping at the line we pushed on thru Belington, into the woods, around Girard Hill, to our right, and another hill to our left, emerging from the dense forest, at a turn of the road to the left, found the timber in front felled, forming a strong abatis, with the Rebel works in full view, having complete command of the road as it curved to the left around the mountain. Could see persons moving about the works and camp in an excited manner, and momentarily expected fight to commence, but were much relieved when we saw the Stars and Stripes, float from the enemies flag pole. Gen. Morris learning that the enemy had likely evacuated, had sent a company in advance. When we saw our Old Flag, hearty cheer after cheer made the welkin ring. Passed the works, then the deserted camp to a second line of works at the foot of the main mountain, where we found the road obstructed by fallen timber. Not far from the Rebel camp were several newly made graves. Were many tents and four or five Cannon spiked, beside other things of value. The encampment and fortifications were in the open fields of large farm far up the side of Laurel Hill. The road and opening at several places were commanded by Rifle Pits and places for artillery. At the first obstruction in the road, were joined by some Artillery, — Barnetts Ohio — and then pushed on to summit, finding and removing many obstructions of timber from the road. Then down the Southern slope to a clear sparkling stream, where the column, consisting of 7th and 9th Ind. halted, when a rush was made for the water. When some one called out poison!

Henry Washington Benham, first in the 1837 West Point class, led the pursuit of the Confederates to Corrick's Ford.

poison!! The boys stopped for a minute, but being very thirsty soon concluded there was not poison enough in the so call Southern Confederacy to effect such a stream.

While resting here General T. A. Morris and staff came up. Then a rapid march of about four miles brought us to the foot of the mountain near Leedsville, here the 7th halted in an old orchard at edge of timber while bridge over Leeds Creek was being repaired. While here scouts reported that the Rebel column, in their hasty retreat, had followed the Pike to near Beverly, had about faced and retraced their steps to Leedsville where they had taken the Rowlsburgh Pike. At this place we took supper, two crackers and small piece of meat. Moving short distance to our left along a road we stopped for the night. Without Coats, Blankets or bedding, hunger, fatigue, excitement and a pelting rain with no shelter robbed us of rest and sleep, fires were built and we stood around them trying to warm our chilled bodies, looking and longing for the first peep of day.

Saturday July 13, 1861. During the early part of the night the remainder of Gen. Morris' Brigade arrived. By four o'clock we were on the move. The 14th Ohio in the lead. The 7th Ind. next followed by the 9th Ind. Close after the Ohio troops was one section of Artillery. All under the immediate command of Capt. H. W. Benham of the Regular Army, and member of Gen. Morris' staff.

A few miles of rapid marching brought us to a considerable stream which we waded. Reaching the Rowlesburg Pike we turned to the left, and followed that, coming in a few miles to a Rebel encampment of the night before. Supposed to have been the rear guard of Cavalry. Going a short distance were halted. Some said for breakfast, but that was scarcely necessary, as we had but one small piece of bread. After resting for a time we pushed on through the village of New Interest and two miles beyond where the enemy had turned to the right upon a mountain road, following this country road, had gone but a short distance when we found it obstructed with large trees recently felled.

A drizzling rain commenced about six o'clock; which by ten was a drenching storm and so continued for several hours. A detail of men with axes were sent to the front. We were evidently gaining on the enemy who now began to throw away articles of weight, or of little value, and as we pressed them closer, they left Tents, Trunks, Knapsacks, Clothing and Blankets. The Van and Rear guard frequently exchanged shots and Rebel axes forming barricades, and Union axes removing answered to each other. A squad were driven from their fire while cooking their breakfast. A banner taken was born back along the line, and very much increased the exhilaration of the jaded troops.

The tramping of the retreating and advancing columns worked the clay road into a sticky mud. This became thin with the heavy rain till it ran down the Mountain side in sluggish streams after us. We passed wagons broken or fast on trees or in the mud. The harness having been cut from the team. Several wagons had been tumbled down steep places. Some times going down for hundreds of feet.

Soldiers on the march.

About noon came to Shavers Fork, or main branch of Cheat River. At a point near Kalers ford. While walking along the bank in the pelting rain, some one started the familiar old Hymn, "On Jordans Stormy banks I Stand." It seemed in some respect so appropriate that the regiment at once joined in the song till the hills and rocks echoed and reached the exalted strain, but the casting of "a wistful eye beyond" showed signs of the enemy at bay, and the singing ceased suddenly when an orderly came up hastily and said the Rebels were in position but a short distance ahead. The step was quickened and when we reached the ford could plainly see the enemies wagon train across a meadow less than one mile away. Wading the cold swift running mountain stream waist deep we were pushing to the front when Captain Benham ordered us to form on the river bank, and to cross in line of battle to our left, and to advance toward the rebel right, as some of the enemy had been seen on the side of the Mountain. When near the center of the stream, our Captain while facing the Co., and stepping backwards, holding his sword in a horizontal position, the hilt in his right hand and the point in his left, and saying; "dress to the right boys," fell backwards over a rock and disappeared; when he came up, spouting water like a whale, no amount of discipline could have prevented a dozen or more voices from saying, "dress up, Captain, dress up."

While we were forming and crossing the river the 14th Ohio assisted by the Artillery, were engaged in a brisk skirmish at the front, in which the enemy were driven from their position at the next ford. We were recalled and ordered forward. As we crossed the river at the second ford, we met an Ohioan from the skirmish line, a ball had struck his musket near the muzzle, breaking the ramrod and forcing the gun against his head, and cutting an ugly gash from which he was bleeding profusely.

Leaving the second ford the enemy formed half mile back on a hill and in some timber, commanding the valley and road over which we must pass in our advance but as we approached, they again retreated following their wagon train closely.

Just after crossing the river the third time we found a large invoice of tents, knapsacks, trunks, clothing and other valuables, evidently thrown from wagons; envelopes, paper and many other items of trade indicated that in the rout some sutler had been sacked. From this on the sides of the road were strewn with the debris to lighten loads.

The rush and excitement was so great that few stopped to secure trophies, not even blankets or coats, then and during the campaign so much needed.

The column was on a double quick, when a prolonged, hideous yell was heard at the front, accompanied by a few shots, and followed by regular volleys.

The enemy had halted at Carricks ford, where the road was blockaded by their stalled teams. They had taken position on the right of the ford, across the river upon an almost precipitous bank, from fifty feet at their right to eighty feet in height at their left, completely commanding the valley, ford and road; their right protected by a rail fence, and the left by low bushes. When our skirmishers advanced on a brisk run along the low level bank of the river, being half hidden by trees at the waters brink, they were at the first mistaken by the enemy for some Georgians whom they knew to have been placed in ambush to the right of their first position and cut off by our rapid advance. When the 14th were well under the bluff, the rebels raised and giving one cheer for Jeff Davis, followed by the fearful yell, which we had heard, opened a heavy fire with musketry and artillery. The 14th Ohio halted and facing to the rear stood their ground, giving several round volleys in

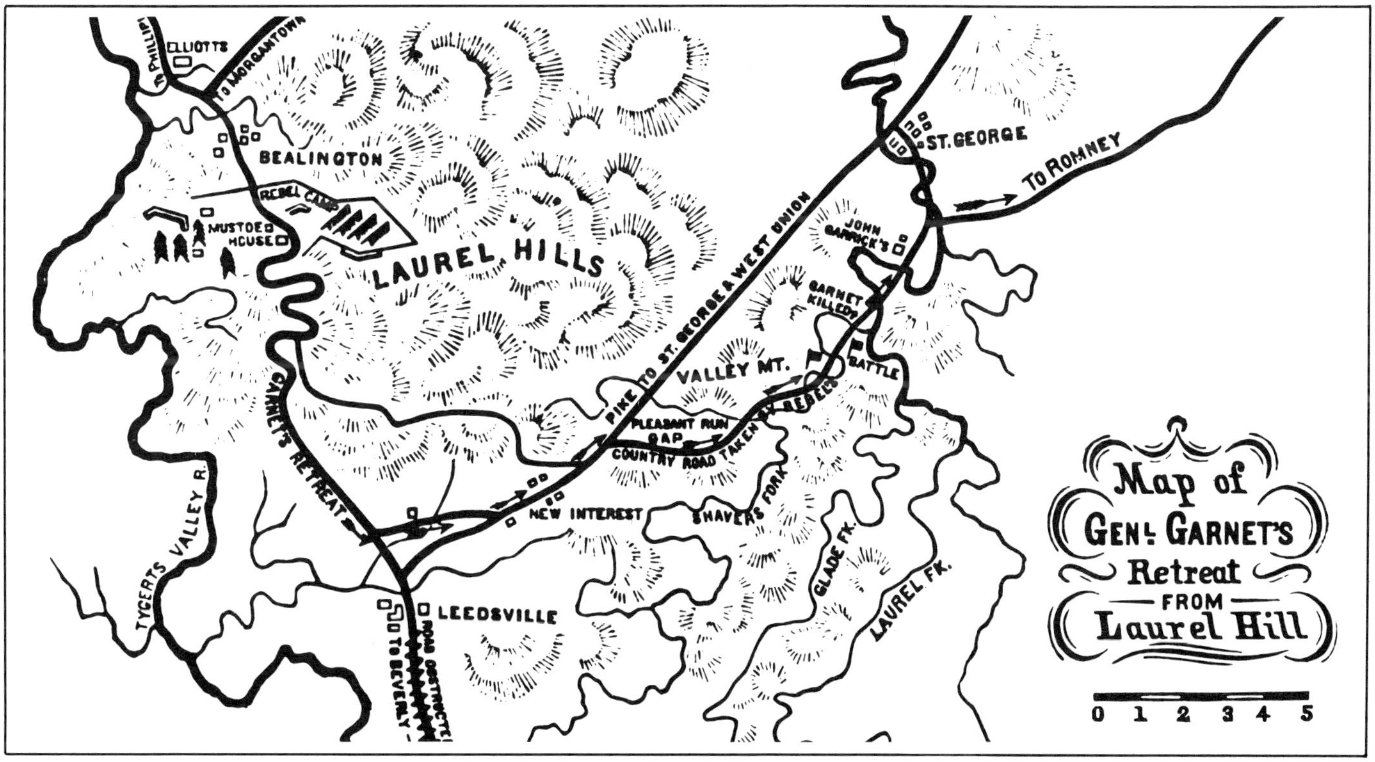

The Union pursuit of the Confederates — from Laurel Hill to Corrick's Ford.

return. Our Artillery took position farther back in the meadow, for better range, and opened at once.

The fighting in front quickened our pace to a run, before reaching the 14th, were met by Captain Benham and ordered to the right across the river, and obliquely up the bluff in an attempt to turn the rebel left. At the foot of the hill the Col. dismounted, and we at once began the difficult ascent, so steep that we had to cling to bushes. Just as we started, some one reported to Benham, who was then placing the 9th Ind. which had come up, that it was impossible to climb the bluff; and when our right had climbed almost to the top, and Co. "H" were about half way up, orders came for us to form in the river and march down to the ford, under close cover of the bluff, and turn their right. Letting go all holds, we were with out much ceremony soon at the bottom, and again forming in a swift current so deep as to necessitate the holding up of cartridge boxes. We then marched some distance down stream, directly under the fire of friend and foe, when we reached the road and were taking position, the enemy fled in great confusion, leaving on the field one cannon *(spiked by Lieut Washington who had proposed the cheer for Jeff Davis, and led in the yell.)* twelve or thirteen dead and many wounded.

At this place we captured about forty loaded wagons and most of the teams. The advance wagon had stuck fast in the narrow passage up the right bank, thus preventing the passage of the rest. These wagons contained only tents, camp equipage and private baggage. Many Trunks and boxes had been opened, and apparently special articles taken and the rest hurriedly abandoned. The enemy had overshot our forces inflicting a loss of but two killed and six wounded, one dangerously. On the battlefield back of the cannon I found a Lyman Cobb Pocket Lexicon, which had once been the property of Chas. T. Smith and Frank R. Smith of Nelson County Va. and bore marks of having been used at both Columbia and Alleghany Colleges at some time. It has also the name of John Jordan Cabell, Meadow Bluff, Greenbriar Co. Va. It is unique in some respects. In many words where C. is now the terminus, K. is used, as "Publick," "Comick," "Rustick" etc. Each Margin contains a proverb, as "Eloquence is the language of nature."

Having no coat or vest, and being wet and somewhat chilled, I picked up a pair of linen pants which I drew on my arms and across my back.

Just as the engagement closed the Sixth Ind. came up followed closely by the remainder of the brigade, under Gen Morris. Our move to the rebel right in an attempt to flank their position, while the 14th Ohio under Col. Steadman, engaged them in the front, had placed us in the advance in the pursuit and we pushed on rapidly maintaining a running skirmish with the rear guard to the next ford half mile distant, where Gen. Garnett, having placed sharpshooters behind some drift wood near the bank, and some fragments of regiments at a turn of the road some thirty rods back; was attempting to rally a force sufficient to delay our crossing and further advance. The Seventh formed as they came up, under an irregular fire from the ambush to which the regiment responded with spirit. In this irregular fire Gen. R. S. Garnett fell mortally wounded, — it is said from a shot by 1st Sergeant Birm-

The death of Confederate General Robert Garnett.

ingham of Co. "A." One brave Georgian stood near the Gen. when others fled, and like a true hero died by the side of his gallant commander. When Gen. Garnett fell, the remainder of the rebel force fled in confusion. We crossed the river the fifth time, and continued the pursuit. Captain Benham and Major Gordon, who had known Garnett in the regular Army, stopped and cared for the remains of their old companion in arms.

About one mile from the scene of the last conflict, we filed to the right and halted near the loghouse in an opening overlooking a large valley plantation, with the river at the farther side, at the foot of a "sugar loaf" shaped mountain of considerable heights. It was now Two o'clock p.m. and still raining. The valley through which we had pursued and engaged the enemy in a running fight, was from one half to one mile wide, mostly in cultivation or meadow with mountain walls on either side. The river sweeping in a rapid current over a stony bottom from side to side; crossing the valley at an average of every mile.

We had marched from four o'clock in the morning with but a morsel of bread for breakfast, and but few and very brief halts; had crossed two or three ranges of mountains; most of the time in a drenching rain, had waded Cheat river five times; been under fire three or four times, and were wet to the skin and mud to our ears. Yet through all this there was a cheerfulness of spirit, far beyond any reasonable expectation.

As soon as we halted, some foragers were sent out. After a time one of Co. "H" returned, bearing on his shoulder a sheep, which was soon dressed and divided. We had neither pots or pans, and were without bread or salt. The boys were soon broiling pieces on sticks or ramrods.

Jim Dean, the wit of Co. "H," who had occasioned many a hearty laugh during the day, now came to grief, he declared that he always detested mutton, and taking a half broiled bit between his thumbs and fore fingers, and opening his lips as wide as possible, tried to eat the meat with out touching or tasting it, saying "dinged if it wasn't eat sheep or die."

Some of our troops passed beyond us, and our scouts are said to have followed the fleeing fugitives about six miles. On account of the exhausted and half starved condition of the troops, rendering rest imperative, we bivouaced for the night.

Fresh beef was issued about dark, and although we were without salt, the broiling upon sticks continued until a late hour; then, having dried our clothing somewhat, we crept into some unthreshed wheat straw, with a hope that we might rest and sleep, but the rain continued, really growing worse, and soon our straw and clothing were wet and our bodies chilled, compelling us to spend another night standing around our fires.

On Cheat River, Sunday July 14, 1861. Our situation afforded us but little rest and less sleep last night. For breakfast and dinner we had fresh beef without bread or salt. Report says the enemy fully fifteen miles in the advance, and rumor says Gen. McClellan has ordered us to return to Belington, as Gen. Hill from Rowelsburg, is expected to intercept the enemy. Certainly further pursuit on our part seems almost impossible.

Remained in camp until near three o'clock p.m. when we moved out, and waded Cheat River four times, and arrived at St. George at dark, where we were each given one cracker and a small piece of pork for our suppers. During the afternoon I turned my left ankle and sprained it badly.

Near where we crossed the river the second time, the rebels had taken the road toward Romney. A small scouting party followed several miles, and returning reported that they had found twelve abandoned wagons, which were secured by a detachment of the Sixth Ind.

St. George, Western Va. July 15, 1861. Were called very early and ordered to be ready to march at day break. In the entire absence of baggage and commissary store, little preparation was needed, and we very patiently awaited for the order to march, for with sore feet, stiff limbs, benumbed bodies, heavy eyes and aching heads, and insatiable hunger gnawing at our vitals, we were loath to start. The order came at sunup and not having had one morsal to eat, we started. My ankle had troubled me very much during the night, so much so that I did not sleep. Passing through St. George, we waded Cheat River for the tenth time; then a smaller stream and turned to the left, and followed up a small stream which we crossed frequently, going on and on, until we passed over a range of mountain, following a road which became only a bridle path, then down and on down until we reached the Beverly and Rowelsburg Pike, which we followed to the left for an hour and stopped at noon for dinner, where rails were abundant and where we were given more fresh meat. This time we were given some salt. Report says the Cattle were sent from Beverly by Gen. McClellan. Weak & weary from hunger and climbing, and from a diarrhea induced from fresh meat without salt or bread, many lay down for the rest and sleep, having no relish for a dinner without bread.

About two p.m. we started on our wearisome way following the pike for two or three hours, came to the place where we left it on Saturday in our pursuit of Gen. Garnett. Here we turned to the right and followed a road over the foot hills of Laural Mountain, passed one large and very neat farm, with good buildings, and a number of slaves who looked in wonder at us as we passed. After a time we turned abruptly to the right again, following only a path by this time the boys were so fatigued as to cause a cessation of all joking, and quarrells and disputes were quite frequent. At the point where we last turned to the right was an old log hut, in which lived a very old man who said we would save many miles by leaving the wagon road and following the path. Our officers thought it a kindness to go the shortest road and save as much marching as possible. For some distance our way was marked by a path, but by dark this was lost, and hungry weak fatigued and foot sore we climbed up the steep rock or Laurel covered sides of the mountain, clinging to bushes or clamboring over the rough stone. At almost every tree, log or stone were one or more who had stopped from sheer exhaustion to rest, but while some were resting others were pushing on up, and thus we were passing, resting, and then in turn passing on and again resting, and being again passed. Men and horses fell and tumbled about some rolling over and over. Notwithstanding orders to remove

Private Josiah Marvel, 7th Indiana Volunteer Infantry Regiment.

the caps from our guns, one soldier failed to do so, and slipping fell and accidentally discharged his piece, the bullet struck and killed an Ohio Lieutenant. Finally we reached the summit and regained the pike where a halt was made to allow stragglers to come up. Many were the doubtful blessings heaped upon the Old Man of the log hut, and not a few pronounced fearful imprecations on him, even consigning him uncerimonously to a very warm place, while others with the keenest irony insisted that he was a good man assuredly a Union man, who in the very goodness of his heart had sought to befriend us.

After a short rest we resumed our march, and slowly dragged ourselves down the western slope of the mountain through the old rebel camp of Laurel Hill, now occupied by loyal Virginians, to our camp near Belington, where we arrived after ten p.m. and found a good supper awaiting us, to which we did full justice, having had nothing to eat during the day except some fresh half cooked beef.

Had marched during the day thirty five miles, save a very few gained by climbing the trackless side of the Mountain.

Belington Va. Tuesday July 16, 1861. Supper over last night, we lay down to sleep, and slept as sleeps a little child. Though if judged by our movements to day, most of us would be thought of as hundred years old.

Some have sore toes, others scalded or blistered feet, some have stiff limbs and others lame backs; and all enough to complain of. By keeping the sock on my sprained ankle wet yesterday, I managed to get to camp in tollerable condition, and reasonable time, but I find it very much swollen today. Camp is exceedingly quiet, and but little done but to eat and sleep; although some have put out a washing, thinking that we shall be ordered home soon.

Belington Va. July 19, 1861. Since the 16th quiet has reigned in camp; nothing occuring of sufficient interest to note. Gen. McClellans forces have advanced to and beyond Beverly, up the valley, and a large number of his weapons have passed this place on route to Webster and Grafton, which place are now the depots of supply for Western Va. Boys are getting quite well rested and are becoming very anxious to be off for home, as our time of enlistment is so nearly out. Have all been busy these days of leisure and waiting, writing letters to friends at home, and recounting to one another the many adventures, hairbreadth escapes and incidents of interest of our late campaign. Newspapers have been filled with glowing accounts of our wonderful achievements. It seems that too much cannot be said by the papers in praise and commendation. From them we suddenly learn that we have suddenly become heroes.

Report says the remnant of Gen. Garnetts forces are making their way in small detachments in direction of Winchester. About sundown orders came for the 7th to pack up, and be ready to march at three oclock tomorrow Morning. This order was received with marked demonstrations of joy. The tents and other baggage were soon in the wagons.

Saturday July 20, 1861. About ten o'clock last night, we lay down hoping to get at least a forty winks nap, but it soon began to rain being with out shelter except Rubber

Blankets. I procured two fence rails upon which I placed my blanket, and lying down drew my Rubber over me, and being secure from the rain enjoyed perhaps two hours sleep.

We were up, breakfast over, and started on our return march by three oclock A.M. The Boys are in fine spirits, and notwithstanding the rain has made the road slippery, we marched at a very rapid gait, and passed through Phillippi at 7 A.M., then passed our old camp on the hill overlooking the town, and a mile or two beyond, where we stopped on the right of the Pike, and pitched our tents. Rumor says we will here await cars at Webster for home.

The fatigue of the hurried march has been greatly lessened by many stirring songs and witty speeches by the way.

Sunday July 21, 1861. This morning I was called to go on fatigue duty unloading Wagons at Phillippi. Returned at three p.m. and found the regt. ready to start for Webster, where we arrived at sundown.

Monday July 22, 1861. It was about 4 o'clock A.M. when we entered box cars at Webster, for Grafton, where we stopped a few minutes to take on the sick of the Regt. Were at Fairmount at sunup and at 9 a.m. stopped at Glen Easton, for an East bound train, and arrived at Benwood, on Ohio River, four miles below Wheeling and rested until dusk, when we crossed over to Bellaire, Ohio. The day has been clear and beautiful, made doubly so to us, for our journey has been one Grand Ovation. The glad hearted loyal people, gathering in large numbers at every village and station to give us a passing welcome, greeting us with songs, flowers, and hearty words of commendation and thanks for having assisted to drive armed secession from their borders.

Bellaire Ohio, July 23, 1861. Last night we were in camp on a level common just west of town, awaiting the arrival and departure of our train. After talking over the many pleasant incidents of the day and our triumphal journey, and speculating somewhat as to the probable route and greeting by the way; had lain down to rest and sleep the surest sleep of warrior veterans, fully assured by the events of the day, of a pleasant journey, and a hearty reception by many friends at home, and of the approval of a grateful people.

About twelve o'clock, there was a quiet stir about camp, and it was whispered that the Federal Army, in front of Washington City, had gone out against the Rebels at Manassas, and that a great battle had been fought on the Banks of Bull Run, and that the Union Army had been defeated, with very great slaughter and driven in a demoralized condition back in to the fortifications about the Capitol, and that the rebels had followed in strong force to the very gates of the City, and now threatened the very existence of the government. That the rebels had been very brutal toward prisoners taken and especially barbarous in their treatment of the wounded. There was soon a confusion of voices over the entire encampment. Men stood around in groups and talked of the probable result, to the Union, of our National defeat, wondering if the Capitol could be saved. Many fearing it would end the war and establish a Southern Confederacy.

Major-General George McClellan, United States Army.

As the Men talked and speculated, the excitement grew and although the disappointment was great, it was soon discovered that there was a strong and growing feeling, that if needed we ought to turn our faces eastward and go in further defence of the Union and the Constitution; and I have no doubt but that if the President, whom we already regarded with much favor, had asked it, the entire regiment would have gone as one man to save Washington City.

There was no more sleep for the 7th at that place. The defeat at Bull Run became the all absorbing topic of conversation, and thus the early morning hours passed, until daybreak when we boarded a passenger train for Columbus. For some unaccountable reason our train went very slow, and it was 11 o'clock when we reached Zanesville, and 4:30 p.m. when we arrived at Columbus; where we were given a good supper by the Citizens. It was after 6 p.m. of 23rd when we left Columbus and near 2 a.m., 24th when we arrived at Cincinnati. All day we could observe the effect of the defeat at Bull Run, upon the citizens. They thronged with less enthusiasm about the train at stations, and there was little or no demonstrations. Many faces wore the expression of deepest despair, evidently our achievements in Western Va. were lost sight of in the terrible defeat and humiliation of Bull Run, and face, speech and manner said plainly it was not Western Virginia alone, but the entire Union of All the States that the people wanted saved. Old men who had enjoyed the benefits of the beneficent government under the Union as it was for more than three score and ten years, talked in faltering tremulous tones; and with tears in their eyes, for the fate of Washington City, and the Union yet hung in the balance.

New troops are being rushed to the capital and enlistments are being urged.

Arriving at Cincinnati, we marched to the Lawrenceburg and Indianapolis depot, where the Regiment were furnished passenger coaches except for Captain Scotts Co. of Martinsville. He was told he would have to crowd his Co. into the already well filled cars, and out the platforms and steps, but he stoutly refused to allow his men treated in such manner, and ordered them to stack arms saying they would wait for the next train. Two Cos. are from Lawrenceburg where a stop was made, and time given for a greeting of friends.

Two Cos. being from Greensburg, we made another stop there and were furnished a good breakfast, and a cordial greeting which made every soldier feel welcome whether he enlisted at G. or not. Arriving at Shelbyville, Captain Blairs Co. was warmly welcomed, as were the entire Regt. Arrived at Indianapolis at one o'clock p.m. We marched to the Market house where we found a dinner and a large concourse of citizens — friends and strangers — awaiting us. Many and earnest were the words of commendation. Dinner and greetings over, we marched to camp north west of camp Sullivan and during the afternoon pitched our tents again. This was more quiet and restful, than on train, but we cant understand why we may not go home.

Many of the boys had bought evening papers and were busy reading or listening to the news from Washington City and elsewhere.

The papers are filled with accounts of retreat from Bull Run, of the disorganized condition of many Brigades, Divisions and of Companies, and the confusion of mind of many of the officers; and that as the troops arrive they are

Rest, relaxation and rumors.

Where the big decisions were made during the Civil War — War Department on the left, Navy Department on the right.

being placed about Alexandria Va. and in front of Washington, to the very best advantage for the defense of the Capitol.

General Geo. B. McClellan, our commander in the Campaign in West Va. has been called to the Capitol. There are very severe criticisms of several officers and small bodies of troops.

Just before "Taps" for "lights out" our mess observed their usual season of scripture reading and prayer.

July 25, 1861. Our camp was rather quiet last night. We had been on the move almost continuosly since leaving Grafton West Va. about 5 A.M. on the morning of the 22 inst. We had certainly earned a nights rest and sleep.

The news boys were in camp early and met with a good sale of their papers, for we were anxious for the latest news; especially from about Washington. Most of the Regiment remained close about camp all day expecting that we would be discharged; as the term of our enlistment is now out.

Several friends of Co. "H" came up from Franklin to day, and seemed well pleased with our work in West. Va.

The evening papers were much sought after and eagerly read. The news is of much the same tenor as yesterday. The administration and the citizens of Washington are very much disturbed lest the rebels might get near enough to throw shells into the city. Over the country generally, enlistments go forward briskly; for the defeat at Bull Run has awakened most of the north to a clearer realization of the facts of real war.

For the few of our squad the day closed much as yesterday did; which has been our practice when possible since our first evening in camp, more than three months ago.

July 26, 1861. Many rumors are afloat this morning as to when we will be paid and mustered out.

Our officers got permission for the several companies to go home for a very few days, and we started for the Depot at noon. On reaching Franklin, we were given a hearty welcome.

Very soon after reaching town a Levee or a large social gathering at the Hall was arranged for this evening.

As my old Gray suit is now worn to holes having been of a poor shoddy material, I started for home. Not chancing to find any conveyance I walked the three miles. I found a hearty welcome, and was soon togged out in my best and on my way back to the party.

The party was well attended. Most of the young people and many of those older were present.

A good string band was present and rendered some excellent music. A Quartett of the Company sang several patriotic pieces, among them, "The Sword of Bunker Hill," the words and music of which they had found in a house in Phillippi, Barbour Co. West Va.

The evening was spent in conversation and in promenading about the hall. It seemed to be the purpose of our entertainers that no soldier should be left long with out a companion.

The affair was a very pleasant one, and I am sure was much enjoyed by the soldiers.

Comrade Jos. E. Boswell, my most intimate chum in camp and campaign whom I had first met in that hall on the morning when we left for camp, was not with us, he having gone home from Indianapolis.

Saturday July 27, 1861. I spent last night with my friend James M. Bone. The forenoon was spent about the store or on streets where I met many friends and acquaintances. Conversation centered about our campaign, the battle of Bull Run and enlistments over the north.

The morning papers state that General McClellan had reached Washington City. The Administration have commissioned him a Major General in the U.S. Army, have by order formed the Military district of The Potomac, including all north eastern Va, the District of Columbia and portions of Maryland, and have placed him in command.

In the afternoon I went out home with father where there awaited me the most appreciable of all welcomes.

Father and others were eager to hear details of the campaign and battles.

I could not wonder at fathers interest in the incidents of the campaign, for he had told me when I first spoke of going how much he wanted to go into the Blackhawk war, but was rejected.

Sunday July 28, 1861. We all attended services at Hopewell church where I met many whom I have known from my childhood. Many being relatives on both my father's and mother's side of the house. Here too, I found myself some what of a hero; more perhaps for the reason that I am the only one of the church and community who had enlisted.

Several young men of near my own age seemed more especially desirous to know something of the service and of camp life.

I returned home, and with us one family who lived farther on. During the afternoon two or three near by neighbors dropped in for a short time, which is quite the unusual thing for this neighborhood.

Monday July 29, 1861. I went to town early where I met most of the officers and members of the company. While many incidents of the service were related; still with soldier and citizen the topic most talked, was the war and enlistments.

The papers are well filled with accounts of the great awakening of patriotism in all the north. The Eastern, Middle, Western and far Western states are astir; and flags and fife and drum are much in evidence in most communities. And yet there are some places little interested, and apparently as in this community some who are bitterly opposed to any further prosecution of the war; and there are in many towns, as in this a newspaper in which very mean unpatriotic things are said. I find there is already talk of raising another company here.

Tuesday July 30, 1861. As our furlough holds good only for to day, we were at the Depot on time, and soon off for Indianapolis and in camp in due time.

Camp was now a dull place for us. As soon as the Regimental and Company officers could make return of arms and accouterments and camp equipments and make settlement of all accounts and make out Pay Rolls we were ready for discharge.

We were mustered out late on the 2nd of August, and having signed the pay rolls, were paid and handed our discharges on August 3rd and went to Franklin by train in the afternoon, It was 9 o'clock p.m. when I reached home.

Several members of the company, were, at the time of enlistment, students in the Franklin College, some of whom were to graduate in May or June and others in lower classes. The graduates were given their Diplomas as though present. This group during the campaign had their tent inscribed AJAX. and were an interesting squad frequently entertained themselves and us with very eloquent addresses or recitations or with heated debates of questions of current interest.

Among them was Thos. J. Morgan, afterward a Lieut. in a company in 70th Ind. Inf. and later adjutant, of which Regt. Benjamin Harrison, was the first Colonel afterward a Brigadier General and Brevet Major Genl. and still later President of the U.S.

T. J. Morgan, later was commissioned Colonel of the 14th U. S. Colored troops, commanded a Brigade and was for gallant conduct in battle Breveted Brigadier. Comrade Jos. E. Boswell an undergraduate of the College, did not return to school, but became a Lieut. and Captain, in another Regiment, and after the close of the war was chosen Sheriff of Marion County Indiana.

Comrade George F. Herriott, of our church, a former student in the College, became Captain of a Co. and later Major of a Regt. and comrade Thomas A. Jeffery, also of our church group, was chosen as the first Second Lieut. of Company "F" of the new 7th and later became First Lieut. and afterward was commissioned Captain of Co. "F," and served to the close of our enlistment.

My chum Comrade Jos. E. Boswell, left us at Indianapolis for his home just north of the city, and I saw but little of him afterwards. John W. Hutchison and James T. Alexander, with whom I went when we enlisted returned to Franklin, and afterwards saw much service in later Companies and Regiments; as did all of the Three Months Men of Company "H," as far as I recall.

This closes my record of my first enlistment, although but little more than three months we had learned something of the Art of War, and made much history and with others had opened the way for much more far reaching history, for we had inaugurated not a war for emancipation, but a war in behalf of humanity.

Indiana's Benjamin Harrison — Civil War Brevet Brigadier-General and United States President, 1889-93.

A Review of the Early Campaigning For Western Virginia

As Billy Davis learned in July 1861, the victory at Phillippi did not end the struggle for west Virginia. On the political front, 25 county governments in western Virginia had stated their intent to secede from the state of Virginia. Also encouraging, the local citizens appeared enthusiastic toward the Union army's occupation of their land.[1] Nevertheless, complete success for the North would be achieved only when the Confederate troops were driven from the region.

General George Brinton McClellan, one-time brilliant West Point cadet and former president of a railroad, proposed to his superiors a sweeping strategic plan for dealing with western Virginia (and way beyond). General-in-Chief Winfield Scott rejected McClellan's plan as unrealistic.[2] The reason was simple — Washington did not have a well-defined strategic plan for occupying west Virginia. This was not just a west Virginia problem. The United States government had not developed comprehensive military goals by June 1861.[3] McClellan's (and Governor Dennison's) "grand" plan, however, was to protect the B&O Railroad, drive the Confederate troops southward, and occupy as much of Virginia as possible.

McClellan arrived at Grafton on June 22, 19 days after the Battle of Phillippi. He announced to his troops he had "heard that there was danger here. I have come to place myself at your head and to share it with you." Less brashly he notified the assistant adjutant general in Washington that he intended to gain "success by maneuvering rather than fighting," also, he would "not throw these raw men into the teeth of artillery and entrenchments, if possible," and, furthermore, he would "not. . . move until everything is ready."[4] Not surprisingly, as the war continued, Abraham Lincoln characterized McClellan as slow and timid when aggressiveness was required. But in June 1861, McClellan appeared to Lincoln and all the nation as a military savior.

The Confederates, in the meantime, were not idle. Colonel Porterfield was censored for his conduct at Phillippi and General Robert Seldon Garnett was given command of western Virginia. Garnett immediately built two strategically located camps — one on Rich Mountain and the other 12 miles north at Laurel Hill. These posts commanded all the major east-west, north-south roads in the region.[5]

McClellan planned to sever Garnett's supply route and his line of retreat by first destroying the Confederates' southern-most position at Rich Mountain. Then McClellan would be between the outnumbered rebels and their supply base to the south.[6] To sustain themselves, the Confederates would have to fight their way out — toward the south! The other possibilities: capitulate, or stay and fight a superior force until wiped out. Whichever, McClellan would achieve his objectives.

Hero of two wars, 6'5" General-in-chief Winfield Scott — by 1861 he was just "Old Fuss and Feathers."

McClellan, in an effort to disguise his strategy, had Brigadier General Thomas A. Morris (including the 7th Indiana) move toward Laurel Hill as a ruse. Billy Davis described in detail the sparring and the feinting which took place between July 7 and 11 near Laurel Hill.

On the night of July 11 McClellan's main body attacked Rich Mountain. After a brief engagement, the Confederates retreated down the mountain. Most of these Confederates were captured as McClellan's men blocked their effort to make it north to the rebel camp at Laurel Hill.[7]

Garnett's troops at Laurel Hill were also blocked — north and south — and his position was now untenable. Garnett took to the mountain paths which lead him to the northeast and his death on July 13 at the engagement of Corrick's Ford. To the north, McClellan had used the B&O in a failed attempt to encircle the Southerners. The Confederate foot soldiers, now without leadership and hemmed in on three sides, abandoned their materials and fled 25 miles to the Allegheny Mountains.[8]

"Our success is complete, and secession is killed in this country," McClellan reported to the War Department.[9]

The 7th Indiana at Laurel Hill

Earlier in the campaign when the battle at Rich Mountain was fought, Billy Davis was a part of the diversionary forces at Laurel Hill.[10] Historian Orville Thomson thought Laurel Hill "would pass muster as a very respectable mountain in Indiana."[11] A contemporary historian

The Battle of Rich Mountain, July 11, 1861.

described Garnett's 150-acre camp as a beautiful location: "Directly east of the camp rose Laurel Mountain [Hill]. The enormous trees were just coming into full leaf due to the cold, wet Spring which had lingered into June, and the azaleas glowed with color and the mountain laurel and rhododendron made a solid bank of bloom in the laurel thickets."(12)

The Union camp was located on farm land 200 yards west of the six-house village of Belington. As the Confederates came forward, four units of Federal troops rushed forward to positions behind fences, logs, blackberry briars, whatever.(13) Thomson said the 7th and 9th Indiana were always at the post of honor (up front) for all four days. When the Union troops advanced, the Confederates, if necessary, could take cover in a dense timber on a hillside. Between the two lines were two low, wooded hills; one was named "Girard's Hill" in honor of the Hoosier soldier killed there. It was on these hills where most of the skirmishing took place.(14)

First one side would come out of their lines and make a demonstration, then fall back. Then the other side would advance its skirmishers, or make a flanking movement. This went on for four days. One eyewitness reported that cannons were fired about 500 times.(15) In General Morris' official report he recounts that the enemy advanced once to as close as ¾ of a mile. Then on July 11, Rich Mountain was captured and Garnett knew it was futile to try and hold Laurel Hill. Although Morris executed the ruse successfully, there was a cost — four dead, six wounded, one missing.(16)

Action at Corrick's Ford on July 13, 1861.

On To Corrick's Ford

When Confederate General Garnett heard the results from Rich Mountain, he wasted little time in evacuating his Laurel Hill camp. In the midnight darkness of July 11, Garnett passed through Leadsville heading south. Learning that the Yankees had blocked the road, he turned around and headed back to Leadsville. Now his plan was to march northeasterly, pass around the northern end of Cheat Mountain and head south using the mountain as a screen.(17)

Strangely, the Union command did not start its pursuit until four in the morning of July 13. General Morris knew early on the 12th of Laurel Hill's abandonment. Billy recorded that the boys wandered over Laurel Hill on the 12th, examining the old rebel camp. Garnett, at the time, was escaping unmolested.

Robert Selden Garnett, first general officer killed in the Civil War.

The situation changed as 1,800 Yankees started a pursuit. Of great consequence to both sides, heavy rains fell, the narrow roads were almost impassable for wagons and artillery, and the creeks were out of their banks. Garnett's force of about 3,000 men made 25 miles before stopping. They had been over mountain spurs, around steep hillsides and across four fords.(18)

Billy's description of the drenching rain and the road conditions of July 13 may have been understated. Daniel Howe, a comrade in the 7th, wrote that he slipped twice on the slimy boulders while crossing the mountain streams.

"I had gone clean under and rolled over on the bottom, gun and all."[19] Thomson recalled the many times the streams were forded — ice cold water, usually waist high.[20] H. W. Benham, Captain of Engineers, officially reported the conditions to his superiors: "[F]or nearly the whole time the rain was pouring in torrents and the clayey [sic] roads almost impassable in many places."[21] A contemporary author wrote of the mud tugging at the boys' heels, of staggering, of slipping down, and of mud becoming like thick tar.[22]

If the Union troops were tired, the Confederates were near exhaustion. Their march had included the hike to near Beverly, then the reverse march for a total of about 15 extra miles. Garnett was aware that Union General Morris' men were closing in on his rear guard. Hundreds of trees were felled to impede the Federal advance. Garnett contested each stream the Union troops attempted to ford. The Confederates, however, had additional cause for desperation — they feared that somehow the Northerners would bypass them and cut off their line of retreat.[23]

At Corrick's Ford on the Cheat River, four miles from where the Confederates had bivouacked the first night, many wagons became stalled in either the river or on the muddy banks.[24] Captain Benham engaged the 14th Ohio and his own artillery in a little skirmish. Garnett, meanwhile, decided to take a more favorable defensive position about 150 yards back from the ford. Billy Davis provided a detailed account of the Union movements at what has been labeled the Battle of Corrick's Ford. General Garnett had ridden back from the head of the column to take his position at the next ford with 10 sharpshooters. (As Billy pointed out, there was more than one ford being contested in this battle.) The Union lines came forward and concentrated their fire on General Garnett and his sharpshooters. Outgunned, Garnett began to move back when he was mortally wounded with a bullet in the back. An aide tried to lift Garnett on to a horse, but could not. Consequently, the first general officer to be killed in the Civil War would be left to his enemy.[25] Private Howe, a former student at Franklin College, passed by the corpse and later wrote that Garnett was "the finest looking officer I had ever seen."[26]

The rebels, for the most part, would eventually reach their camps at McDowell, Virginia. Billy and his comrades returned to Belington — they were going home — their three-month enlistment would soon be over.

The Confederates lost 50 men at Corrick's Ford while Union Captain Benham reported his losses as "two killed, and six or seven wounded, one dangerously."[27]

To many participants, the early battles in west Virginia represented a form of carnage. Little could these young men understand that someday historians would record these engagements as minor Civil War skirmishes.

The newspaper reporters likewise lacked perspective. Regardless, fairness was expected. A young reporter for the Cincinnati *Gazette*, who had given a full account of the Rich Mountain Battle, was taken to task for giving too much credit to the Indiana regiments. Later the reporter, Whitelaw Reid, published a "correction."[28] (Billy recorded later, under the date line of July 6, that Reid had "materially augmented our numbers and greatly strengthened our position.") As the war continued, Reid became an exemplary war correspondent.

Another reporter, this one with the Cincinnati *Times*, got caught up in the excitement of reporting the war. At Corrick's Ford, George P. Buell picked up a musket and made a charge with the 7th Indiana.[29]

After the Battle of Corrick's Ford, the newspaper reporters felt an obligation to inform the Northern readers who was to blame for the Confederate getaway. Reid, who disliked "The Little Napoleon," reported that McClellan was to blame: "And this is the culmination of the brilliant generalship which the journals of the sensational persuasion have been besmearing with such nauseous flattery."[30]

Whitelaw Reid, war correspondent for the Cincinnati Gazette.

The Union victories in western Virginia were given full attention by the reporters and their readers. Here was the evidence that the rebellion was going to be quickly crushed. Then the Battle of First Bull Run (or Manassas) occurred. The New York *Times'* headlines of July 22 and 23 sounded the alarm: "The Greatest Battle Ever Fought on this Continent," "Fearful Carnage On Both Sides," "Disaster to the National Army," "90,000 Rebels In The Field," "But 20,000 of the National Forces in Action," "A Panic Among the Teamsters and Civilians," "The Retreat of Our Forces on the Eve of Victory," "Exaggerated Statements of Our Losses," and then a clarifying (?) headline on July 24, "The Victory of Sunday, and How it Was Lost."[31] In time, the First Bull Run Battle would be put in perspective, but in late July the misinformation and overstatements would create a panic atmosphere throughout the North.

END NOTES

(1) Warren W. Hassler, Jr., *General George B. McClellan: Shield of the Union* (Westport, 1974); pp. 6, 12. Similar background information can be found in: Stutler, *West Virginia in the Civil War;* Boem, *The Civil War in Western Virginia.* For more information concerning the Battle of Phillippi and its significance, see Eva Margaret Carnes, Editor, *Centennial History of the Phillippi Covered Bridge 1852-1952* (Phillippi, 1952); Chapter III, "The Battle of Phillippi" by Mary R. Hoge.

(2) *Ibid.;* pp. 5-7.

(3) James M. McPherson, *Battle Cry of Freedom: The Civil War Era* (New York, 1988); p. 333.

(4) *The War of the Rebellion: A Compilation of the Official Records of the Union and Confederate Armies* (Washington, 1880-1901); series I, v. II, pp. 197, 199. Hereafter these documents will be cited as *ORs*.

(5) Stutler, *West Virginia in the Civil War;* p. 28.

(6) Hassler, *General George B. McClellan . . . .;* pp. 14-15. McClellan told General-in-Chief Scott this would be a repeat of the maneuver at Cerro Gordo, one of Scott's masterful movements in the Mexican War.

(7) Stutler, *West Virginia in the Civil War;* p. 29. For a detailed description of the battle of Rich Mountain, see Jack Zinn, *The Battle of Rich Mountain* (Parsons, 1971)

(8) Richard O. Curry, "McClellan's Western Virginia Campaign of 1861," *Ohio History,* a publication of The Ohio Historical Society (Columbus, 1962); v. 71, n. 2, p. 94.

(9) *ORs*, series I, v, II, p. 204.

(10) Boem, *The Civil War in Western Virginia;* p. 53. General Morris had fallen out of favor with McClellan because he had asked for reinforcements while at Phillippi. McClellan let Morris know that if he ever asked for reinforcements again, he would be sent back to Indiana. Almost providentially, McClellan would become renowned as the Civil War general who never thought he had enough troops and was always pleading with his superiors for more, more, more.

(11) Thomson, *Seventh Indiana;* p. 28. Also Kemper, *War Papers;* p. 127 for discussion of the Laurel Hill affair.

(12) Carnes, *The Tygart Valley Line;* p. 71. The camp's description can also be found in *The Soldier of Indiana;* p. 48.

(13) *Ibid.;* p. 97. For a detailed account of the activities at Laurel Hill, see Fritz Haselberger, *Yanks from the South* (Chelsea, Michigan, 1987); pp. 189-214.

(14) Thomson, *Seventh Indiana;* pp. 27-29.

(15) Carnes, *The Tygart Valley Line;* p. 99.

(16) *ORs*, series I, v. II, pp. 218-219 (General Morris' report.)

(17) Boem, *The Civil War in Western Virginia;* pp. 73-74. Boem also points out the possibility that Garnett could have marched south through Beverly as the Union forces had not yet occupied Beverly. In defense of Garnett, the first report he received indicated that the Union troops were in Beverly. Boem, however, believes Garnett should have confirmed the situation before heading back to Leadsville.

(18) Haselberger, *Yanks from the South;* pp. 195-196.

(19) Howe, *Civil War Times;* p. 13.

(20) Thomson, *Seventh Indiana;* p. 32.

(21) *ORs*, series I, v. II, p. 222.

(22) Haselberger, *Yanks from the South;* p. 195.

(23) *Ibid.;* p. 197-198.

(24) *Ibid.*

(25) Boem, *The Civil War in Western Virginia;* p. 78.

(26) Howe, *Civil War Times;* p. 13.

(27) Haselberger, *Yanks from the South;* p. 199 for the Confederate casualties and *ORs*, series I, v. II, p. 223, (Captain Benham's report) for the Union losses.

(28) J. Cutler Andrews, *The North Reports the Civil War* (University of Pittsburgh, 1955); p. 106.

(29) *Ibid.*

(30) *Ibid;* p. 108. McClellan blamed his subordinates for slowness in the matter.

(31) Eugene P. Moehring and Arleen Keylin, Editors, *The Civil War Extra* (New York, 1975); pp. 36, 38, 39.

PICTURE CREDITS

—49— *The Tygart Valley Line*, courtesy, Barbour County Historical Society.

—50— *The Soldier of Indiana.*

—51— Courtesy, USAMHI.

—52— Same.

—52— Miller's *Photographic History.*

—53— *The Soldier of Indiana.*

—54— Courtesy, West Virginia University.

—56— Indiana Historical Society

—57— Courtesy, The Louis A. Warren Lincoln Library and Museum.

—58— Miller's *Photographic History.*

—59— Courtesy, USAMHI.

—60— Miller's *Photographic History.*

—61— Same.

—62— *Harper's Pictorial History of the Civil War.*

—62— Courtesy, West Virginia University.

—62— Miller's *Photographic History.*

—63— Courtesy, Library of Congress.

CHAPTER 5 AN UNDERCURRENT OF ANXIETY AS TO THE FUTURE

"BETWEEN ENLISTMENTS."

The days following the 3rd of August, when we were discharged were restless days for me; spent about town for the most part. Our campaign in West Va, under General George B. McClellan, having been a success; and the Battle of Bull Run, having been a serious defeat, placing Washington City in great danger of capture by the rebels, was occasion for the administration to at once call Gen'l McClellan, to the Capitol, where he was placed in command of Washington, and all the troops of the vicinity.

The papers said that he found every thing in a bad condition. He at once began the work of properly placing the troops already there and by every means trying to bring order out of chaos. It was said in the papers that he at once began to build Forts and to throw up fortifications to defend the capitol, and to gather war materials of every kind needed by a well organized and thoroughly equipped army; and to prepare for a long struggle. They say that McClellan superintends all the work of fortifying. Much of it personally; frequently going in the night to inspect work being done on some of the Forts. He also looks to the placing of the new troops as they come in.

The papers are filled continually with these matters and also from other places in the seceded and border slave states, so that war and enlistment were the topics of most conversations.

There were a number of social parties and a picnic or two, most of which I attended and enjoyed. And I took two or three days to visit with some relatives in Greenwood, ten miles north.

Two companies were being recruited in Johnson County, at the head of one was Samuel Lambertson a Merchant Tailor of Franklin. At the head of the other was George W. Allison, editor of The Franklin Jeffersonian. Lambertson, in politics had of late years been a Republican, and Allison and his paper had been Democratic, but when Sumter fell party names and line were lost and they, like most of our citizens, were for the Union, first last and at all times, and at any cost.

Thomas A. Jeffery, a comrade of Co. H in the Three Months Service and myself decided to enlist with Lambertson and his friends; and at once began a recruiting work.

The first recruit that I secured was John C. Henderson a school mate and near neighbor. I found him chopping in a large body of timber near fathers farm. After a few statements on my part, and a number of questions on his part answered by me as best I could, John said you put my name down for me; and I will finish this job if I can, but mind you I am ready any time.

Most names then enrolled were from town and near vicinity, from about Amity, five miles East of South and from the vicinity of Trafalger and Nineveh, both west of South of Franklin. Jeffery and myself began to work in Hopewell neighborhood, three miles west of Franklin.

A meeting of the company was called and an election of officers held; resulting in the choice of Samuel Lambertson as Captain, George G. Smith as First Lieut. Thomas A. Jeffery as Second Lieut. and David Holmes, a school Teacher as orderly.

The young ladies of Hopewell met and decided to make a silk flag for the new Company. Little sewing parties were held and the Flag was soon completed.

The Government at Washington urged the Governors of States to hasten forward enlistments, and to send troops to the front as rapidly as possible.

Governor O. P. Morton of Indiana urged all companies now in course of formation to hurry into camp. Our Officers were pressed to go to camp at once.

It was decided that our Company should go into camp at Indianapolis on Thursday, Aug. 29th and every member had been notified.

It was arranged that our Company should meet at Hopewell on the 28th Aug. to receive the Flag; and the people of the neighborhood planned a picnic for the occasion.

Mr. John H. Vannuys (whose son Samuel Watson, and some of his nephews, and others, some of his near neighbors, and several of them members of his class in Sabbath School, were members of the Co;) invited the Company and the neighbors to a grove near the north west corner of his farm at a point just one mile north of the church.

The grove was a beautiful place; and the day was ideal for a picnic. There was a large attendance of members of the company and their friends. A platform and a long table had been erected, and a very fine dinner was spread.

The table was fairly loaded with a bountiful supply of the good things of the farms around. There were substantials for the hungry, dainties for the delicate and tarts for the most fastidious.

An 1881 stylized illustration of the John H. Vannuys farm.

The soldiers were given the place of honor at the table. By the side of Captain Lambertson was Rev. John F. Smith, pastor of Hopewell Presbyterian Church who invoked the Divine blessing upon president Lincoln and all in authority, upon the Army, upon the nation, and upon the table comforts before us.

The dinner was duly discussed in detail in a most practical manner. Soldiers and citizens seemed in fine spirits. Some one facitiously suggested that we do justice to all the samples before us, and each determine which samples he would ask "Uncle Sam" to issue to him individually. Some one said if that is done, wont the boys live high! This being questioned and the Captain being appealed to, said with a placid smile, certainly, they will; Lieut. Smith thought it was doubtful, and Jeffery and I thought it was more than doubtful.

When the dinner was well over, Mr Vannuys who seemed to be somewhat in charge, called the people together and asked quiet for a little time. Captain Lambertson called the company into line and said the orderly will call the roll. David Holmes 1st Sergeant then called the roll in a clear strong voice, when all present had answered "here," he turned and said "Captain, all present or accounted for." The Captain said "you will keep your places for a while."

Then the young ladies came forward carrying the beautiful flag made by them, and mounted the platform. Miss Mary E. Vannuys, then stepped forward and, presented the Flag, in the following appropriate and patriotic address.

"Soldiers, defenders of our homes and firesides we are here to day for the performance of a duty at once sad and yet pleasant. Sad because we must bid farewell to our brave friends and relatives. It may be for years and it may be forever. But pleasant, because we see you are willing to go to the post of toil and danger when duty demands you, and ready to imperil your lives for your sisters, your wives and your mothers. And it is pleasant because our hearts can go with you. The cause in which you have enlisted is so holy we can conscientiously follow you in every danger with our sympathy and prayers.

It is not for us to engage in the bitter strife of the battlefield, nor face the rifle ball, nor bare our breast to the brandished steel. It is little we can do, but you work, we'll cheer, and as a pledge of this, we present you with this flag.

It is the work of our hands. We solemnly ask you to guard it well. But we would not presume to teach you your duty, for that you know and we are confident you will perform it.

Take this flag, bear it, bear it proudly and in the tempest of battle and the din of arms and the shrieks of the dying and the wounded, look up to that banner and know that the hands which set in order those stars and stripes are raised to heaven for you. That our hearts are poured out in supplication at the throne of grace. That the God of battles will be with you, shield you and be your exceeding great reward.

We know that this our hearts gift will not be disgraced in your hands. We know that you will never suffer traitorous hands to defile this humble but sacred pledge of our love.

Should the staff be broken and the flag fall to the ground, we are sure there will be some one in this company, who Jasper like will spring forward in the hottest of the strife and bravely raise it to heaven from whence it gathered all its hues. Under such a banner, but with fewer stars our fathers fought and died; you will not forsake it now.

Yes, though we tell you weeping, we say to you go, and in the name of your God set up your banners. Go, and the God of Israel go before you as a pillar of cloud by day and a pillar of fire by night. Go, and may our happy hearts ere long welcome you to our now desolate homes and firesides.

But if any of you fall may it be said of you as of the brave and lamented Ellsworth, "He died while his country defending."

Again commending you to the god of battles and the God of peace, we bid you an affectionate farewell."

At the close of Miss Vannuyses address, Capt. Lambertson took the Flag and said, we accept this flag. I will ask Lieut. Jeffery to speak for my self and the company. Lieut. Thomas A. Jeffery then came to the stand and spoke as follows in response:

"Ladies of Hopewell, In behalf of the Franklin Riflemen, I receive this flag, a proud Banner that was borne aloft and defended so gallantly by our fore-fathers during the dark and eventful days of the Revolution of Seventy-Six; and which has been for us so many years the golden ensign of Constitutional liberty. That glorious old flag which has ever been the shield of the American Citizen, whether in foreign lands or on the broad seas. I say I receive this flag as one of the strongest evidence that you are not idle spectators of the gigantic struggle now being made to preserve the best nation on the earth from the destruction that has been threatened it by traitors to the government.

If we should ever be called to enter into deadly conflict with the enemies of that flag; our arms will be nerved for its defense; when we remember that it was the handiwork of the fair ladies of Hopewell; and that with it we have the sympathy and prayers of such self sacrificing and patriotic ladies.

So far as in us lies this banner shall have the post of honor in the field and when hostilities shall cease, and traitors learn to war no more, against our land and humanity, with the smiles of a beneficent providence we hope to return this flag from many a victorious conflict

"Our hearts can go with you."

with the enemy. It may be all tattered and torn, but with out a stain of dishonor. As you have said we soon may be separated, but I hope not forever, but you can rest assured that where ever we may be, that you have presented us with a token that will never be forgotten by us, while memory lasts.

We may soon be called to the tented field, there to meet in deadly conflict with those that would seek to destroy this government, and trample that flag in the dust which has been their shield and protection ever since the days of their infancy. Let memory be dethroned; Let us be lost to all that is good and noble when we can say we know not the emblem of our fathers liberty.

I thank you again for this holy manifestation of the interest and good wishes you have toward the Franklin Riflemen and the cause for which we are ready to stake our lives and our sacred honor. Long may that banner triumphantly wave over the land of the free and the home of the brave."

Following Lieutenant Jeffery's address Captain Lambertson proposed three cheers for President Lincoln, then three for Gov. O. P. Morton, and three for the Flag and the Union, all of which were given with such volume as to make the woods ring. Then Mr John H. VanNuys, proposed three cheers for "our boys," "The Franklin Riflemen," to which the citizens responded, so heartily that the welkin rang.

The Captain called a meeting of the company at 9 o'clock, tomorrow a.m. in McClellans Hall in Franklin, ready to start for camp at Indianapolis.

We then broke ranks and all turned again to the several pastimes of the day. The "boys" were full of hope, and enthusiasm ran high.

There were several new enlistments during the day especially during the afternoon, many of them were young men of Hopewell and Shiloh church neighborhoods.

The people too seemed to enter into the spirit of the occasion, and to vie pleasantly with each other in favors and encouragement to the volunteers; and yet there was, quite apparent, an under current of anxiety as to the future, first, there was the parting and then the uncertainty of return, and of general results.

This was quite evident throughout the day, perhaps most noticeable among the young soldiers and their lady friends. My best girl was there: and some folks thought there were several of her, but could not make out which one was her. I will now admit there were about a dozen of her; and it is proper to say here, that the most of her got married before I returned.

Some of the "boys" went home early to prepare for going into camp tomorrow. The day had been a very pleasant one. Father and the family were there. I went home with them. And thus ended my stay about home between enlistments.

"It is little we can do."

Hoosiers Respond to the Civil War

Indiana ranked second nationally in the number of men it provided for the Union cause. The patriotism was evident from the beginning when 12,000 men came forward to answer the initial call for 4,683. Indiana soldiers were at the first land battle on June 3, 1861 (Phillippi) — and at the last on May 12, 1865 at Palmetto Ranch in Texas. It was officially recorded that Indiana contributed 196,363 men, or 74 percent of those who were eligible for service. Over 7,000 died or were mortally wounded on the battlefields, and another 19,000 died from "all other" causes (primarily diseases). In other words, about one out of eight died.[(1)]

The typical Hoosier soldier was 22 years old, 5'8," blue eyed, light complexioned, and had either sandy or dark hair. Near "average," Billy at the time of his enlistment was 23, 5'6," blue eyed, light complexioned and brown haired. Seventy-one percent of Indiana soldiers indicated "farmer" as their former occupation.[(2)] Billy would be an exception.

On the home front, much was made of southern sympathizers and disloyalty. By war's end, however, patriotism in Indiana may have reached its highest point. At least President Lincoln's popularity increased from 51 to 53 per cent in the four war years and Governor Morton doubled the Republican plurality for his office in the same period.[(3)]

The Civil War had a marked effect on the lives of the folks at home. The daily hardships certainly were not lessened. The farm wife, for example, in addition to the traditional tasks of cooking, birthing, nursing, gardening, milking, churning, washing, mending, etc., was now managing, plowing, and harvesting. The work of being a soldier's wife far exceeded the work of being a soldier. Then, whatever the difficulty — and the loneliness — women were counted on to lift the spirits of their loved ones in uniform.

The war years had another effect on women. For the first time, women were being accepted in the male-dominated work force. Women began to teach in public schools, work in factories and provide professional health care.[(4)]

In August 1861, everything was of historical significance. A nation was facing its greatest crisis. Each of 31 million people was nearing a major personal milestone. The future was going to be determined by men and their guns. Billy Davis sensed the sentiment at Mr. Vannuys' picnic when he wrote, "The boys were full of hope and enthusiasm ran high." And for those who were not soldiers, they "vie pleasantly with each other in favors and encouragement to the volunteers."

"But if any of you fall . . ."

William Black — a wounded Civil War soldier.

END NOTES

(1) William F. Fox, *Regimental Losses in The American Civil War 1861-1865* (Dayton, 1985); pp. 526-536 — for the statistics. There were (at least) two methods to determine these national rankings. Indiana is number two in either computation. One method requires every enlistment be adjusted or equated to a three-year enrollment. The other method is a simple calculation based on total enlistments, regardless of length of service, and regardless of how many times one man enlisted. Civil War statistics must be treated with caution. For discussions of Indiana's contribution, see the Indiana history publications which cover the Civil War period. Particularly Thornbrough, *Indiana in the Civil War Era 1850-1880* which establishes the tone of patriotism.

(2) Carl A. Zenor, "Indiana Goes to War," *Indiana and the Civil War* (Indianapolis, 1961); p. 10. Based on samples of vital records analyzed after the war.

(3) Patrick J. Furlong, *Indiana An Illustrated History* (Northridge, California 1985); p. 80. Also (for an exaggerated narrative of War Governor Morton's accomplishments): Charles M. Walker, *Sketch of the Life, Character, and Public Service of Oliver P. Morton* (Indianapolis, 1878).

(4) Donald F. Carmony, "War and the Emancipation of Women," *Indiana and the Civil War;* p. 26. Another significant change was the turnaround in life expectancies. Until the Civil War, men statistically outlived women. By 1900, women were outliving men by two years and the gap has been widening ever since.

PICTURE CREDITS

—66— *Johnson County Atlas,* courtesy, Johnson County Historical Society.

—67— Miller's *Photographic History.*

—68— *Harper's Pictorial History of the Civil War.*

—69— Miller's *Photographic History.*

—70— Same.

CHAPTER 6 A VERY DISAGREEABLE GLOOMY TIME

Franklin, Indiana. Thursday Aug. 29, 1861. At an early hour this morning the home good byes were spoken and father and I started to town. My outfit consisted of one quilt, underwear, a book or two, and several useful articles.

There were many people in town, seemingly most of the friends of members of the Company were there to see them off.

Early in the afternoon Captain Samuel Lambertson's Company — The Franklin Riflemen, met in McClellan's Hall; and at two p.m. formed and marched to the Baptist Church, where we were addressed by the Rev. John L. Jones, a veteran of the war of 1812, after which the young Ladies of Franklin presented Captain Lambertson with a beautiful Bouquet. We were then escorted to the Depot by Thirty four young ladies dressed in white and each wearing a Red, White and Blue Scarf.

We soon stepped onto the cars and at once started for Indianapolis, waving a farewell to a large crowd of friends who had assembled to see us off. The run to Indianapolis was soon made. We then marched to Camp Morton, which we reached about sundown. Quarters were soon assigned us and rations drawn. After supper the Hopewell contingent and several from Franklin and Bethany neighborhood met in our Bunk and were led in a scripture reading and prayer service by Comrade James M. Bone. And thus began our first night in Camp.

Camp Morton, Friday Aug. 30, 1861. Camp was very quiet for us new arrivals. We had no drill, but were interested in seeing others drill or attempt it, and in seeing the novelties of camp life yet most of the time was spent in our new quarters in conversation or in reading the Daily Papers.

Late in the Afternoon we were moved to another at the South west corner of Camp Morton.

Saturday Aug. 31, 1861. This too has been a very quiet day. Drilled some the forenoon. The commissioned officers and some of the non commissioned officers spend most of their leisure time studying the Tactics. Many of us privates spend our leisure time reading some books we brought with us. I have Twelve Lectures to young Men, by H. W. Beecher. Capt. Lambertson and Lieut. Smith went to Franklin this afternoon.

Sunday Sept. 1, 1861. There has been no drilling to day, and it has been very quiet in camp. A gentleman from the city gave a Temperance Lecture and distributed some Temperance Tracts.

Rev. Mr Stevens, a Presbyterian Minister of Indianapolis preached an excellent sermon in the afternoon.

We met again for reading of scriptures and for prayer and thus closed our first Sabbath day in camp.

Monday, Sept. 2, 1861. Lieut. Jeffery took the company out for a drill practice this forenoon. He like myself, having been members of Co. "H," 7th Regt. Ind. Vol. Inft. in the Three Month's Service.

About 11 o'clock a.m. Capt. Lambertson and Lieut Smith, came into camp bringing several recruits to the company. Thomas Hill came as a cook for Messes No. 5 & 6.

I obtained a pass and at 4 p.m. started for Franklin and then walked out home, which I reached at a late hour. I found Grand father and Grand Mother Davis from Clark County, Ills. there. The evening was very pleasantly spent; for it had been several years since any of us had seen our Grand parents. The evening was more especially interesting to me for the reason that Grand-father had been a Soldier in the war of 1812 and stationed about Detroit, Mich.

Tuesday, Sept. 3, 1861. The early morning was spent visiting home folks and my Grand parents. I then went to see my sister Mary Ellen in her home; then I hurried to town and took the train for Indianapolis at 10 a.m. and reached camp before noon. At 2 o'clock Captain took the Company to the Canal bathing. While there I let down into a hole, and went under, being unexpected I strangled, I struggled, and called for help, and was taken out by comrade Wm. G. Allison.

Late this afternoon, James Gavin, Adjutant of 7th Ind. of the Three Months Service, came over and asked officers to take this company into a reorganization of the 7th Regiment. The officers agreed to do so. At the usual

James Gavin, Lieutenant-Colonel of the 7th Indiana — Colonel from November 27, 1861 through April 23, 1863.

time we had our little prayer meeting and retired. I felt especially thankful that I had been spared from drowning.

Camp Morton, Wednesday Sept. 4, 1861. This morning our old Adjutant came with an order for us to move to Camp Dumont. Capt. Lambertson being officer of the Day in this camp we could not go. During the day Samuel V. List, Samuel W. Vannuys, George K. Covert, Richard V. Ditmars and a Robert Sloan came as recruits to our Company. They are all from Hopewell neighborhood.

Camp Dumont, Thursday, Sept. 5, 1861. We were up early this morning preparing to move, and as soon as Captain Lambertson was relieved from duty as officer of the day, we started for Camp Dumont.

When we arrived we were assigned our place. Tents were furnished and we began at once to pitch them and found ourselves quite awkward at the work.

We learn that the Seventh Regiment Indiana Volunteer Infantry was organized September 2, 1861 with Ebenezer Dumont colonel of the reorganized Regiment, with Lieut. James Gavin Adjutant of the 7th in the Three Months Service as Lieutenant Colonel, and Captain John F. Cheek of Company "D" in the old Regiment as Major, and Lieut. John M. Blair as Adjutant.

The Officers of the reorganized Regiment were Mustered into service September 2nd 1861, by Lieut Col. Wood of the United States Army. We learn too, that we are to be Company "F" in the new Seventh. Up to this time we have called ourselves the "Franklin Riflemen."

The following is a full Roster of Co. "F," with some incidents related to each as I now recall them. [See Appendix A.]

Camp Morton, Sept. 5, 1861. Continued. Just at dinner time Mr R. T. Overstreet and wife and Mr L. W. Fletcher and wife of Franklin, came into camp with baskets well filled with good things. We had not been in Camp long, yet long enough to relish such things and we were grateful to our friends for remembering us so kindly.

This afternoon blankets were issued to us. Mr Willis D. Jones, and his sister in-law, Miss Kate Alexander called for a short time. Our evening service of prayer was observed and we retired.

Camp Dumont, Friday, Sept. 6, 1861. This is a beautiful morning. Several friends of members of Co. "F," came early in wagons, with a full days supply for our Mess tables.

Lieutenants Smith and Jeffery went to Franklin this afternoon, consequently we drilled but little. Many of the boys in camp get the Daily Papers, Morning and Evening and in that way we keep informed of the state of new enlistments and of the movements of our several armies.

Camp Dumont, Saturday Sept. 7, 1861. Early this morning John H. Vannuys esq. and wife and Mr Peter Ditmars and wife of Hopewell neighborhood and others from South of Franklin, came in. This afternoon several of this co. went to J. H. Vanjens, in the City and bought Revolvers.

We called at the Merrill Book Store where we met Mr J. H. V. Smith, to whom several of us had gone to school. He kindly went with us to Odd Fellows Hall from the top of which we had a fine view of the city.

Camp Dumont, Sabbath Sept. 8, 1861. This morning most of our mess arranged to go into the City to Church. Started at ten A.M. to the Third Presbyterian church. This was their Communion Sabbath. Heard a good sermon and enjoyed a very helpful service, and at close returned to camp. After dinner a number of us went to a near by grove and resting in the shade read some books we brought from home. Later in the P.M. Rev. A. C. Allen, a former Pastor at Hopewell preached. This evening a number of us went again to the Third Presbyterian church.

Camp Dumont, Monday, Sept. 9, '61. The day passed with little worth noting. Most of the boys who went home Saturday returned today, which makes this look like a Company and not a squad.

The Daily Papers supply much interest in camp.

Quite a number of friends of members of the Regt. were in camp today.

Camp Dumont, Tuesday, Sept. 10, '61. Early this morning friends from Shiloh and Hopewell neighborhood came in wagons; and friends of a large group of comrades from South of Franklin, and some friends of a squad of Co. "F" from Boone County west of Indianapolis came in also, and so it is almost every week day. We learn from the papers that such is true in Camp Morton and the several Rendesvous over this and other states.

Almost every one visiting our camp come to see some relative or friend; and so it is over all the north; it seems as though they felt that they were not doing enough for the volunteer soldier; an indication that the patriotism of the country is thoroughly aroused.

The streets of Indianapolis in 1854 — Odd Fellows Building on far right.

The "streets" of Camp Morton in 1863.

The coming of so many visitors makes of every camp a social center. Young ladies do not hesitate to visit a camp that they may meet their best gentleman friend if he has enlisted, and to encourage him. Almost every noon the several messes spread down blankets and a sumptious feast is furnished.

In the afternoon I went to the city with some lady friends from Franklin and while there I met Lieut. Col. Gavin who said he thought we would go to the front soon.

Camp Dumont, Wednesday, Sept. 11, '61. Last evening we drew Shirts Drawers and Socks. It was raining this morning and continued until noon. We spent the time marking our new property. After dinner I went to get a Revolver repaired, and while there met a comrade of the Three Month Service; and we went to the State House to the State Library, and had an interesting time looking at War Relics from Mexico and other bric a brac curio and in examining books.

Camp Dumont, Thursday Sept. 12, 1861. There was some fog this morning, but it soon disappeared leaving a clear sky. Comrade James R. Dunlap, Benjamin G. Trout, John H. Vannuys, Samuel Watson Vannuys, Richard V. Ditmars, Gabriel M. Overstreet, Samuel V. List, Abraham I. Canary, George K. Covert, John C. Henderson, and myself went to a studio in the city and had a group picture taken.

When we returned to camp from the Studio, I was much pleased to find my Father, and my Sister Martha and my brother Daniel in camp, they brought full baskets and the table was already spread. This was my time for special joy and rejoicing. As my father was well acquainted with most of the Johnson County boys it was a great day for him.

We received our Coats and Pants this afternoon, getting a good fit was almost out of the question. We were ordered out on our first Dress Parade at five o'clock this afternoon. The Adjutant read an order that all Volunteers having Revolvers or Pistols must send them home, as they would not be allowed to take them. Our Mess assembled for a short service.

Camp Dumont, Friday Sept. 13, 1861. This morning I was detailed for camp guard duty, the first in this camp. Early this morning a squad of Hopewell folks came in. They had not forgotten the baskets. Had a pleasant time to day when off duty, at 5 p.m. bid my friends good bye.

We have had very little Company and no Regimental drill up to this time, and yet there is talk that we will go to the front soon. At dusk went on guard not far from the Regimental wood pile and caught a citizen taking some wood; called the Corporal of the guard and sent my captive to headquarters.

About nine P.M. Lieut. Col. Gavin, rode into camp and ordered us to get three days rations and be ready to march at 4 o'clock tomorrow Morning. We are querying what we can do without guns and ammunition.

Soon it began to rain. At ten we marched to the Armory in the City and drew guns, accouterments and ammunition.

Camp Dumont, Indianapolis, Ind. Saturday, Sept. 14, 1861. I was called at 4 A.M. and sent to Headquarters for guard duty. Ours is the only regiment in this camp. At break of day I was relieved from duty and went to the Co. and was relieved of further duty at nine A.M. Rained hard all forenoon. At 11 A.M., went with my friend Wm. H. LaGrange to the Depot. He thinks that he will enlist and come to our Company, as there are so many of his friends and acquaintances in this Co. After friend LaGrange left, I went to the studio for a picture for a friend.

After dinner we put our bedding, clothes and other belongings in to bundles to move. Cleared off about 3 p.m. Orders came to be ready to march at 6 p.m. At Sundown John H. Vannuys, Esq. bid his son Samuel Watson and the rest of us good bye.

At dusk we started for the Lawrenceburg Depot and left Indianapolis near ten p.m.

(It is proper to note here that Wm. H. Lagrange, mentioned above as likely to enlist soon, was very soon there after taken down with Typhoid fever and was dangerously ill for a month or two. The fever settled in his legs causing fever sores and making him something of an invalid to this writing, March, 1913.)

Cincinnatti, Ohio, Sunday Sept. 15, 1861. We arrived here at 8 A.M. after the arrival of the other half of the Regt. we started on our march to the Marietta-Cincinnatti Depot. Went North to Fourth St. followed that to Pike and Pike to Front and Front to the Depot.

At 2 p.m. we started for Marietta. At the train a light haired young man standing at the car door, asked Captain Lambertson if he might go in his Company. The Captain said yes, come on, and extended a hand and lifted him into the Box Car. His name was John M. Johnson, said he was sixteen years old, his home was in Cincinnatti, he was a student of the City High School. *(He was of an amiable*

Guards along the railroad.

A Cincinnati apple vendor.

By the mountain and by the shore.

disposition, and soon became a favorite with the Company and more especially of Captain Lambertson. He served through the three years, was seldom sick and never seriously so, I think he missed no marches, and I believe he failed but once to be on the firing line. That was at Second Bull Run, on Aug. 30th 1862, and then because his shoes gave out, went to pieces. He was because of faithfulness of service promoted Corporal and then to Sergeant, and was discharged September 20th, 1864, at end of enlistment.)

Our course was up the Little Miami River Valley, with a rough broken country on our right and left, we next came to rather low flat lands and then to some nice rolling country. At ten p.m. we left Chillicothe, Ohio.

On the Train in Ohio, Monday, Sept. 16, 1861. I slept several short naps last night, but did not rest much. Daylight found us in a very broken country. Some fine scenery. At 8:30 we came to a large hill or Mountain where two engines were used to move our train and there was much switching and backing in order to get to the top, we were at times apparently on the side of the mountain, and when we were over much the same process was necessary to get us down and to the River at a point opposite Parkersburg, West Va. where we waited for a Ferry Boat to carry us over, and at twelve o'clock we stepped on to the sacred soil of Va. At 3 P.M. we took train and at dark started towards Grafton. Passed through several Tunnels during the night.

On the Train, W. Va. Tuesday Sept. 17, 1861. Day light found us at Clarksburg, soon after leaving the town we came to and entered a Tunnel, said to be a mile long in which it was indescribably dark. Bridgeport came next then the Village of Webster, about five miles south of Grafton where we arrived by 9:30 A.M.

We were soon off the train, formed a line & stacked arms for the first time. The Tents arrived and were soon pitched after a fashion, for we are not yet experts.

There came up a heavy thunder and rain storm before all the tents were up.

We soon had our first dinner as real soldiers fully armed and equipped in a real camp in the enemies country; or what was the enemies country when the war began.

The most noted incident of the afternoon was a serious mishap Comrade Wm M. Kelley while making Tent stake, and although right handed was using the axe in his left hand and cut off his right index or trigger finger. *(He was discharged for disability September, 18, 1862.)*

I think that most of the boys wrote home this afternoon. I wrote a letter to my father.

This inhospitable introduction to Virginia has lengthened some faces somewhat. Late to day we received our Knapsacks and Caps.

Our little band met in a prayer service and retired.

Webster, W. Va. Wednesday Sept. 18, 1861. This was a gloomy morning. After breakfast we began to prepare for moving. Contrary to orders several of the boys of the Regt. fired their muskets, thinking there was nothing to try them out at a mark.

Our time was spent this morning packing our clothing and trinkets in our knapsacks and strapping our blankets in a roll on top of our knapsacks.

Three new men came from Franklin to this Company to day. We started at 3 p.m. on our march toward Phillippi, and stopped at dusk three miles short of Phillippi, and when the wagons came, we soon pitched our tents, and after supper, being much fatigued from carrying such heavy loads over muddy roads, lay down to rest, and thus ended our first march.

Near Phillippi, W. Va. Thursday Sept. 19, 1861. Up early and had breakfast over when orders came to strike tents and get ready to march; we were soon ready and started at 8 a.m. A walk of two miles brought us to the hill where the 7th camped through the most of June in the Three Months Service. One mile farther we came to Phillippi, W. Va. where the Civil War began, on the early morning of June 3, 1861, when the first Federal Volunteers — The Seventh Ind. Vols. — met the first Confederate

A Phillippi street about 1861, looking north.

Volunteers in battle; true it was not much of a battle, but it was the first.

Not many troops here now, and but few citizens. We trudged on our way resting frequently. Passed through Bealington, where we camped during the first week of last July. Are but few houses. At 5 p.m. reached Laurel Hill and camped for the night. Visited the Fortifications and the graves of some of the Rebels killed last July.

After prayers in our mess we retired.

A Little History and a Statement. It is not amiss to state here that during the Three Month Service while we were camped on the hill north of Phillippi; Col. Dumont, then in command at that point, wanted information as to location and strength of the rebels at Laurel Hill and Vicinity.

Dr. W. B. Fletcher of Indianapolis, Surgeon of the 6th Ind. and John Hartman Wilson, a citizen of Bealington at north foot of Laurel Hill; offered their services and were accepted. They started on June 27th, and after a few days, were able to report position, plans of Fortifications and strength of the enemy, and that Gen'l R. G. Garnett, a Virginian, graduate of West Point, class of 1841 was in command. This was more possible on their part because Wilson was acquainted and knew all the roads bridle paths and streams of the vicinity.

Bealington in 1861 was a village of half dozen houses. Now at this writing 1913, it has several thousand people, has two or more Railroads, and a number of Iron Furnaces, Coke Kilns and other large Factories. Coal and Iron ore are mined extensively here abouts.

I wish to state that Mr John Hartman Wilson, the scout and spy mentioned above has for many years been a citizen of Iola, Kansas and a neighbor of mine.

Laurel Hill, W. Va. Friday Sept. 20, 1861. Started early for Beverly. Crossed the remaining and higher portions of Laurel Hill, wended our way down the South Eastern slope and stopped at noon near Leedsville, on the spot where the 7th stopped on night of July 12, when following the Confederate Genl. R. S. Garnett and his forces.

After an hours rest we started and soon through Leedsville, a village of five or six houses strung along the Phillippi Beverley Pike at the point where the Rowlesburg Pike leaves the former. Our course was up Tygarts Valley, with fine scenery on our right and left. About sundown we went into camp East of the River and just North of Beverley.

Fifty Years later. In 1861, Leedsville was but a Village on the Pike just East of Leeds Creek, in a very beautiful and especially rich valley.

At this writing — 1913 — it is the large and important city of Elkins, so called, for Senator Steven B. Elkins.

The City has several Railroads, many Iron Furnaces, Steel Rolling Mills, and other large business Enterprises.

The Mountains of this portion of W. Va. are full of Coal and Iron Ore. When in that vicinity in Dec. 1861, we saw one place in Laurel Hill near the river where an eight foot Vein of Coal was in sight.

What a fine opportunity for investment at close of war.

Near Beverley, W. Va., Saturday Sept. 21, 1861. Awakened early and found it raining; got up and began ditching our tent to prevent being drowned out. After breakfast, I went to town, found it is small but well located in a beautiful valley surrounded by Mountains all covered with Cedar, Pine and Oak and other valuable Timber.

Frequently when it is raining in the Valley the Sun will be shining on the mountain tops. Still raining at bed time.

After singing and prayers we laid down.

Near Beverley, W. Va. Sunday Sept. 22, 1861. It was still raining this morning. Laid some flat stone about our tent so as to keep out of the mud a little.

About ten o'clock came orders for a hurry up dinner. We had dinner, packed up and were soon ready.

Started at noon, carrying our guns and accoutrements, Knapsacks etc, we plodded on through the mud resting frequently.

Our course continued up Tygarts Valley River, thr'u' a very beautiful valley with the finest scenery. The valley has evidently been long settled, judging from the permanent character of the improvements, shown by the large substantial houses and barns, in the number of orchards and quality of some of the fruit. A muddy tiresome march brought us near to Huttonsville at sundown, the village consists of a half dozen houses at the foot of the Mountain and near the river. The clouds cleared away by dark.

Huttonsville, W. Va. Monday, Sept. 23, 1861. Judging from the amount of Rations, Forage and ammunition stored here it is evident that this is a base of supplies for a considerable army; perhaps for the coming winter.

Started early, our route was still up Tygarts Valley River. Crossed a small swift stream said to be "Elk Water," and stopped near noon in a narrow valley with the river at our left, with the mountains every where in view.

It appears as though we are the advance post of this Elk Water encampment. Pitched our tents, ditched around them, got dinner, dried our blankets and clothes and disposed ourselves as comfortably as possible. In the afternoon I called in the Camp of the 17th Regiment Ind. Vol. Inft. and found a number of friends. Retired after prayers.

Subsequent Events. It is well to mention here that the 17th Regiment, was shortly there after ordered to the South West, and took an active part in Kentucky and Tennessee, in 1863. East Tennessee in 1863. Against Atlanta, 1864. Campaign after Hood 1864, and Wilson's raid in Alabama and Georgia in 1865.

Elk Water, W. Va. Tuesday, Sept. 24, 1861. Last night was cool. This is a beautiful morning, clear and calm. About noon the Regiment was called out on general Examination and Inspection.

Comrade A. I. Canary is sick today. Dress Parade at 5 p.m., the first in Virginia.

Elk Water W. Va. Weds., Sept. 25, 1861. We had our first Battalion or Regimental drill this afternoon and Dress Parade again at 5 o'clock. Many of the boys were much broken from the inclement weather and the hard marches through the mud from Webster to this place. A prayer service was held in our tent again this evening.

Elk Water, W. Va. Thursday Sept. 26, 1861. To day was much as yesterday in camp, except that it began raining about sundown. Comrade Robert Sloan who has been complaining since the 24th is much worse today.

Friday, Sept. 27, 1861. Rained all last night. About two this afternoon a detail of twenty five from this company in charge of Lieut. T. A. Jeffery were called for to go on picket about three miles out. We found a small stream near so swollen that we could not cross except on horses.

We trudged through the rain and mud and about sundown arrived at the Picket Post up a narrow gulch two or three miles from camp. The greatly increased volume of water from so much rain so nearly filled the narrow valley that we scarcely found standing room.

We at once went about putting up a brush bivouac open on one side for a fire in front, while this was being built a large branch fell from an overhanging tree and stuck into the ground just where I had been standing but a few seconds before. When our change of pickets were placed we put our fire out and gathered into our brush tent. We all had a round of picket duty during the night.

Saturday Sept. 28, 1861. Last night was rainy, cold and dreary almost beyond description, we got very little sleep, for our teeth chattered together most of the night, and we are a sorry looking lot of boys this morning, after our first night on picket.

About nine A.M. our breakfast came to us and it was a good one. We had no dinner; but about 3 p.m. Lieut. Smith of Co. "F," came out with twenty five more of our boys to relieve us. Col. Dumont came with Lieut. Smith and returned with us.

Once in camp we soon had a good supper.

Comrade A. I. Canary, who had been sick since the 24th inst. was taken to the Hospital this evening.

So much rain has raised the river and washed out part of our breast works, and ran our Quartermaster to the hills. The 3rd Ohio Regt. had to move to higher grounds. Evening: The clouds have cleared away, and it is getting much colder.

Sabbath, Sept. 29, 1861. This was a beautiful morning. As soon as breakfast was over, Comrades R. V. Ditmars and Jesse Y. Demaree took breakfast to our comrades on the picket line. I went to the Hospital and found Comrade A. I. Canary, some better. Returned via the Hospital of the 17th Ind. and found my friend Langton of that Regt. improving.

This evening when our pickets came in they had sent out a foraging party and secured an abundance of fresh beef. J. M. Bone and J. C. Henderson and others went foraging and failed to return; it is thought they must have gotten lost.

One of the 13th Ind. Vols. was buried today with Military honors. It is said he died from fever. There are many fever patients in the hospitals now.

Camp Elk Water, W. Va. Monday, Sept. 30, 1861. Comrade J. M. Bone, J. C. Henderson, and three or four others mentioned yesterday as not having returned from a foraging party, came in this morning. Said they had been lost.

Where rumors "float."

Was clear this morning. We went out and drilled for two hours. I did not feel very well.

Another member of the 13th Ind. was buried to day. He too, died from fever. I did not go on Regimental Drill or Dress Parade. Robt. Sloan, A. I. Canary and W. G. Allison, are some better today.

Camp Elk Water W. Va. Tues., Oct. 1 1861. Last evening a rumer floated into camp, that we were to move at twelve. It proved to be incorrect, but while on drill this A.M. orders came to prepare for marching at noon, drew two days rations and at two p.m. formed lines and started toward Huttonsville, where we forded the river, after a march of two miles came to an old Rebel camp of a month ago, when Gen'l J. J. Reynolds, and his forces were cut off by Gen'l R. E. Lee, which was the occasion for sending us to the front so hurriedly.

Near dark we stopped for the night at the foot of Cheat Mountain. Here we found plenty of rails for a booming fire.

Cheat Mountain, W. Va., Wedns. Oct. 2, 1861. Started at 5 A.M. Soon commenced raining and continued until noon. When we reached the Summit about noon we went into the timber to our right and prepared dinner, and each group or Mess built a bivouac of brush with one side open, in front of which we built rousing fires.

After dinner and when our building was done, some of us went about Headquarters on the summit and found it, as we thought strongly fortified.

A heavy breastwork of logs and earth had been built and a wide and deep ditch or moat had been dug in front. There were many Cannon in the Fort, some were very large, Siege guns, we supposed, and in front of this the timber had all been felled with the tops out away from the Fort and the limbs had been cut so as to leave a sharp point toward the attacking force, this a soldier said was called an abatis.

The large guns in the Fort had full sweep and range of the road and all possible lines of approach.

The 9th Ind. Col. Milroys Regiment was in the Fort and had done most of the work of fortifying.

Drew, fresh beef, salt, beans, and sugar later in the after noon, and being well tired out we laid down early.

Greenbrier Va. Thursday, Oct. 3 1861. We were called at twelve last night and marched at two A.M. We soon crossed Shavers Fork of Cheat River. During the night when going down the mountain we halted from some cause and Sergt. James A. Holmes, laid down to rest and rolled off and went down some twelve or fifteen feet and lodged on a narrow shelf. Some time was spent in getting him up, he was not hurt much.

We marched rapidly and about seven A.M. crossed Greenbrier River, and were now on the eastside of the Alleghaney Mountains where the water flows to the Ohio River, through the Great Kanawha river and not through the Mononghela river.

Soon after crossing the Greenbrier we filed to the left and "Slung Knapsacks," and soon came in sight of the

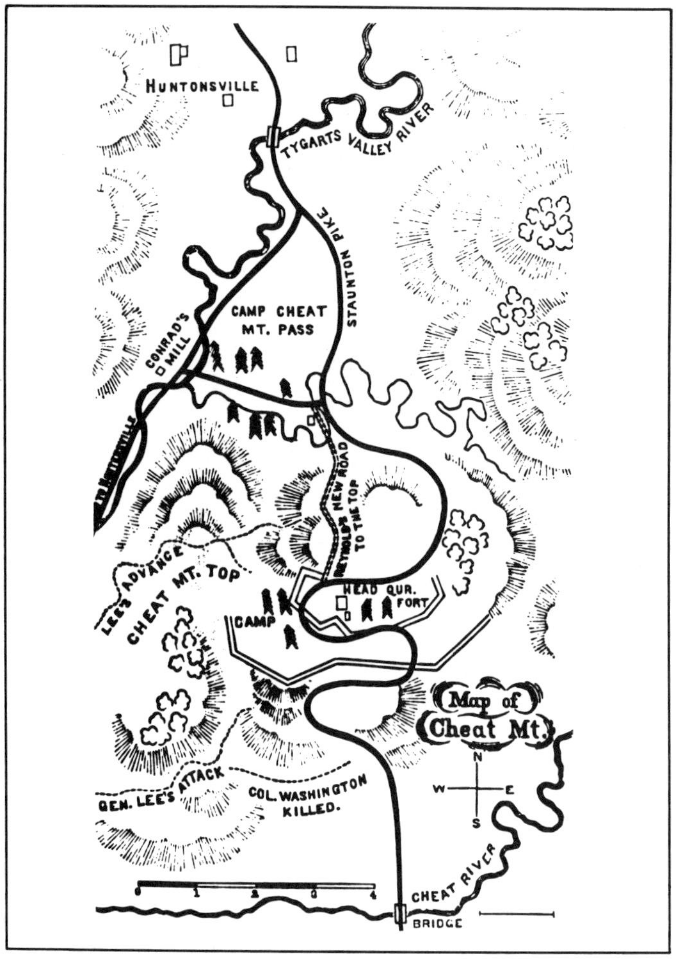

The Cheat Mountain region — a series of engagements had been fought here September 10 through the 15th — Camp Elkwater was seven miles west of Cheat Mountain.

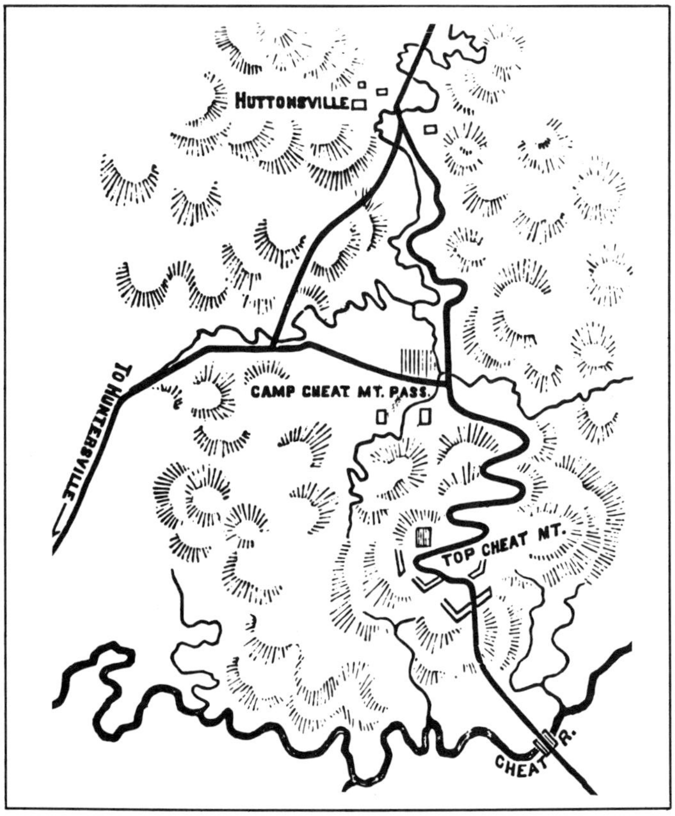

The Cheat Mountain summit and fort.

Rebel camp. A strong line of skirmishers were thrown forward by Col. Milroy, who was opposed by three rebel regiments. We now started in on the double quick, going to the left of our Artillery, somewhat nearer the Rebel works and laid down behind a fence, and saw the enemy file into their trenches.

After half an hour or more we moved into the timber, it was said to prevent a flank movement, after standing there for some time we filed left and went across a meadow to the rear of our batteries on the mountain side nearly east of the Rebel camp and works. We crouched behind the stone and fence for shelter. Col. Dumont, ordered us to lay low; and shoot every Rebel that showed his head. Many shots were fired, but apparently to no effect because of the distance.

When the enemies shells began to fall close about us we moved out in good order. Our Artillery ran out of ammunition and about noon we left the field. The 7th went up a hollow and rested a while and then moved leisurely back to our knapsacks, and thence to Cheat Mountain Summit, where we arrived about dark, tired enough with marching and our first days battle to lie down and rest. Drew two days rations.

Cheat Mountain Summit. W. Va., Oct. 4, 1861. Started early this morning, but had not gone more than two miles when an alarm was sounded at the Fort, we turned and double quicked almost back to the summit, and finding that it was a false alarm caused by the coming in of Col. Milroys Regt. which had stopped in ambush last night. We turned and plodded on through the mud and stopped near the foot of the mountain for dinner and an hours rest.

During the afternoon we waded Elk Water and Tygarts Valley River; and at dusk halted in our quarters at camp Elk Water well tired out.

After Supper, and prayers in our Mess we retired.

Camp Elk Water, Saturday, Oct. 5, 1861. Nothing of importance transpired to day. We were all quite willing to remain near camp.

Sunday Oct. 6, 1861. This has been a beautiful day. This afternoon three Infantry regiments one Cavalry regt. and two pieces of Artillery went to the front on reconnoisance. Had two sermons here in camp.

Monday, Oct 7th, 1861. Nothing of note. The main topic of conversation continues to be the last battle. Our very narrow escapes, etc, etc. No two appear to have seen things in the same light, yet every one is sure he is correct. The probable where abouts of our winter quarters is becoming a vital question with us. Some think we will be taken to Indiana, others say if so, what of the Rebels and West Va. If we stay here how can we be fed and comfortably sheltered, are some of the questions debated.

Tuesday, Oct. 8, 1861. This morning the three Inft. Regts and other troops who went out front reconnoitering on the 6th inst came in and reported that the Rebels had evacuated their camp and burned much property. This afternoon we went out on regimental drill and dress parade. Strict orders were read regarding time for Co. and regtl Drill, and Dress Reveille, Tattoo and Taps.

Robert E. Lee

Wednesday, Oct. 9, 1861. Had Company drill for one hour before breakfast; then Officers drill followed by Company drill from ten to Eleven & half. A.M. In the afternoon Company drill from one to two thirty, p.m. and Regimental drill from three to four p.m., followed by Dress Parade.

Mail came, brought many letters and papers.

Camp Elk Water Va. Thurs. Oct. 10, 1861. It was announced early this morning, that Company "F" were to go on picket. Commenced preparations at once. About 9 A.M. we started, went up the river two miles, here we halted and told this would be Co. headquarters. Most of Mess number two and some others stopped here. The rest of the Co. were placed up the river on our left and up a hollow on our right.

Myself and others went out and got chestnuts and apples. After dinner eleven of us went up the valley four miles where we found an abundance of apples on very tall trees, the trees were old and had been planted close together. Found some pumpkins and corn on our way back, and on our arrival at Company Headquarters, we found that others of the Mess had foraged a lot of Mutton. We had a great feast.

Guards were carefully stationed, and we laid down to rest and dream.

Friday, Oct. 11, 1861. Last night Lieut. Jeffery appointed me Corporal of guard and at twelve I got up and relieved J. M. Bone as Corporal and stationed the guards from that till day break.

The day was passed with but little duty, but with much feasting. Commenced raining near dark and rained very hard until Midnight, then turned very cold.

Saturday, Oct. 12, 1861. This morning all of our Mess but six returned to camp. In the afternoon the Regiment moved about one mile down the river to Headquarters, found it a pleasant place to camp. Pitched our tents with a Street in the center again. About dark the six of our mess left on picket came in. At the usual hour met in prayer.

Camp Elk Water, W. Va. Sunday, Oct. 13, 1861. This was a beautiful morning. We had no drilling to day. Chaplain Kiger is sick, therefore no preaching. I received two letters and a large Map of Virginia. Wrote two letters, one to Miss A. L. the other to Mr J. L. Jones jr.

Monday, Oct. 14, 1861. This has been a pleasant day. We drilled the regular hours and had Regimental drill and Dress Parade. The topic in camp talk is whether we are to stay here this winter or not.

Tuesday, Oct 15, 1861. This is very fine weather. Guess this must be the "Indian Summer" of this Mountain Wilderness. Lieut. Col. James Gavin, left for Webster on his way to Indianapolis.

Rumor says that Col. Dumont has been or will soon be commissioned a Brigadier General. This afternoon Co. F graded their Street, then went on Regimental Drill and Dress parade. Major John F. Cheek in command.

Wednesday, Oct. 16, 1861. Was detailed early this morning as one of six from Company F. to repair our Earth works where damaged by the high waters, recently.

There were fifty of this Regiment in charge of Lieut. Pattison. We worked until night.

Thursday, Oct. 17, 1861. Were up early, while at breakfast we were called into line for roll call, and then went out on morning drill. I took charge of the Second Plattoon. Spent the usual hours drilling to day. Commenced raining before dark. No mail yesterday or today.

Friday, Oct. 18, 1861. Were called early for roll call and drill, found it almost clear. Captain Lambertson and Lieut. Smith, both sick. Lieut. Jeffery is Officer of the guard. Sergeant J. A. Holmes, took charge of and drilled the company. Mail came in this morning bringing much news.

Camp Elk Water, W. Va. Sat. Oct. 19, 1861. We were called early as usual. This is a beautiful morning. Captain said this would be "Wash Day" in the forenoon for all who needed to use the day for that purpose, but be ready for Regimental drill and dress parade in the afternoon.

Sunday, Oct. 20, 1861. Commenced raining about dark but soon cold and quit raining. No drill to day. I wrote three letters one to Father, one to Albert B. Lagrange and one to Mr Daniel C. Lagrange. Had Dress parade at the usual hour. Nothing for me in todays mail. Closed the day with a prayer service.

Monday, Oct. 21, 1861. Was detailed this morning to work on the Hospital. We got but little done. A private of Company "B" died last night and was buried this afternoon with military honors.

Tuesday, Oct. 22, 1861. Did not rest well last night got a pass this morning got some sasafras roots for a round of Tea. Drilled this afternoon. Commenced raining again about dark.

Wednesday, Oct. 23, 1861. Reveille sounded early and we crept out to find it raining, and it drizzled constantly till noon. Comrade S. W. Vannuys and I climbed a high hill in the afternoon and got some Winter Green, and dug some Laurel Roots.

Captain Lambertson and Lieut. Smith quite sick today. Comrades R.V. Ditmars and W. G. Young are very sick. When it quit raining it turned colder and some snow fell. Received a letter from home containing some stamps.

Thursday, Oct. 24, 1861. Helped to build a chimney and Fireplace for Capt and Lieuts. Also one in a small room for Lowe Young & Ditmars. Moved the latter to that room. Much rejoicing over the coming of two recruits to Co. F, they were Adrain Shafer and James M. Brown.

Camp Elk Water, Friday, Oct. 25, 1861. This morning we looked out on a white frost upon every thing. There were many red noses and much rubbing of hands over and about the fire all forenoon. After roll call Co F went out on Company drill. After breakfast we remodeled the chimney and fireplace in the Small room where Ditmars, Young and Lowe are. They are no better today.

Procured some Sods preparatory to raising and making our tent more comfortable.

No mail today.

Saturday Oct. 26, 1861. After the morning drill, Lieut. Jeffery told us there would be no more drill this forenoon; that we must wash up and clean in and about our tents and shine our guns. Tent number ten went to work and by time for regimental drill in the afternoon had

Harper's titled this, "The Mountain Region of Western Virginia."

built a fire place and had raised our tent two feet, with a sod wall under it. Ditmars, Young and Lowe no better. Capt. Lambertson and Lieut. Smith a little better.

Sunday, Oct. 27, 1861. At roll call Lieut. Jeffery told us to prepare for Inspection of Arms at 9 A.M. and for hearing the Articles of War read all of which was done at the hour named. This afternoon wrote a letter home, and received four, one from a Cousin in Andrain County, Missouri. He says plainly that he favors the South, that he is opposed to war; that if he were to go into the army at all, it would be to do battle for the confederacy; that he was sorry that I would go into the army, especially that I was fighting against my relatives.

At dark went to sit up with Comrades David B. Lowe, R. V. Ditmars, and W. S. Young, they are improving some, but Lieut Smith has been very sick to day.

Monday, Oct. 28, 1861. The sick are some better this Morning. I went on guard at 9 A.M. Scouts came in with lots of Cattle and Sheep and two Rebels all captured while out foraging.

Camp Elk Water, W. Va. Tuesday, Oct. 29, 1861. Was relieved from guard duty at 9 A.M. Wrote a letter to my friend Miss Jennie ______. Went out on Inspection. Lieut. Slemmer of Fort Pickens fame, now a Major in our Regular Army, was the Inspecting Officer. He complimented us on our neat soldierly appearance, and for our efficiency in the Manual of Arms. After Supper twenty five of Co. F under Lieut. Jeffery, went out one mile west of camp on picket. The post was up a small hollow.

A Personal Reminiscence. The Miss Jennie — to whom I wrote the letter mentioned in today's record was Miss Jennie ______ of Hopewell. She was one of the several young Lady friends whom "I left behind me." We had agreed to write each other, and at least two letters each way had passed. Our letters were letters of friendship purely until her last to me, and that too was in just a "friendship tone" except the last sentence where she said "But I must close lest I love you to much." When I read that it almost took my breath for a minute. I wondered if any of the boys in the tent had seen that line, it was folded at once and nervously placed in my pocket. I at once left the tent and went up the side of the mountain when I read the letter again and again especially the last sentence.

The letter was then pinned in my inside Vest pocket on the left side. I sought a quiet place every day for the reading of that letter. I had never before received a letter of that kind, but I became deeply interested at once; and fully responsive in sentiment. Every thing appeared in a new light to me. The mountains never seemed so beautiful. I dared not speak as I felt therefore I said nothing to my mess mates. I wanted very much to answer at once. I was sure a fine speech was called for from me; but that was a new subject to me. I was without experience along that line. I seemed to be living in a kind of dream land. At times I wished the war would close so that I could go home.

Sometimes I wondered if I could get a Furlough for the winter, hoping the war, this cruel war would be over soon; I would wonder the Rules of War didn't allow a

Robert H. Milroy, Colonel of the 9th Indiana Infantry.

soldier to go home whenever he wished; especially those in my condition.

And thus ten days passed; ten days of some delightful dreams, along with puzzling questions.

The answer was now due. Sitting at our little improvised Desk in tent number ten, I read the letter again, and when I came to that line I stopped suddenly; scales must have surely fallen from my Eyes; for I saw clearly that what had been **LOVE** to me, was really **BORE**. I sat dumb, even to my self, while the air castles which I had built, tumbled into one heap and vanished.

At first I felt undone; but after a little time; when my mind became composed, I managed to write Miss Jennie ______ of Hopewell, a real "friendship" letter, just the same as before.

Wednesday, Oct. 30, 1861. Near ten this A.M. our breakfast got to us and it certainly tasted good. We were told last p.m. by the pickets whom we relieved that Bear and Deer had been heard and seen here, but they did not come around last night. Several of the boys went out on a scout but found nothing. But little mail today.

Thursday, Oct. 31, 1861. Comrade Robert Sloan and I went out quite early on a Scout of our own and climbed a very large hill, and then climbed trees, but could see nothing but Mountains, with Cheat Mountain in the distance across valley to the East. We saw fifteen or twenty wild Turkeys to day, but Geo. K. Covert was the only one to get a shot and that at long range.

Near sundown the relief picket came and we returned to camp; and found the sick some better.

Camp Elk Water, Friday, Nov. 1, 1861. Comrade J. H. Vannuys was not well last night. Comrades R. V. Ditmars, and W. S. Young are enough improved to come to the tent. D. B. Lowe and Lieut. Smith are some better. Received two letters, one from Miss S. A. L. one from Cousin D. G. McGee of Greenwood, Johnson County, Indiana.

Camp Elk Water, Sat. Nov. 2, 1861. Near dark last p.m. it began and rained all night. Went on guard at nine A.M. Rained all forenoon, and drizzled afternoon and evening.

Sabbath, Nov. 3, 1861. Stood guard in the rain from three till five A.M. Was discharged from guard duty at nine A.M. Rained all day. Wrote letter to my friend A. N. Covert, of Hopewell, Ind.

Nothing by mail for me. No preaching today.

Observed our usual prayer service at the close of the day.

Monday, Nov. 4, 1861. Very cold this morning. Could see snow on a Mountain three or four miles to the north.

The sick of this Company except comrade W. H. Snedicker, are some better. Nothing else to-day worthy of note.

Tuesday, Nov. 5, 1861. Cleared off and was warmer. I was detailed this morning to work with the Hay and Corn in the Quartermasters Department. Quarter Master Johnson has been away for a little time but returned today.

Wednesday, Nov. 6, 1861. Commenced raining last night about dark and rained all night and has rained all day. Had roll call at eight p.m. No mail to day.

Thursday, Nov. 7, 1861. Clear and cold. The mud has become so insufferably deep that men were detailed to

Joseph J. Reynolds, former Colonel of the 10th Indiana Infantry, commanded a brigade in western Virginia.

William R. Rosecrans commanded all the Union forces in western Virginia in the fall of 1861.

haul stone and pave about Headquarters and the Quartermasters tent. A lot of Clothing, Nails, and Axes came to day.

Camp Elk Water, Friday, Nov. 8, 1861. Had an interesting debate in Company "F" last evening. Question Resolved, "That it would not be wise policy on the part of the Government to try to keep troops here during the coming winter." The affirmative gained the decision — of course.

Went on guard at 5 p.m. in place of I. N. Watkins.

This morning came the sad word announcing the death of our friend John Graham of Co. "D" 17th Regt. Ind. Vols.

Saturday, Nov. 9, 1861. Last evening Lieut. Col. James Gavin, came in from Indiana. Our camp is full of rumors, some of them quite vague. The one most likely is that Col. Dumont, had been commissioned Brigadier General and Lieut. Col. James Gavin has been made Colonel of the Regiment.

Sunday, Nov. 10, 1861. We are getting quite anxious for word from home. I received a letter from my brother-in-law, Elisha Vannarsdall. All are well at home.

Monday, Nov. 11, 1861. All was quiet in camp, wrote a letter to my friend and school mate Wm. H. Lagrange and one to Robert E. Henderson. Mail again to day, one letter for me from home.

This afternoon a detail of twenty five Mechanics was called for from each company. Late in the day I was detailed for Cattle guard. Went near the river. Was on duty with young Thompson of Greensburg, Ind.

Tuesday, Nov. 12, 1861. Came in from guard early for breakfast and learned that a Telegraphic Dispatch had been received stating that the Federals had taken Fort Beaufort and were bombarding Charleston, S.C. About dark a Despatch came stating that the Federals had taken three Confederate War Vessels and a lot of provisions.

Four prisoners were brought into camp today.

Wednesday, Nov. 13, 1861. Yesterday's news confirmed. Nothing else of note to day.

Camp Elk Water, W. Va. Thurs., Nov. 14,1861. This morning comrade Alban Hendricks requested that I should go and chop logs in his place. I went and we chopped all day in the rain.

Mr Wm H. Fisher, of Bethany Presbyterian church neighborhood, near Whiteland, Johnson Co. Ind. came in today for a visit with his four sons, James M., John H, and Thomas H, of Co. "F," 7th Ind. and Wm. H. of Co. "D," of 17 Regt. Ind. Mr Fisher brought many things and much good news for members of the Co. from home folks.

Friday, Nov. 15, 1861. Last night comrade W. H. Snedicker died of fever. Went out and chopped logs for Winter Quarters, until noon, when it began snowing and raining. At two p.m. attended the funeral of comrade Snedicker, a volley was fired over the grave. Rained and snowed all afternoon.

Thomas Hill our Mess Cook was taken quite sick to day.

Saturday, Nov. 16, 1861. Snowed all night and was six inches deep on our Mess table this morning. It is a very disagreeable gloomy time. Some of the boys have the blues; and some I think are really "home sick." One comrade in particular, whines much of the time and now and then boo, boos, if any comrade sympathizes with him very much. Most of our Mess — his closer companions have taken to laughing at him which keeps him angry, and he doubts as to whether we know what Father, Mother, Brother Sister and home means. It really appears cruel.

(Addendum. It is proper to add here that the "home sick" comrade mentioned above pulled through all right, and afterwards often laughed over the matter and declared that at the time he thought us little above

Inspector General Adam J. Slemmer complimented the 7th on their "neat soldierly appearance."

savages, and he often said if we had all sympathized with him he believed he would have died there. It is well also to say that altho taken prisoner at Port Republic, Va. and taken to Lynchburg, Va. he made his escape and returned to the Regt. and continued with the Company to the close of the Three Years Service and was honorably discharged on Sept. 20th 1864. He afterwards reenlisted for three years, was given a clerical position and was discharged at the close of the war.)

Sunday, Nov. 17, 1861. Very cold this morning. Mr W. H. Fisher mentioned on Nov. 14, started for his home today. I was detailed to work on Hospital to day. Thomas Hill very sick with fever.

(Addendum: I think it is well as a matter of history to say here that the Mr. W. H. Fisher, mentioned above and on the 14, Nov., enlisted and went as Captain in the 70th Regt. Ind. Vol. Inft. of which Hon. Benjamin Harrison was Colonel, then, commissioned as Brigadier, then Brev. Major General, afterwards was a United States Senator from Indiana; and afterwards, from March 4th 1889 to Mar. 4th, 1893, was President of the United States.

Captain Fisher's fifth and youngest son, Joseph enlisted along with the captain. Of these five sons James M. of Co. "F" was wounded at Petersburg, Va. June, ____ 1864. Died in Hospital near Washington, D.C. July 3, 1864, and was buried at Arlington, Va. John H, of Co. "F" was wounded at ____ and again in the Wilderness Va. May 6th 1864, and lost an arm. Thomas H. was wounded at Bull Run, August 30th 1862, and died near Washington, D.C. Sept. 17th, 1862 and was buried at Alexandria, Va. The Captain and his sons Wm H. and Joseph, returned to their home at the close of the war. Such was the Patriotism of that family and the results.)

Monday, Nov. 18, 1861. Last night at Roll call, a shouting was heard in the 3rd Ohio Regt. This morning we learn that they are to leave this Camp to day. About nine A.M. they started for the North, a happy lot of men. It is said the 6th Ohio, will go tomorrow.

Camp Elk Water, W. Va. Nov. 19, 1861. This morning the 6th Ohio started. They left their tents standing, and now our Regt. have to guard them. Was one of a detail to go to day and cut roads and carry logs out of the brush to haul for building a Hospital for our sick. Large mail to day but nothing for me.

Wednesday, Nov. 20, 1861. Raining this morning. Was again detailed for work in the Quartermasters Department.

Yesterday the sick were moved from the upper Hospital to Secessionists house near our camp. General Dumont having ordered the Rebel to move out so that the house could be used as a Hospital.

Thursday, Nov. 21, 1861. Comrade S. W. Vannuys assisted in the commissary in my place while I wrote some letters. Mail came, but nothing for me. Have to note these days except the sick and their care.

Friday, Nov. 22, 1861. I went again to day to work at the Q. M. Dept. Were Invoicing and boxing Shirts, Drawers, Knapsacks, Haversacks and other commissary Stores. All the details at work about camp. We are evidently preparing for something, but what is it, are we to go or stay?

Camp Elk Water, W. Va. Sat. Nov. 23, 1861. A large detail began to day to put up Winter Quarters, which makes it look very much as if we are to remain here for the winter, which if so is very disappointing to all of us.

The mail brought good news from the Great Naval Expedition to the coast of North & South Carolina.

Comrade Thomas Hill improving slowly and comrade Corporal James Featheringill is some better.

Sunday, Nov. 24, 1861. Snowing very hard this morning. The house builders were excused from work today. No news of any kind in camp. Snowed hard all day. Very difficult to keep ourselves at all comfortable in our tents for our wood is nearly all green. This weather is very trying on the sick.

Monday, Nov. 25, 1861. Is still snowing this morning. There is quite a stir about Headquarters. Many rumors are afloat about camp, one to the effect that we are to go North soon. Perhaps the general wish is father to the rumor. Report says that Gen'l Dumont will go in a few days. The Pay Master finished paying the Virginia Regiments today.

Tuesday, Nov. 26, 1861. A train of wagons left this morning loaded with ammunition, said to be going only to Huttonsville.

The pay master came this afternoon. The ammunition train returned this afternoon having gone no farther than Huttonsville, where they unloaded; which makes it appear very much as though a strong body of troops are to remain about Elk Water and Cheat Mountain Summit this winter. We are afraid that the 7th may be a part of this force. We signed the Pay Rolls this afternoon.

Wednesday, Nov. 27, 1861. It was raining at day break. Company "A" was paid off first then "C" and "K" Gen'l Dumont, left camp about ten A.M. Adjutant John M. Blair accompanied him, Captain Ferry also accompanied the General. General Dumont is going to the S. W. where he had been assigned the command of a Brigade. It is understood that Captain Ferry and Lieut. Blair are to be members of his Staff. It is said that Gen'l Dumont's commission, when issued was dated back to Sept. 3rd, the next day after his commission as Col. of reorganized 7th Regt. General Dumont, for bravery and efficiency on the Battlefield, was Breveted a Major General of Volunteers. *He was afterwards elected as a Representative in Congress, and was active in Reconstruction Days.* Co "F" were paid this p.m. I received $25.55 for 2 months Sept. and Oct. The sick require much attention.

Camp Elk Water W. Va. Thurs, Nov. 28, 1861. Commissary Department issued two days provisions this morning.

I bought a Can of Peaches and some Cakes of the Sutler, in order to get a Five Dollar Scrip changed, so that I might pay some small debts.

All the Quarter Masters Stores were Invoiced to-day and turned over to the Virginia Troops. It now looks as though we are to leave this region. Comrade James M. Bone, of our Mess is very sick to day.

Friday, Nov. 29, 1861. It rained all day. We are preparing to start for Webster tomorrow. I am sending a Twenty Dollar Gold piece to my father, by Lieut. Geo. S. Smith, who will attempt to go with us to Webster, on his way home. Comrade Bone very sick again to day. A private of another Company "sauced," Colonel James Gavin, who knocked him down, and then sent him to the "guard house." Still raining at bed time.

A West Virginia Update

While Billy was "between enlistments" during the summer of '61, the struggle for west Virginia continued. McClellan's July proclamation of total victory had been premature — the fighting moved to the Kanawha Valley.

On July 17, former Virginia governor Henry Wise attempted to hold a Confederate position at Scary Creek, 15 miles west of Charleston. After a determined stand, Wise retreated with his 800 men in the face of Union General Jacob Cox's force of 1,200. On July 25 Cox entered Charleston and on July 29 he occupied Gauley Bridge to the east. Once again, the campaign for west Virginia appeared to have been won by the Yankees.

The Confederate authorities decided not to give up so easily. Robert E. Lee would take command of all the Confederate forces in west Virginia. And to be sure this region was held, he was assigned an additional 15,000 men. Lee would be facing the newly appointed Federal Commander, William S. Rosecrans. (On July 22, the day after the Union army fiasco at Bull Run, General McClellan had been summoned to Washington and Rosecrans was given command of what would become the Department of Western Virginia.) One of Lee's subordinates, John Floyd, another former governor of Virginia, won minor engagements at Cross Lanes on August 26 and Carnifex Ferry on September 10. However, these victories were of little consequence.[1]

General Lee personally operated farther to the north. His initial battle of the Civil War occurred on September 12. After much planning, Lee attacked the fortified Union forces on Cheat Mountain, near Huttonsville. Measles, twenty straight days of rain, lack of coordination and an exaggerated estimate of enemy strength resulted in Lee's first loss. Skirmishing in the area continued until the night of September 15 when Lee ordered a retreat. Lee's previously esteemed reputation was scarred and he was reassigned to a theatre where there was no serious fighting.[2] (Lee's and McClellan's record in west Virginia would not be an indicator of history's final judgment — quite the contrary.)

The "Battle" of Greenbrier River

After the Cheat Mountain affair, the Confederates took up positions on a hill overlooking the crossing of the Parkersburg-Staunton Pike on the Greenbrier River. Billy and the 7th arrived back in western Virginia about this same time and camped at the old Cheat Mountain fort. On

Henry Wise

John Floyd

Two former governors of Virginia turned Confederate military leaders.

Jacob D. Cox commanded the Department of the Kanawha in western Virginia in 1861.

October 3, the battle of Greenbrier was fought. Although Billy may have had a limited perspective, he adequately described this minor engagement. First, the Union boys advanced but found they could not dislodge the Confederates from their positions. Then, the Yankees returned to their camps. That was the battle.

The Union field commander reported the engagement as a successful armed reconnaissance and estimated rebel killed and wounded at 300 (actually 35). The Confederate commander estimated he had inflicted casualties on his enemy totalling 250 to 300 (actually 43).(3) Billy wrote on October 7 that, "No two appear to have seen things in the same light."

Chaplain Kiger

A curiosity of Billy's journal is his infrequent references to the regimental chaplain, Father Kiger. It was mentioned on Sunday, October 13, 1861 that the chaplain was sick and no services were held. However, on most Sundays, Kiger's name is not noted. Almost dutifully, Billy recorded his attendance at religious services or even the informal prayer gatherings. Yet, Chaplain Kiger's name is seldom mentioned.

Orville Thomson, the sarcastic regimental historian, may have offered some explanation: "Father Kiger was surely a good, and at one time may have been a useful man; but if so, was now a 'has-been.' He served one valuable purpose, however — when the regiment saw the old bob-tailed pony and its venerable rider coming into camp it had occular demonstration that the long-looked-for-and-much-prayed-for paymaster was not far off."(4)

Thomson also recorded the story of a confrontation the chaplain had with the regimental commander while impatiently waiting for his personal baggage to be loaded on to a train: "The chaplain was standing guard over his baggage, [which was] somewhat short of a car-load, while the loading was going on, and unable to get any attention from the quartermaster, he appealed to the Colonel, whose caustic reply was: 'I think if we had a little more chaplain and not so ______ed much baggage, we would get along better.' "(5)

In fairness to Father Kiger, chaplain scoffing was a favorite pastime of Civil War soldiers. The most common complaint had to do with the chaplain's absence or neglect of duty. The "Holy Joes" were ridiculed for poor sermons and gun-shyness, as well as being too old.(6) There may have been a fragment of truth in the criticism. Some chaplains were physically incapable of keeping up with "the boys." Others were ill-suited for the work, lacking in training or education, or too lazy to perform their duties.(7)

The preponderance of Civil War chaplains, however, answered their calling with efficiency and devotion. They comforted and counseled whenever the need. They asked for strength and they prayed for the souls of soldiers.(8)

Disease

There were 10,000,000 cases of sickness during the Civil War. An estimated 225,000 boys in blue and 164,000 boys in gray died of sickness. One out of every 65 Union soldiers was killed in action; far worse, one out of every 13.5 died of disease. In this war, microbes were more dangerous than bullets.(9)

Certainly those, like Billy, who were in western Virginia in the summer and fall of 1861 were not safe from disease. In the Union armies (in west Virginia) during the four months of July-October, there were 20,279 cases of disease and 150 deaths caused by disease. The total number of troops, at any one time, during that period ranged from 10,000 to 25,000. One medical historian cited the most common diseases as dysentery, diarrhea, malaria, typhoid fever, rheumatism and measles. (Before the end of the war, 44,500 Union soldiers would die of dysentery and diarrhea.) When Billy and the Federals struck at the Greenbrier River on October 3, 1861, they were at about half strength — dysentery had prevailed. A measles epidemic had passed but, with the coming of cold weather, respiratory infections would strike.(10)

At the time, there was little understanding as to why there was so much sickness. Some thought it was all due to the "sickly months," or excessive rains, or fatigue; one officer even guessed hygiene. General Thomas Morris from Indiana thought the diarrhea was caused by eating fresh beef without bread and salt.(11) This was also Billy's conclusion.

Today there is considerably more knowledge about the contributors to many camp diseases. The rural background of most recruits prevented any previous exposure to communicable diseases. Camp and field sanitation was usually neglected by the officers. Many times, soap was not available nor even felt to be necessary. Latrines were not used or controlled. Rats, dogs and cats ran through the garbage. The cold and wet weather contributed. There was a lack of understanding concerning nutritious food. There were shortages of wholesome food and good water. Hospital facilities and medical supplies were inadequate. And (particularly, in western Virginia) the terrain was usually ill-suited for sanitation purposes.(12)

Unknown to medical science at the time, bacteria was the primary offender. Dr. Paul E. Steiner, author of *Disease in the Civil War,* wrote, "In 1861, the existence and importance of pathogenic microbes was still unknown. The concept of living, subvisible, self-multiplying, invasive organisms . . . as the cause of disease had not yet been accepted."(13) Agony came to the Civil War soldier in many sizes and shapes.

END NOTES

(1) Curry, "McClellan's Western Virginia Campaign of 1861," *Ohio History;* pp. 94-95. For a detailed account of the Scary Creek engagement, see Terry Lowry, *The Battle of Scary Creek: Military Operations in the Kanawha Valley April-July 1861* (Charlestown, 1982); pp. 107-133.

(2) Stutler, *West Virginia in the Civil War;* pp. 95-99. For a detailed account of the Cheat Mountain engagement see Jack Zinn, *R. E. Lee's Cheat Mountain Campaign* (Parsons, reprinted 1984); pp. 126-178.

(3) *ORs;* series I, v. V, pp. 220-221, 223 and 227. These are the official reports of Brigadier General J. J. Reynolds (from Lafayette, Indiana) and Brigadier General H. R. Jackson.

(4) Thomson, *Seventh Indiana;* p. 46.

(5) *Ibid.*

(6) Wiley, *The Life of Billy Yank;* p. 264-266.

(7) James I. Robertson, Jr., *Soldiers Blue and Gray* (University of South Carolina, 1988); p. 176.

(8) *Ibid,;* p. 178; and Wiley, *The Life of Billy Yank;* p. 267.

(9) Stewart Brooks, *Civil War Medicine* (Springfield, 1966); p. 106. Also, for the chances of war, see E. B. Long, *Civil War Day by Day* (Garden City, 1971); p. 710-712.

(10) Paul E. Steiner, *Disease in the Civil War: Natural Biological Warfare in 1861-1865* (Springfield, 1968); p. 56.

(11) *Ibid.;* p. 61.

(12) *Ibid.;* p. 60, and Brooks, p. 108-110.

(13) Steiner, p. 4.

PICTURE CREDITS

—72— Courtesy, Mary Selch (great-granddaughter of Colonel Gavin).

—73— Courtesy, Indiana State Library.

—74— Courtesy, University of Georgia Library.

—74— Miller's *Photographic History.*

—75— The Lloyd Ostendorf Collection.

—76— Miller's *Photographic History.*

—77— *The Tygart Valley Line,* courtesy, Barbour County Historical Society.

—79— Courtesy, National Archives.

—80— *The Soldier of Indiana.*

—81— Miller's *Photographic History.*

—83— *Harper's Pictorial History of the Civil War.*

—84— Courtesy, USAMHI.

—84— *The Soldier of Indiana.*

—85— Miller's *Photographic History.*

—85— Courtesy, USAMHI.

—87— Both courtesy of the Library of Congress.

—88— Courtesy, USAMHI.

—89— Courtesy, Library of Congress.

Former judge Henry R. Jackson estimated the Confederate losses at the "Battle" of Greenbrier River.

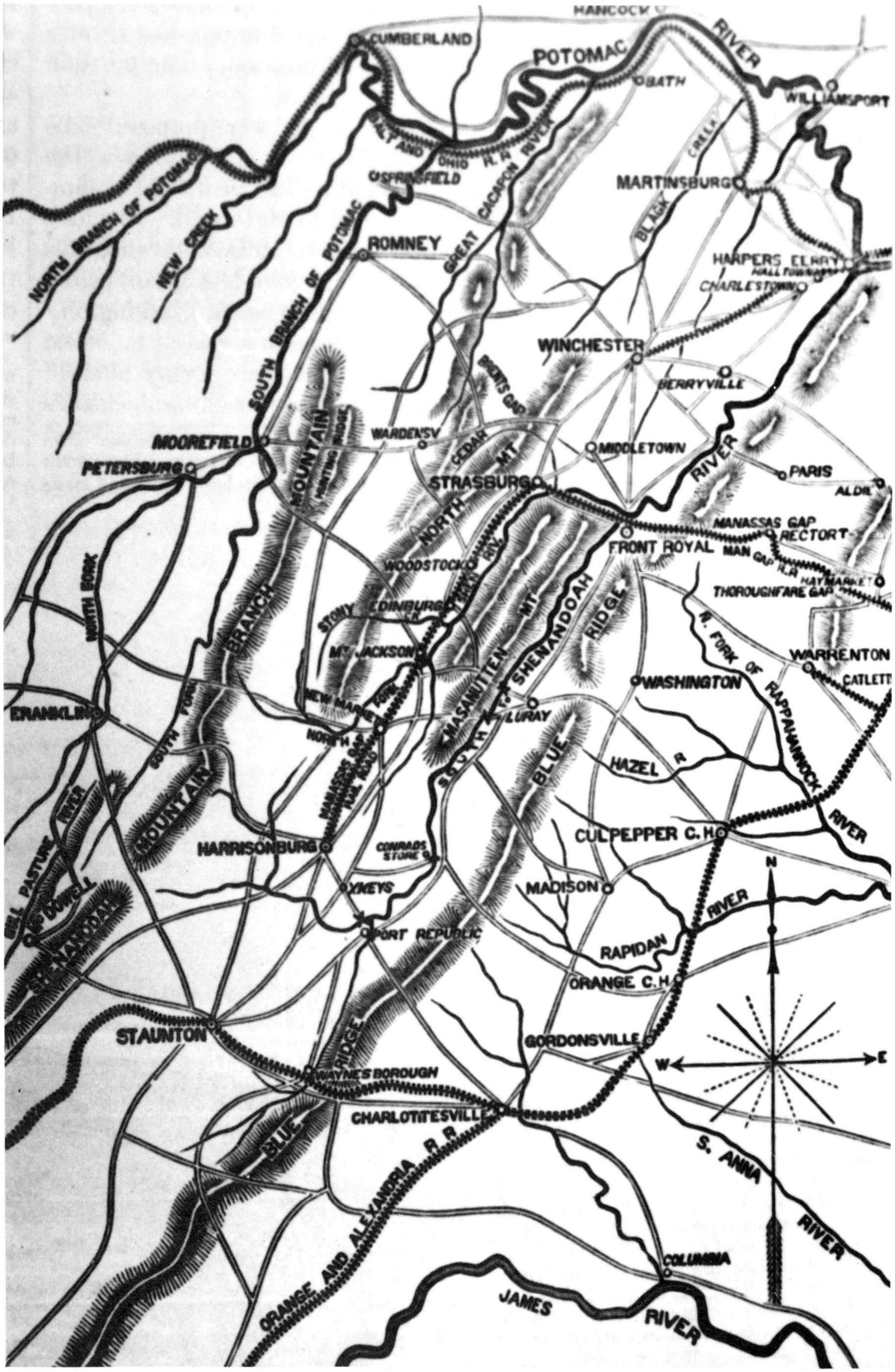

The Shenandoah Valley — between the Alleghenies and the Blue Ridge.

CHAPTER 7 WAS IT REALLY NECESSARY?

Saturday, Nov. 30, 1861. We were up early packing and getting ready to start. Ate our breakfast by the light of burning barrells from the Quartermasters Department.

At day light we began to arrange the sick in our tents and in the Hospital as comfortable as possible and to provide from the Sutlers stock some dainties and appetizing rarities for them. Comrade Hill was taken to Comrade Bones tent. Comrades Elisha Adams and ________ Brown, and ________ Dragoo, and others were taken to the Hospital. It commenced snowing about the time we got up. Tents were struck, rolled and the wagons loaded.

All things being somewhat ready we pulled out for the north about nine A.M. While we were glad to be going, it was sad to leave so many of our Comrades and Messmates in the Tents and Hospital.

We had not gone far till we were Mud to our knees, and all who wore shoes had wet feet. Myself and a number of the Co. and Regt. had boots. At Eleven half past we halted at Huttonsville, and stopped about one mile north for dinner.

It is evident from the amount of ammunition and commissary and Quarter Masters supplies of every kind carefully stored at Huttonsville that it is the intention to maintain a strong force near here during this winter in order to hold the advance gained during the summer and fall.

After an hours rest we trudged on through the mud and water, and near sundown halted at the Bridge within two miles of Beverley, Rails were soon procured for fires and straw for beds. When we had the mud cleaned somewhat from our clothes we dried them, and lay down to sleep — if we could. It was getting colder. We were without tents or shelter of any kind, and thus I spent the last day and evening of November, 1861.

Near Beverley, W. Va. Dec. 1, 1861. Many slept cold last night, consequently we were up early. We marched on after breakfast one mile beyond Beverley and stopped for dinner. Drew rations for the day. It is very cold and raining some. As soon as dinner was over, we started again, we did not follow the roads except over the hills.

We soon separated into squads, some with a commissioned or non-commissioned officer and others with out. Rained all afternoon. After passing the Rowlesburg Pike, near Leedsville, we turned to our left across a large valley, we soon came to a new road which we followed after passing the second large farm house, stopped for the night near some hay and straw stacks.

As it was still raining our squad put up a sort of open front hay and straw shed and covered it with our Gum Blankets, and built a fire of rails in front.

After a supper of hard bread and fat meat we rested.

Near Laurel Hill, W. Va. Dec. 2, 1861. Spent a cold night with little rest or sleep. Made some Coffee and after breakfast started taking another road to avoid the worst place over Laurel Hill. At eleven A.M. reached the top of the Hill, and at one p.m. were at Bealington.

Near two miles north of Bealington, we halted for the night; with plenty of rails and straw near. All our mess did not get in.

We made a very comfortable looking hut, commenced snowing late this afternoon.

Two Miles North of Bealington, W. Va. Tues. Dec. 3, 1861. Bought some Pies and Cakes from citizens for our breakfasts. After breakfast we started on toward Phillippi, the road was frozen and very rough. We reached Phillippi, about 3. p.m. and took quarters in a small room on the west side of Main Street. Gathered in wood and then looked out for supper, some dropped in on some citizens, while others feasted on Pie and cake. Boys not near all up.

Phillippi, W. Va. Wednes. Dec. 4, 1861. Bought some cake and with milk I had made out my breakfast. Went to the country and got a good supply of Milk for our Mess. The stragglers keep coming in sick, hungry and much fatigued. Comrade Samuel V. List, whom we were obliged to leave on the way yesterday came in this afternoon, sick and worn out. All the company wagons came in this afternoon. Found a place this afternoon for Lieut. Smith, S. V. List, R. V. Ditmars, S. W. Vannuys, J. C. Henderson and myself to sleep in house before a good coal fire, by far much the best we have found since our enlistment.

An army on the move.

Phillippi, W. Va. Thurs. Dec. 5, 1861. Last evening after we had gone to bed a report came that we would march at 6 A.M. this morning. Got up early and spoke for early breakfast for four, and made arrangement to leave Comrade S. V. List, at a private house near.

During my service about Phillippi, last summer I made several acquaintance among the people which has proven pleasant and helpful to myself and others at this time.

We started before sunup. The ground was frozen, making the road very rough, and the marching very hard.

Arrived within one mile of Webster Depot near noon where we halted, about the middle of the afternoon the wagons came in; a detail was at once sent to load the wagons and all our baggage etc, on to the cars.

It turned warmer to day and is thawing during the afternoon. At dark we are standing in the mud around small fires awaiting orders to board the train. It was Seven p.m. when we formed line and marched through the mud and climbed into a lot of Box Cars.

And here closed a Mid winter campaign of six days from Camp Elk Water to Webster. I think by odds the hardest campaign of my three year service.

On The Train W. Va. Friday, Dec. 6, 1861. About nine o'clock last P.M. we left Webster. Soon passed Grafton. Tried to sleep but it was too cold in the box cars. About day break we came to the North Fork of Potomac River at a small town, Piedmont, and about ten A.M. arrived at Cumberland, Md. and soon ran down to Green Spring Run, where we left the train and were marched to a Meadow where we stacked arms. Soon Col. Gavin said that we must occupy the cars to night.

Passed through some beautiful country to day. Hills and Mountains always in sight and covered with Cedar and Pine.

Green Spring Run W. Va. Sat. Dec. 7, 1861. Last night five Companies were ordered to go by train about ten miles down the road, they returned this morning, did nothing but lie in ambush all night. Two Cavalry Companies came here today, they are to go to Romney, they say. Col. Gavin went to Romney today to see Gen'l Kelley. We suppose it will soon be known where we are to go.

Green Spring Run, W. Va. Sunday, Dec. 8, 1861. The report is circulating this morning that we are to go to Springfield about eight miles out on the Romney road. About noon we were ordered into line with Gun, Knapsacks etc. the wagons had started and were ready when the Col. got a dispatch from General Kelley, for the 7th to pitch tents here. We were then marched into a field and our place having been assigned us, we soon had our tents up, straw was procured and everything made as comfortable as possible.

We got a large tall tent with but one pole, that in the center, reminds us of pictures of Indian Tepee's.

Green Spring Run, W. Va. Monday, Dec. 9, 1861. Nothing was done in camp to day, except to ditch around our tents, and to arrange otherwise for our comfort. I commenced again to day in the Quarter Masters Department.

Dress Parade at 4 p.m.

A Querry: I mention above that I commenced again today to work in the Quartermasters Department. I was first by regular detail on the 5th Nov. sent to work in the Q.M. Dept. since which time I have several times been called there to assist.

I never knew why, but I suppose having clerked in a General Merchandise Store and acquainted with the running of Invoices and caring for stock, was a reason.

I have often wondered if there was a thought of making me Quarter Master Sergeant, for I was there frequently when it is not mentioned in my Diary. If that was the thought or purpose it was broken into on the 17th, Dec. when I was obliged to go to the Hospital with fever. If so, that little attack of fever and two weeks in Hospital at Cumberland Md. was very fortunate for me for it kept me with my comrades and in line of promotion.

Tuesday, Dec. 10, 1861. We received a large mail this morning. Two letters for me. We had Company drill in the forenoon and the afternoon and Dress Parade at the usual hour.

Wednesday, Dec. 11, 1861. This morning orders were given at roll call to have all cooking utensils at the car as soon as breakfast was over. Soon orders came that all who were able must arrange to march. About Nine A.M. we were called into line and marched to the cars, and at Eleven A.M. we started down the road; soon crossed the south branch of the Potomac. Passed through some rugged country. About noon halted at the Little Cacapon River, where we left the cars and at once placed out Pickets. Company "I" was left at Camp. Companies "E" & "F," stopped at this place and the rest of the Regiment went down to Great Cacapon River, to guard the road and to assist in rebuilding the Bridge. The distance is said to be twenty five or thirty miles.

Little Cacapon River, W. Va. Thurs. Dec. 12, 1861. Was rather cold for us last night. This forenoon a large train load of Bridge Timbers already framed went down to Great Cacapon River.

Little Cacapon River, W. Va. Sunday, Dec. 15, 1861. Nothing worthy of note for several days. We are here on out post duty, we are with out our Tents, and have much picket duty to do. Not feeling well I was allowed to come to camp this afternoon.

Green Spring Run, W. Va. Monday Dec. 16, 1861. Was very unwell and laid in my tent all-day.

Green Spring Run, Va. to Cumberland, Md. Dec. 17, 1861. This Morning Dr Banta, said I was in danger of fever and gave me six powders to take at stated times. This afternoon I was ordered to arrange for going to Cumberland Md. to Hospital. Was soon in a wagon on my way to the R.R.

About dark the train started for Cumberland. The Hospital was full, we were put into a room temporarily until the next morning when we were taken to comfortable quarters in the National Hotel.

Cumberland Md. Wednes. Dec. 25, 1861. I suppose I must have had a severe attack of fever, for I find that I have neglected my Diary for a full week. Feeling some better to day I wrote two letters and walked out to mail them.

Cumberland, Md. Sunday, Dec. 29, 1861. Nothing worth noting has transpired since the 25th. I have been improving steadily and gaining strength. This afternoon I

The streets of Cumberland, Maryland, circa 1860s.

walked out over town. Saw the Court House, The Roman Catholic Church, and two other Catholic buildings, and other churches and fine buildings about the city. I reached the Hotel after an hours walk very much fatigued. I laid down and interested myself in reading a sketch of the life of the late Col. and Hon. Senator, E. R. Baker of ______ who was killed at Ball's Bluff on ________.

Cumberland, Md. National Hotel Hospital, Dec. 30, 1861. This morning while at breakfast I was tapped on the shoulder, on looking up, I found it was Corporal Wm H. Dawson of Co. "F." He brought me three letters and much word from the Company. When the Doctor came in I asked him if he would allow me to go to the regiment. The request was granted and a Hospital Discharge was given me. I arranged during the day to start at eight A.M. tomorrow.

Cumberland, Md. Tuesday, Dec. 31, 1861. Was up early and got my breakfast and made my way to the R.R. Depot.

The train started at Nine A.M. Comrade G. M. Overstreet is with me, he too has had a siege of fever and is returning.

We arrived at Green Spring Run in due time and found that there were none of our wagons there, Comrade Overstreet and I started to walk to Springfield, eight miles distance. We walked all the way and carried our Knapsacks for six miles.

On arriving in camp we found the boys in tolerably good health. We found Mr John H. Vannuys of Hopewell, father of Comrade S. W. Vannuys. He came out for a brief visit with his son, and acquaintances in the Co. and to bring out many donations of useful articles for members of the Company from their friends at home. The box of donations have not yet arrived.

While I was at the Hospital the company had received word of the death of Lieut. George S. Smith. About two hours before we reached the Company Lieut. T. A. Jeffery, had been promoted to First Lieut. and Second Sergeant James A. Holmes, had been chosen Second Lieut.

Found the boys in good spirits. Was glad to find floors and stoves and straw in the Tents.

Lieuts. Jeffery and Holmes treated the Company to Oysters, making the last evening of the year 1861, a very pleasant one. And thus I spent the last day and evening of the year 1861.

Springfield, W. Va. Wednesday, Jan. 1, 1862. This was a bright, clear morning. Breakfast was soon over. Many in this tent were busy writing letters to friends. I wrote two, one to home folks. All the boys enjoy this first day of the New Year.

Our Mess had sent to Cumberland a day or two ago and purchased a set of Chessmen. This afternoon I made a Checker or Chess board, and with Comrade Wm G. Allison, as my instructor, took my first lesson in Chess. — at bed time the usual prayer and service was held.

Thursday, Jan 2, 1862. Weather is still crisp and cold. A court martial has been in session for two days, a Dress parade this afternoon the decision of the court was read, there were three culprits, they, under guard, were marched in front of the Regt, two had the word "Thief" written on card board on their chests and backs. A third was to do duty for two weeks under guard 'policing camp,' with ball and chain attached to one foot. There was a strong wind to day.

Friday, Jan. 3, 1862. This morning Esq. John H. Vannuys, of Hopewell, went to Green Spring Run, where he found the supplies that he brought from Johnson County, for many of the boys of Co. "F." — The several boxes were opened at once and distribution made. Each one was anxious to see what there was for them. Some got Quilts. Some got blankets or comforts. Others got warm shirts and drawers for underwear, wool socks and mittens and almost every one got numerous smaller articles. There were many useful articles for Members of the company from Boone Co. Ind. I got a pair of boots from father and three pair of wool socks and a pair of wool mittens, all home grown, home spun and home knit; a lot of dried peaches for sauce, and a supply of paper, Envelopes and stamps, for myself, and a pair of wool Mittens for Comrade Wm Thompson who is from Boone Co. Ind. Other Boone Co. boys received articles for their comfort.

Saturday, Jan. 4, 1862. Very cold and disagreeable today. Snowed all last night. Every thing was quiet till about one p.m. were told to leave the tents standing and to prepare to march at once. About this time a squad of Cavalry, who had gone to the front this morning came in and reported that they had been attacked and their Captain had been killed or wounded and taken prisoner. The long roll was sounded and the 7th started very soon. The convalescent did not go. I was one of those left in camp.

Springfield W. Va. Sunday, Jan. 5, 1862. I went last night at the request of Doctor Banta, to assist at the hospital. We were busy all night caring for the sick; keeping them well wrapped, and suffered from the cold ourselves.

The regiment returned to camp at noon, had gone only to Green Spring Run. Said they had suffered very much with the cold.

Monday, Ja. 6, 1862. Esq. J. H. Vannuys, father of comrade S. W. Vannuys started home this Morning. It has been a great pleasure to have Mr Vannuys in our tent and in the company for a few days, and a great help in our prayer service and during the quiet of the Sabbath day.

Mr Vannuys, takes with him the good will of Co. "F" and many letters to our friends, and as many trinkets whittled out by the boys with pocket knives, Letters and souvenirs to be left at the J. L. Jones & sons Store, where I used to Clerk. Friends would be notified by the papers.

Springfield, W. Va. Tuesday, Jan 7, 1862. Two Cavalry Co's and fifty six unmounted scouts from the Regt. went out on the Winchester Road. Heavy details were made this morning to build some breast works. The Cavalry and the foot scouts under Captain Waterman returned and reported no enemy found.

Wednesday, Jan. 8, 1862. The Cavalry went scouting again to day. Continued work on our line of defenses. Camp is full of reports of fighting at Winchester and in Kentucky. One report says 18,000 Confederates are coming through here to attack Romney. Much excitement prevails.

These men from the 3rd Indiana Cavalry fought in the east.

Thursday, Jan 9, 1862. Lieut. Col. Cheek, returned to day from a visit home on a Leave of Absence. A thousand rumors are afloat in camp. One to the effect that there are 12,000 Secesh marching on this place.

The Cavalry and Scouts went out this Morning. A Company of Cavalry from Romney, came at 3 p.m. and returned at ten p.m. Our scouts did not see any thing of the large attacking party.

Springfield W. Va. Friday, Jan. 10, 1862. Last evening Co. C. went to the breast works and remained there all night. Another large detail was made this Morning to continue work on our fortifications.

All was quiet until about dark when orders came to draw and cook two days rations, there is much excitement in camp and many rumors. One that Winchester has been taken. Had orders at ten p.m. to roll blankets, pack knapsacks, and strike tents. Good fires were built to sit or stand about, but at best we suffered with the cold.

Saturday, January 11, 1862. Could not sleep last night because of the cold. Cavalry came in about 11 p.m. and reported "all is well." Several Regiments from Romney came in last night. Our camp is full of rumors. Commenced raining about noon, at 3 p.m. it rained so hard that most of the regiment went to town for shelter. W. S. Young, G. M. Overstreet, J. C. Henderson and myself remained in camp, put up a shelter, at 4 p.m. there was a false alarm.

Springfield, W. Va. Sunday, Jan. 12, 1862. This is my 24th Birthday. At one o'clock orders came to be ready to march in half an hour, we packed our knapsacks, and into town. I was not feeling well, the Captain secured me a place in the rear of a loaded wagon. At 3 A.M. the regiment formed and started for Pattersons Creek Station on the B&O R.R. on the Potomac river. At daylight were in the village of Frankfort, built of logs — houses are. One wagon was overturned and another had the tongue broken. Arrived at Patterson Station at ten o'clock A.M. Soon the regiment came in, stacked arms and began to prepare for dinner. Several of the boys are almost sick with colds and all are very tired. This is a river bottom and apparently dead level. Tents were soon up.

Comrade B. G. Trout, went to the hospital at Cumberland this evening with the measles.

Patterson Station, W. Va. Monday, Jan. 13, 1862. Rained some last night, was colder this Morning, and grew colder all day. I put pockets in Comrade J. H. Vannuy's Overcoat to day, as I had done in my own and for several others. Caught more cold during the day. Mail came. Nothing for me.

Tuesday, Jan. 14, 1862. Began to snow last night and has snowed all day. Comrades G. K. Covert and J. E. Graham, came in to day from hospital at Grafton, W. Va. Gen. Lander is now in command of this brigade, and has ordered that each regt. shall place a guard around their camp.

Wednesday, Jan. 15, 1862. Snowed all last night. I was detailed this morning, as one of the camp guard, commenced to rain when at guard Mount. Comrade James R. Dunlap was taken to Cumberland hospital to day with the Measels. — Major B. C. Shaw and Lieut. T. A. Jeffery, went to Cumberland to day, got the regimental mail, but left it in a store. Rained all day. Rumor says we are to move tomorrow.

Thursday, Jan. 16, 1862. This has been a beautiful day, the sun has taken most of the snow all off, leaving it wet everywhere and very muddy about camp. Orders came this afternoon that we would be called early tomorrow from hospital.

Our Tent, has adopted a Rule that every one must clean his boots good before stepping inside, and take their boots off and set them near the door, just inside. Paddles for cleaning and a bootjack have been provided.

Patterson Station, W. Va. Friday, Jan. 17, 1862. We were called at 5 A.M. and told to clean our Muskets, brush

Winter quarters near New Creek, western Virginia.

our clothes, roll our blankets, and strap them to our knapsacks. At nine A.M. a line was formed and the 7. marched to the parade ground where the 7. Ohio, and 1. W. Va. soon came onto the ground, when a Brigade was formed, composed of the 7th Ohio, 7. Ind. 1st West Va. with two regiments to be added soon, to be under command of Col. E. B. Tyler, of the 7. Ohio. This will be the 3rd Brigade of Gen'l Landers Division.

Orders came this afternoon that we keep three days rations on hand and cooked.

Near sundown Co. F and D. of 7. Ind. and two Co's each of 7. Ohio and 1 W. Va., were ordered to report at the station at dark. Soon boarded the train — box cars —, and started for Green Spring Run, where some sesesh have appeared. Near one mile north of G.S.R. two companies were left off, and Co's F & D, were left at Green Spring

Wash day.

A temporary Post Office.

Run Station and the train with the other troops went farther down. We at once deployed across the valley, but found no enemy. Report says that twenty rebels were seen here to day looking for a secreted Telegraph Battery. The train soon came and we returned to camp.

Patterson Station, W. Va. Saturday, Jan. 18, 1862. When we awakened this morning it was raining and continued until noon. The day being very disagreeable, I remained close in our big "Sibley" Tent, tried to play chess, and wrote two letters one to Wm. H. Lagrange, and the other to Miss Jennie Graham, of Hopewell.

Saturday, Jan. 19, 1862. Raining again this morning and kept at it all day. I went on guard at 9 A.M. About 8. p.m. came orders to be ready to march in ten minutes, with one days provisions, at 10:30 boarded a Box car train. At Green Spring Run, G.H.I. & K. got off under command

General Erastus Tyler and his staff. (Guess who rode the big white horse?)

of Major B. C. Shaw, and the six remaining companies went down to South Branch bridge. Forty privates were detailed, twenty five to picket the mountain and fifteen to patrol back to Major Shaws patrol.

Monday, Jan. 20, 1862. Rained all night and until noon. I stood patrol in the timber on the mountain side all night. Early this morning Col. James Gavin and A.B. & C. went down to Pawpaw Station, but soon came back and the regt. returned to camp. It was thought safe to put the train onto the bridge, we walked over and to camp. The "Home Brigade" pushed the drift off and saved the bridge.

Patterson Station, W. Va. Tuesday, Jan. 21, 1862. Rained again this morning, disagreeable getting about camp. Mud is about shoe mouth deep and in many places the consistency of a thin paste or batter. Comrade J. H. Vannuys of our Mess was taken to Cumberland and hospital with the Measels to day. Snowed some this evening.

An Incident Recalled. W. G. Allison was on guard duty yesterday and last night, his hours for duty were from 10 to 12, and from four to six. We had retired early, when he prepared for duty at ten p.m. he pulled F. M. Good's boots on and walked his beat for two hours, came in and pulled the boots off with out cleaning them and set them in their place in the "boot row," and laid down. When called at four a.m. for guard, still disliking to wear his own boots in the deep mud, he put on G. K. Covert's boots for two hours and when off duty, took them off and set them beside Goods' boots and went to bed. When Frank and George got up and saw their boots, each accused the other of having worn their boots during the night and had not cleaned them. Each stoutly denied having been out during the night. Each one protested in the most vehement language that no one else in the tent could put their boots on — for they are both small — just then Allison pretending to waken enquired the trouble, when told, he said quietly; never mind boys, "I wore both pair of boots when on guard, because I did not wish to get mine soiled," but they insisted he could not put their boots on. But he proved it by pulling one boot of each on with ease, having a low instep enabled him to do that easily.

Of course the two wallowed him good, when he said "enough," they let him up, and the incident was ever after a closed one.

Another Incident, at that same camp occurred on a Sunday Morning when the Captain sent the 8th Corporal on a tour of inspection of the tents and men. When he had inspected one tent and its occupants proverbial for their verification to the teaching that "Cleanliness is next to Godliness," and seemed satisfied; the boys knowing that the Corporal was exemplary in his habits, proceeded with much deliberateness to inspect his hands and neck and ears, and then informed him that he was o.k. The Corp. reported that he found tent no. ____ all right, but that he did not care to go there again and on that mission. However, the Corporal was not much offended after all, for all kinds of pranks and jokes were current in the Army.

Wednesday, Jan. 22, 1862. An alarm was caused at 3. o'c this morning by the advance pickets on the R.R. getting scared at some cattle and ran for reserve. One of them fell and discharged his Musket accidentally when they neared the reserves one gun was fired but no one was hurt. The alarm reached camp and "B" & "G," went out to strengthen the pickets. No Mail Yesterday or to day. Our prayer Meeting service was observed.

Thursday, Jan. 23. Was detailed this morning for Camp guard. At ten A.M. the regiment was ordered out in overcoats and with blankets rolled and across the shoulder.

The call was for Brigade drill, when line was formed we executed several evolutions, then formed column by division and wheeled by right and left; marched to the rear, loaded then marched and fired, this round for several times, then charged bayonets and returned to camp. Mail came. I received a letter from Mr S. H. Covert and one from Uncle Isaac M. McGee.

Friday, Jan. 24, 1862. I was not very well last night. At ten a.m. orders came to prepare one meal and with over coats & blankets and be ready to march on call. Later the order was countermanded.

About 4 o'clock the Left wing was ordered to move with two days rations. The regimental scouts were ordered out also. Of Co. "F" five scouts, only two Comrades W. G. Allison and G. M. Overstreet, were able to go. Comrades W. S. Young, John C. Henderson and myself volunteered to go. The scouts were given the first two freight cars and the left wing occupied the rest of the train. It was dark when we started. Co. K was left at Green Spring Run. Co. F. stopped at South Branch Bridge, while G. H. and I went to French's Store, where the scouts got out and formed line. Col. Gavin ordered us forward stating that he and a squad of Cavalry would soon follow.

We started into the country, climbing slowly a long hill side we came to a road leading down a deep gorge, we stopped and a scout reconnoitered and soon reported the way clear; we advanced again soon the Col. and those with him passed us, we trudged on and after a while reached a cross roads six miles from the R.R. and a small hewed log house on one corner. Captain Waterman, our commander knocked at the door and getting no response burst it open and we went in. Friday was now past.

Saturday, Jan. 25, 1862. The room was small and contained no furniture except a few benches and small table. A good fire place occupied the center of one end. Guards were at once placed on the roads each way from the house. Captain Waterman said that if any thing was taken or destroyed it would be at the peril of the culprit.

Soon a light was seen approaching slowly. Report said it must be Cavalry as they could hear the rattle of sabers. We formed in ambush along the fence prepared to give them a volley, by the time we were settled in our hiding place, an old lady and a boy came up; she was carrying a lantern and the boy had a tin pan & frying pan which he was carelessly rattling. We showed our selves in a peaceful way and as it was snowing she could not see the color of our Clothes. Said she had been nursing a sick neighbor and was going home Said she had heard we were coming to day, and was glad to see us, that she had two sons and nephew in Capt. Sheats Co. of Cavalry (Rebel) and wished us success. She had happily taken us to be Secesh.

About 3. A.M. Col. Gavin and his little squad brought in a rebel artillery man whom they had surprised and taken in. Shortly after Pierson and Falkner, Mounted scouts and two or three others, having gone farther out than the Col. returned having captured a cavalry Lieut. and his horse, while he was asleep at his fathers. We now started for camp, the snow was about six inches deep, for it had been snowing since we left Camp, this made it very slavish walking, we reached the Rail road at 4. A.M. As the train had returned to the South Branch Bridge, we laid down and slept some but it was too cold. Day light came. Company F. managed to capture a good sized Secesh hog, which was soon butchered, and when the train came the hog was divided and taken to camp, when we arrived about 3 o'clock in the afternoon. We had had a very hard trip with doubtless good results.

Sunday, Jan. 26, 1862. Last night was clear, windy and very cold. Ground frozen solid this Morning. As the sun shone all day it thawed some. Have marched the three last Sabbaths and have enjoyed the quiet of our tents to day. Observed two prayer Services to day.

Monday, Jan. 27, 1862. Froze again last night. At 9 A.M. got orders for Brigade drill at ten. The 7. Ind. was the first on the drill ground. The 3rd Brigade is as follows: 7th Ohio, 1 W. Va, 7th Ind., 29. Ohio, and 110 Penn. under command of Col. E. B. Tyler, of 7. Ohio. Col Tyler requested the Cols., to drill their regiments as often as possible, he says we must prepare to meet the rebels by bayonet charges, says he has great faith in the bullet but likes the bayonet the best.

Patterson Station, W. Va. Tuesday, Jan. 28, 1862. Was writing a letter when the Scouts were called out, we went with a portion of 7. Ohio, about three miles down the railroad after some forage for the horses and mules. Several wagons accompanied us.

Five rebels were seen but they fled on horseback. Two shots were fired by advance scouts, results not known. Returned to camp by ten A.M. with well filled wagons. Am suffering some with tooth ache.

Wednesday, Jan. 29, 1862. I failed to note on last Monday a Battery of Artillery, which is now a part of this brigade. No news to day relating to matters North or in the South West.

Thursday, Jan. 30, 1862. There is a rumor in Camp that our regt. is going into the Regular service; and another that we are to go to Newport Barracks, Va. There is likely no truth in either. Am still plagued with the tooth ache or neuralgia.

Men of the 110th Pennsylvania — they were in the same brigade with the 7th Indiana.

Soldiering.

Friday, Jan. 31, 1862. Received two letters to day, one from Wm H. Lagrange, a country neighbor boy friend, and one from J. Lewis Jones, one of the firm of J. L. Jones & sons, where I was clerking when I enlisted on April, 17, 1861.

Patterson Station, W. Va. Saturday, Feb. 1, 1862. A snow of six inches fell last night, on a mud foundation of about the same depth. It is very disagreeable getting about Camp, and for that reason camp is very quiet. Those who have or can get a book are able to entertain themselves. Others are playing chess or checkers, and others are writing and many are playing cards.

Sunday, Feb. 2, 1862. This morning orders were given to bundle up and be ready to strike tents at 11 A.M. but orders came at one p.m. that we were not going to day. Rumor said it had been planned to move camp down the railroad ten or twelve miles. Orderly Sergeant David Holmes and his brother Corporal George Holmes, came in from Ohio, after an absence of near two months. George had been in hospital with fever, his brother David got furloughs, and took Geo. home — Morrow Ohio (?) and they remained there until Geo was able to return.

Monday, Feb. 3, 1862. When we turned out this morning we found it snowing. There was not much stir about Camp today, as we expect to move very soon most of the boys are writing letters to parents, or may be to a Sweet heart. An interesting debate was held in this tent last Friday & Saturday nights, and no mention of it made in proper place.

Patterson Station, W. Va. Tuesday, Feb. 4, 1862. All was quiet until 1. p.m. when orders came to prepare for inspection at 5. p.m. but at 2 p.m. we were ordered to prepare three days rations and be ready to march on call. Report said our tents would follow tomorrow. We went to the station at 4. p.m. at dusk took to "box cars" and moved down the river and nine o'clock arrived at French's Store, 11 or 12 Miles below Patterson station.

French's Store W. Va. Wednesday, Feb. 5, 1862. As soon as we were off the cars, fires were built and when we had warmed ourselves, we went into an old warehouse, made our beds on the bare floor and slept very well under two blankets. At day light got up, prepared and ate our breakfast of Coffee and hard tack, and stayed near our fires. A small drove of contraband hogs were feeding near us; some of the boys gave chase; one of them ran across a fire where comrade Wm Gordon was making a cup of Coffee for his canteen, and he caught it. Being a "Secesh" hog; of course it was butchered at once, and divided to our Mess, and was soon over the fire in frying pan or Stew kettle.

Just now orders came for the 7. Ind. to fall in, notwithstanding our heavy loads, most of that hog went with us. When in line we marched out six miles to the cross roads where the Scouts spent most of the night of 24. of January.

When we stacked Arms, the Col. called "Attention 7. Ind. dont let me see you take any of those rails, or touch the Wheat or Straw in stacks there." And at once galloped to a near by hollow and disappeared. Of course the 7th got most of the rails by taking only top rails, and what wheat and straw they could use, and put by a fine supply for the Colonel.

Major Shaw told us to build bivouacs and make ourselves as comfortable as possible.

During the afternoon the rest of our Brigade came up and several other regiments of the division arrived. Having put up good bivouacs of rails with wheat sheaves in the cracks and straw for beds and roof, we laid down at dark and were soon asleep.

Cross Road, Hampshire Co. W. Va. Thursday, Feb. 6, 1862. At twelve o'clock last night we were called from our warm bivouacs to march at one A.M. The 7. Ohio was in the lead and the 7. Ind. close after it. The road lead down a steep rough gorge, at the foot of the hill we started to climb up and over a higher hill or mountain by a more Continuous and rougher road than the one behind us. After a walk of four miles we found ourselves on the bank of Little Cacapon river, here we rested for two hours while a temporary foot bridge was built, upon which we crossed and marched another four miles over another rough road and halted, it was said within six miles of Blues Gap, here we built fires and remained till four p.m. when we formed line about faced, recrossed the river on the foot bridge and reached our Camp at nine p.m. much fatigued and foot sore from our reconnaissance we were soon on our comfortable straw beds and a sleep.

We do not know how many, if not all the regiments of the division took part in this move, but we know that it was intended as a feint, or else a real move to this vicinity of Strasburg, to cut Jacksons line of retreat from Winchester.

Big Levels, Hampshire Co. W. Va. Friday, Feb. 7, 1862. Most of the boys report having slept well last night. Cooking utensils came this morning, and enough rations came for our dinner and about noon provisions came for about one day.

This, we are told is called Big Leavels; is, as we can see, on top of a high ridge of the Alleghany Mts; and that the Log Cabin at the corner, where the Scouts spent much of the night of the 24. of January is the property of one John Phillips, who is the acting Justice of the Peace of this Township, and the Post Master of this community so that our act of house breaking, we had violated the laws of the Great Commonwealth of Virginia and the Laws of the Federal Government which we had sworn to maintain.

Big Levels, W. Va. Saturday, Feb. 8, 1862. Commenced to snow at 8 a.m. Report says that the 13 & 14 Ind. had a fight with the rebels at Big Cacapon river and were victorious and captured three cannon and some prisoners.

Snowed all day, wind high and changeable, and very cold on this high elevation. Comrade W. L. Dunlap was taken to the hospital to day.

Sunday, Feb. 9, 1862. Very cold last night, wind strong from the North. Comrade Wm G. Allison, of our mess is sick to day and was taken to Cumberland to the hospital. He thought that he was perhaps taking the Rheumatism. Draw rations regularly now, but is difficult to prepare them as we have but one kettle for several Messes. Are recovering from our late hard march and exposure, and camp assumes a more cheerful appearance. Clear and very cold.

Monday, Feb. 10, 1862. Last night was, perhaps the coldest of the winter. Had Regimental drill from ten to twelve, and Brigade drill in the afternoon. Drilling in the deep snow with heavy frozen crust on top was a laborious work. Was it really necessary?

Big Levels, W. Va. Feb. 11, 1862. I neglected to record on the 7. Feb. that Just before dark the boys left at Patterson Station came into camp and reported that the troops had all moved to the front, and that Comrades Lawrence Lowe, our Teamster and B. Dragoo, came in from a furlough home and that Elkanah Forsyth, came as a recruit.

Wind blew from the South East to day. Snowed gently most of the day. We must now go near a mile for rails or wood for fires. — One week of very cold disagreeable weather has passed since we came to this bleak place, and we are yet with out tents. We hope for a better show next week.

We are out of paper and Envelopes and cannot write to our friends. Report says that some large battles have been fought in Kentucky & Mo. Very few News papers reach us here.

Camp Big Levels, Wednesday, Feb. 12, 1862. The meager news received to day, confirms the hard fighting in Ky. and Mo. Aus. D. Springer returned to camp to day from the hospital.

Report says the rebels have retaken Romney. About 4 p.m. received orders to cook what rations we had. Soon orders came to draw three days rations, which indicates a movement to morrow. Lieuts. T. A. Jeffery and J. A. Holmes, came into camp from Cumberland. Comrades, Geo. K Covert and Columbus Reynolds not being able to march, were with many others of the Regiment, sent to the hospital at Cumberland.

Winter camp.

Big Levels, Hampshire Co. W. Va. Thursday, Feb. 13, 1862. Up early with orders to prepare to march, which we did with alacrity and gladness, for it had been a hard week on all of us. The order "fall in line" came at eleven A.M. and by noon all the 3rd Brigade was on the march toward the railroad. The road lead down a narrow gorge on the side of a Mountain toward the Potomac river. After a march of five miles over a very rocky road we reached the R.R. and found it "All quiet on the Potomac". We then marched down the railroad four or five miles to Paw Paw station. While at Little Cacapon station, the First W. Va. Cavalry, the Ringgold Cavalry and two Cos. of other cavalry past us. When near the station we turned to the right. Very soon rails and wood were gathered and fires kindled and in a little time each one had a cup of hot coffee, a piece of fat meat and a "hard tack", and this we called supper, and enjoyed it. At and near Paw Paw Station are many troops and it is quite Muddy. It was sundown when we stopped here — Saw several Canal Boats pass down.

Paw Paw Station W. Va. Friday, Feb. 14, 1862. Last night we arranged some rails to sleep on and keep out of the wind. In addition to a severe cold I was plagued with the tooth Ache, and did not sleep much. Were called at four A.M. and had breakfast over by day light. About that time it began to rain but changed to snow but soon was too cold to snow. The wind from the north was fierce. Our Mess No. 5, had just moved out of the wind and had secured more rails for fire when orders came for the 7th to move. Formed line in the road and trudged through the mud and over stones up a small stream on which we passed two small Saw Mills and a small grist Mill in which overshot wheels furnished the power. After a two mile walk we turned to the right into a field on an elevation, with higher hills surrounding it, here we stacked arms some sought for wood while others went back to the nearest Mill for lumber. Soon our tents and baggage began coming in, but it was late at night when our blankets and a tent came, pitched the tent and laid down.

Saturday, Feb. 15, 1862. When we got up this morning it was snowing very hard. Soon some one came and claimed the tent that sheltered us; we give it up and shortly found our own in use in another Co. It was soon up and the floor laid. While some were arranging the tent, others were watching for our knapsacks and cooking utensils, soon the Mess box came and by one p.m. we had all our belongings.

Sunday, Feb. 16, 1862. Morning: All is quiet in camp. Continued quiet through out the day. Much of the time was spent writing home folks to acquaint them of our change of camp and of our welfare. This is called "Camp Cheek" in honor of our Lieut. Colonel, and is located full three miles from Paw Paw, on the "All quiet Potomac." Held prayer Service and retired.

Camp Cheek, W. Va., Monday, Feb. 17, 1862. Comrade Alban Hendricks, of Co. F. died early this Morning and was buried late this afternoon. *Report of the Adjutant General of Ind. shows that Hendricks died on Feb. 11, 1862 of disease, in the hospital at Cumberland. Only hospitals will show.*

Camp Cheek, W. Va. Tuesday, Feb. 18, 1862. Clear and warmer. The report of capture of Fort Henry, on Tennessee river in Tenn. by Federals confirmed. The commander of the fort and many prisoners were taken. It is also reported that Generals, Grant and McClernand, have captured Fort Donolson, on the Cumberland river in Tenn. and many officers and men, with many cannon and other arms and munitions of war. And that Gen. Burnside had taken Roanoke Island, N.C. and rebel forces there.

Camp Cheek, W. Va. Wednesday, Feb. 19, 1862. Commenced to rain and snow this Morning, and continued to snow all day, and turned colder by dark. Comrade, Benj G. Trout came in late last evening and reported our boys in hospital at Cumberland improving. Yesterdays news reports confirmed. Certainly cheering news to us. Am suffering with a severe cold. Wrote letter to Cousin D. G. McGee.

Camp Cheek, W. Va. Thursday, Feb. 20, 1862. Last night was so windy that many tents were blown down. Papers received contain very cheering news from our armies in the South West and from Gen'l Burnsides Expedition. The boys of the 7th Ind. are more cheerful than for some time. Order for Dress parade was countermanded because of high wind.

Camp Cheek, W. Va. Friday, Feb. 21, 1862. About 8 o'clock last evening word came that the rebel Gen. Sterling Price and his army had been captured at Springfield, Mo. Cheering was heard all over camp and the Band played "America" "Hail Columbia" "Star Spangled Banner. Had drill in forenoon and afternoon and Dress parade at 4. p.m.

Camp Cheek, W. Va. Saturday, Feb. 22, 1862. At nine A.M. the 7th Ind. formed line and went down to 7. Ohio, where all the Brigade assembled and were Reviewed by Gen'l Lander, our Division commander, after which the Gen'l, gave a brief address and we returned to camp at four p.m. Good news form the South West confirmed.

Camp Cheek, W. Va. Sunday, Feb. 23, 1862. Thinking there would be no preaching in camp to day, I wrote one letter and had another well on the way to a finish when I was detailed to help to pitch a tent for the Colonel. Was very quiet in camp to day except from an over amount of high wind. While we Hopewell boys have held an evening prayer service when possible since going to camp on 29. of Aug. last, it was deemed well to form A Prayer Meeting Compact. with the thought of maintaining a prayer Meeting Sabbath and Wednesday evenings in camp. All readily so obligated themselves.

Camp Cheek, W. Va. Monday, Feb. 24, 1862. Heavy rain with Thundering until ten a.m. At that time came high winds which made tent poles tremble. Very soon a harder dash came, followed by loud yelling. Looked out and saw that most of the Left Wing tents were down, just then came a harder gust, when the boys sprang to the poles and stakes inside and out and to stay ropes and we managed to keep the tent up, hats caps, pants, coats, shirts, drawers and all manner of Mess apparel could be seen flying in the air. Cook sheds were tumbling, crumbling and scattering, kettles, buckets, pots, pans, cups and every description of cooking utensil and tin table ware were rolling and whirling every where. Many unfinished letters started without signature, direction or stamp. It is safe to say they will never reach their intended destination.

From the prostrate tents could be seen comrades creeping from under the tents half suffocated by the smoke from stoves. Tents when half up were again blown down. This day and this high wind will long be remembered by many of the boys of the 7th Ind. Inft. Turned colder. No drill, no Dress parade.

Camp Cheek, W. Va. Tuesday, Feb. 25, 1862. Last night it seemed unsafe to lie down to sleep, but our tent being well staked and stayed with guy ropes we prepared for bed. After reading a lesson from the Bible, a Hymn was sung and a prayer offered, and we retired.

This morning the wind has calmed down and all is quiet excitement incident to yesterdays tornado, almost every one has an interesting experience to relate. Had regimental drill from ten to twelve; also some practice firing.

Camp Cheek, W. Va. Wednesday, Feb. 26, 1862. Regimental drill in forenoon and more practice firing. Got my first Sutlers Checks to day, being without money had to buy on time, until next pay day. Often buy items from the sutler, but till now have been able to pay.

The Sutler in the regiment is necessary at many times, but an evil because of exorbitant prices charged.

The mail brought us but few letters but many papers from which we are able to glean many particulars of late battles in the South West, that Burnside is still advancing in North Carolina and of advance of Gen'l Curtiss in Arkansas. Report says Gen'l Buell has taken Nashville, Tenn.

Camp Cheek, W. Va. Thursday, 27, 1862. Prayer Meeting was held last evening and a very good interest was shown. This is a beautiful morning, clear and cold, with a

"Wheeled" pontoons.

A pontoon bridge being constructed.

A pontoon bridge in use.

A storage area for bridge parts.

A newly constructed bridge.

strong wind all day by which we were constantly reminded of the blizzard of Monday the 24th. Rumors say the bridge over the South Branch of Potomac river near Patterson Station was burned last night.

Our scouts say they know nothing of Stonewall Jackson coming this way but heard that he had been heavily reinforced at Winchester.

A very high wind today.

Camp Cheek, Hampshire Co, W. Va. Friday, February 28, 1862. Very cold and windy today. Had a General Inspection and Muster of the Regiment, which indicates that the Pay Master May be expected this way soon, and he will be welcomed for most of the boys are out of money.

News papers today state that the Federals have taken Nashville and Memphis, Tenn.

Camp Cheek Hampshire Co. W. Va. Saturday, March 1, 1862. Last night orders came for us to prepare to march with three days rations. The opinion is that it means an advance on Winchester.

Two p.m. a beautiful day. Many conjectures as to our probable destination. We are to carry three days rations, and another three days rations are to be carried in wagons. All the boys are cheerful. Think we will have a chance to do something here in Va. as well as the armies in Ky. and Tenn.

Comrade Ben. G. Trout of Co. F. started home on furlough; sent many letters by him to friends.

During the leisure in camp this winter the boys have whittled out many pipes rings and other small Souvenir trinkets from Laurel root which takes a fine polish. I sent a pipe to father to keep for me; it represents half an egg shell held bowl up in a Crows foot.

March comes in like a lamb, some wind in the forenoon. Orders are to march at four p.m. Started on time. Seventh Ohio, in the lead, the road lead up a hollow for some distance, then up the Mountain side, when on the top we could see a deep narrow Valley with a still higher Mountain beyond. The sun was just setting and we had before us a very fine picture.

For three miles or more we went down a narrow rough, rocky road, at the foot of the Mountain we found the Big Cacapon river swift but shallow; a foot bridge made of wagons drawn in one after the other close enough together for us to step from one to another.

On Big Cacapon, Mar 2, 62. Sunday. We crossed the river with ease and rapidity and are now encamped in a pine and cedar forest one mile south of the river. Pine logs were soon cut and good fires built.

It was difficult to build bivouacs on the Mountain side, but pine and cedar twigs were cut and laid down for beds and we soon laid down to sleep and slept three or four hours and wakened because of the cold.

Sun up Sunday Morning found us standing about our large fires warming one side at a time, and waiting for orders to march, but we didnt miss our cup of coffee and thick fat bacon warmed on a stick over the fire and crackers as a filler.

Noon came and yet no orders, the horizon was dark in the North west. We were without tents, began putting up bivouacs, a heavy snow began to fall soon. Our fires melted the snow as it fell on our brush overhead so that we were nothing better by our work. Although extremely disagreeable the boys are in good spirits. Quit snowing about three in the afternoon and near that time orders came to fall in. It was a disappointment when we about faced and turned toward our old camp. We recrossed the river on the foot bridge of wagons, the snow made it very slick walking over the rough stone and many fell, but we reached Camp Cheek at sundown very much exhausted. We wonder if our move was first intended as a start for Winchester or only a feint, or if we returned because of General Landers sickness.

Frederick West Lander.

The Winter of '61-'62

The situation was not good for the Union cause when New Year's Eve rolled around in 1861. It had been a year of frustration — Yankee morale was low. To the south, the Confederates' spirits were as high as they would reach in the next four years of war.[1] In 1861, the Rebel triumphs had been numerous: Fort Sumter, South Carolina; Harpers Ferry, Manassas and Ball's Bluff, all in Virginia. It was more of the same out west: Lexington, Wilson's Creek and Belmont, Missouri. The few bits of good news for the Federal government had come from western Virginia. Billy had been a part of these "victories" although his most important personal concern remained his day-to-day survival in the camps.

Early in 1862, the military situation changed and morale began to rise in the north.[2] The Union boys won a battle at Mill Springs, Kentucky on January 19. Then came Grant's major victories in February at Forts Henry and Donelson, Tennessee. Also in February, the Confederates abandoned Nashville, Tennessee and the Union troops occupied Roanoke Island, North Carolina. There were rumors of a great advance on Richmond. Encouraging, but this too, would not lessen a soldier's daily struggle for warmth, food and some fun.

The Good Times

Billy Davis' words portray a dismal, dreary existence. Yet, his only protest seems to be that conditions were, at times, "disagreeable." Through it all, there is a sense of camaraderie and strong personal relationships, particularly, in mess number five.

Billy's greatest joy was receiving a letter. Just as he felt it necessary to log the weather conditions, he seemed to record all the letters sent and received. And he did not forget to record the times when there was "nothing for me." His reactions were typical of most Civil War soldiers. The boys would literally "wear out" the letter they received — unfolding, reading, folding — time after time.[3] Mail service for Union soldiers was performed by the Post Office Department, in the same manner it always had for civilians. Stationery and stamps were available from the sutlers (although a military decree had to be issued that sutlers were not to profit from the sale of stamps).[4] Soldiers could mail their correspondence and packages without postage and the recipient was obligated to pay the charges.[5] And mail posted for delivery in enemy territory would be transferred at either Louisville or Nashville. The Confederate government had established a mirror image of the U.S. Post Office Department — even to the point of operating at a financial loss.[6] The most effective method of mail delivery, as Billy related frequently, was the "hand carrying" performed by civilians and soldiers as they travelled between home and camp.

A welcome sight.

To overcome the monotony of camp life, Billy took part in almost all the common diversions: reading newspapers, discussing rumors, singing songs, and playing games. However, it is doubtful he took part in every one of the popular activities because of his religious convictions. The most popular games accommodated gambling, such as, chuck-a-luck (a dice game), poker, twenty-one, euchre and keno. Gambling was commonplace in the Civil War camps — it was said soldiers would bet on anything.[7] Billy, however, never mentions any exchanges of money. He does record participating in the popular games of checkers and chess (and later, watching baseball).

Foraging was also a game of sorts — although many times it was a necessity. This activity was simply stealing from the local residents. Billy's tale of the officer telling the boys "don't let me see you take any of those rails" and galloping off is an often-told example of the implicit approval from above. Even when there was strict discipline and punishment, the boys could usually out-smart their officers.

There were periods of great religious revivals during the Civil War and then there were periods when soldiers lost interest in godliness. Such was not the case for Billy and his comrades. Company F of the 7th Indiana became famous as the singingest and prayingest company in the regiment.[8] Mess number five must have contributed to that reputation by conducting prayer services at least twice each week. And evidently they would sing hymns into the night.

Billy dedicated himself to soldiering, but he also maintained and nurtured close relationships with his family, his friends and his God.

Paper "boys."

A game of chance, perhaps.

END NOTES

(1) Bell I. Wiley, *The Road to Appomattox* (New York, 1977); refer to graphic illustration between pp. 33-35.

(2) *Ibid.*

(3) Wiley, *The Life of Billy Yank;* p. 190.

(4) *ORs*; series III, v. II, p. 315.

(5) *Ibid.;* v. I, p. 383.

(6) Herman Hattaway, "Via Confederate Post," *Civil War Times Illustrated* (Gettysburg, April 1976); v. XV, n. 1, pp. 22, 26. (Not surprisingly, the Confederate Post Office Department received much criticism — some things did not change.)

(7) For more background (and details) on the activities of Civil War soldiers see Robertson, *Soldiers Blue and Gray* and *Tenting Tonight; The Soldiers Life* (Alexandria, 1984); and Wiley, *The Life of Billy Yank* and *The Common Soldier of the Civil War* (New York, 1975). These books are based, in part, on soldiers' letters, diaries and journals.

(8) *Nostalgia News;* October 1, 1978, issue n. 6, p. 14.

PICTURE CREDITS

—90— Map. *Harper's Pictorial History of the Civil War.*

—92— Miller's *Photographic History.*

—93— Courtesy, Allegany County (Maryland) Historical Society.

—95— Miller's *Photographic History.*

—96— Courtesy, Chicago Historical Society.

—96— Courtesy, National Archives.

—97— Miller's *Photographic History.*

—98— Courtesy, USAMHI.

—99— Minnesota Historical Society.

—100— Miller's *Photographic History.*

—102— Same.

—103— Same.

—104— Courtesy, USAMHI.

—105— Miller's *Photographic History.*

—105— Courtesy, USAMHI.

—106— Same.

—107— Miller's *Photographic History.*

—107— Same.

—108— Courtesy, USAMHI.

CHAPTER 8 OUR FIRST REAL BATTLE

Camp Cheek W. Va. Mar. 3rd, 1862. Monday. Commenced to rain sometime last night. Word came early announcing the death of Gen'l Landers. I was detailed for guard duty. The Regiment went to the late Gen. Landers Head quarters to the funeral. Rained all day.

March 4, 1862, Tuesday. Commenced snowing this Morning. Report says that Comrade James M. Bone, who has been home on furlough and recruiting service would return soon with ten recruits for Co. F.

March 5, 1862, Wednesday. A Camp rumor says that Gen. N. P. Banks had crossed the Potomac and in advancing on Leesburg had been repulsed. Report not Credited. We have orders to keep on hand three days rations of Coffee browned and ground.

March 6, 1862, Thursday. — Last night a private of Co. C. died and was buried this afternoon. One John Miller of Co. K having been Court Martialed was reprimanded at Dress parade.

Friday, March 7, 1862. Last evening we were much surprised when Comrade James R. Dunlap of our Mess stepped into our tent, he having been in hospital at Cumberland over seven weeks, went there with Measels. He is looking well and reports the rest of the boys improving.

This afternoon we drew large Gum blankets four of which make a closed tent large enough for four persons. Are eyelets along the edges for strings to join them. In the center of each is an opening through which to put the head when standing or Marching. There is a broad flap which drops over the opening when used as a tent. Query, can we always find poles on which to pitch our Poncho's? Weather cold but calm.

Camp Cheek, Hampshire Co. W. Va. Saturday, March 8, 1862. Early this morning came the order "Roll your blankets" — "Draw three days rations," then "Strike tents." Near ten a.m. started for Paw Paw station. Found that all the troops had gone but one regiment. Halted on the hill side near the R.R. and awaited our train. Comrade Robert Sloan is not well. I am one of a detail to load our baggage on cars. The 7. Ohio left on a train late this afternoon. But little Mail to day.

On B. & O. RR. Paw Paw Station W. Va. Sunday, March 9, 1862. Comrades John C. Henderson and Austin D. Springer and myself made a bed of twigs and then pitched our new Poncho and laid down to sleep. The night was clear and cold this morning every thing was white with frost. We had slept well. At daylight were called to Coffee and breakfast and at sunup were in box cars and on our way toward Baltimore. The first thing noticible was a Tunnell thru which we passed. From our bivouacs yesterday we could see two tunnells, one for the R.R. the other for the Canal. This is a beautiful day, and does honor to blustery March. Trains are passing us hourly some are loaded with bridge timbers, but nothing can be learned as to what is going on below. No mail today.

Opposite Hancock Md. Monday, Mar. 10, 1862. At dusk last p.m. we started down the RR. passed thru one tunnell and over some very rough country, and arrived here at 11. p.m. When we awakened this morning we found it raining.

Quit raining by noon, when the clouds cleared away somewhat of Hancock could be seen.

Opposite Hancock, Md. Morgan Co. W. Va. Mar. 11, 1862. Comrades Thos. H. Fisher A. D. Springer and myself made our bed together on a pile of cross ties and altho the night was cold and a strong wind from the north we slept well.

A very pleasant day indeed. Word came to day giving an account of a Naval engagement at Hampton Roads where the Merrimac an Armored Rebel Steamer attacked several Armored Federal naval Vessells and worsted all and cleared the Roads, and how the little Monitor came to the rescue and sent the Merrimac to Norfolk badly crippled.

While waiting to day for the repair of the Railroad in front, several of our boys got out and dug Laurel Roots

The Paw Paw tunnel for the Chesapeake and Ohio Canal.

from which many small souvenir trinkets were afterward whittled.

Addenda. I now have a Pipe that I afterward whittled with my pocket knife from a block of this Laurel. It represents half an egg shell, held in a Crows foot. Years later I whittled and neatly joined two pieces of this and put a hand hold on the oak stick used as a Cane when escaping from Confederate prison at Lynchburg, Va. in June, 1864. I frequently use that Cane at this date, 1915. I still have a small unused block of this wood.

On B & O R.R. W. Va. Mar, 12, 1862, Wednesday. At four yesterday afternoon the train started again, soon came to Sleepy Creek. At dark were at Cherry Run and the Engine off the track. Started again about midnight, went a short distance below Black Creek in Berkeley, Co. where the train must stop and us walk.

We ate our breakfast before day light. I was detailed to help fill the Locomotive Tank. Carried water in buckets from a pond near the road. While at this the regt started and we had a brisk walk of three miles to over take them. Here workmen were relaying the track. At this place we left the "All quiet Potomac river and started across a most beautiful country, more level than we have seen since leaving the state of Ohio, last Sept.

Farms generally well improved with fine houses and immense barns apparently well filled. Slaves are seen on every farm. Passed the Village of North Mountain, a beautiful picture with North Mountains the Eastern ridge of the Alleghanies as a background. At this village we saw an American Eagle in a large cage.

When within one mile of Martinsburg we came to the wrecks of the B. & O. R.R. Engines and cars assembled and burned by order of T. J. Jackson, (Stonewall) before the battle of Bull run. Halted in Martinsburg at 1. p.m. where we rested an hour for Coffee and dinner. The Stars and Stripes are floating over the fine Court House. Marched on a fine Turnpike three miles south of town and halted near a very large spring, below this spring is a small lake near which are three fine farm residences and large bank barns and slave quarter near.

Big Spring, Berkeley Co. W. Va. Thursday, 13, 1862. Our Wagons came up last evening, and we drew some fresh beef. Were called early this Morning, breakfast over we were told to roll and mark our Extra Quilts and

Working on the railroad — with supervision.

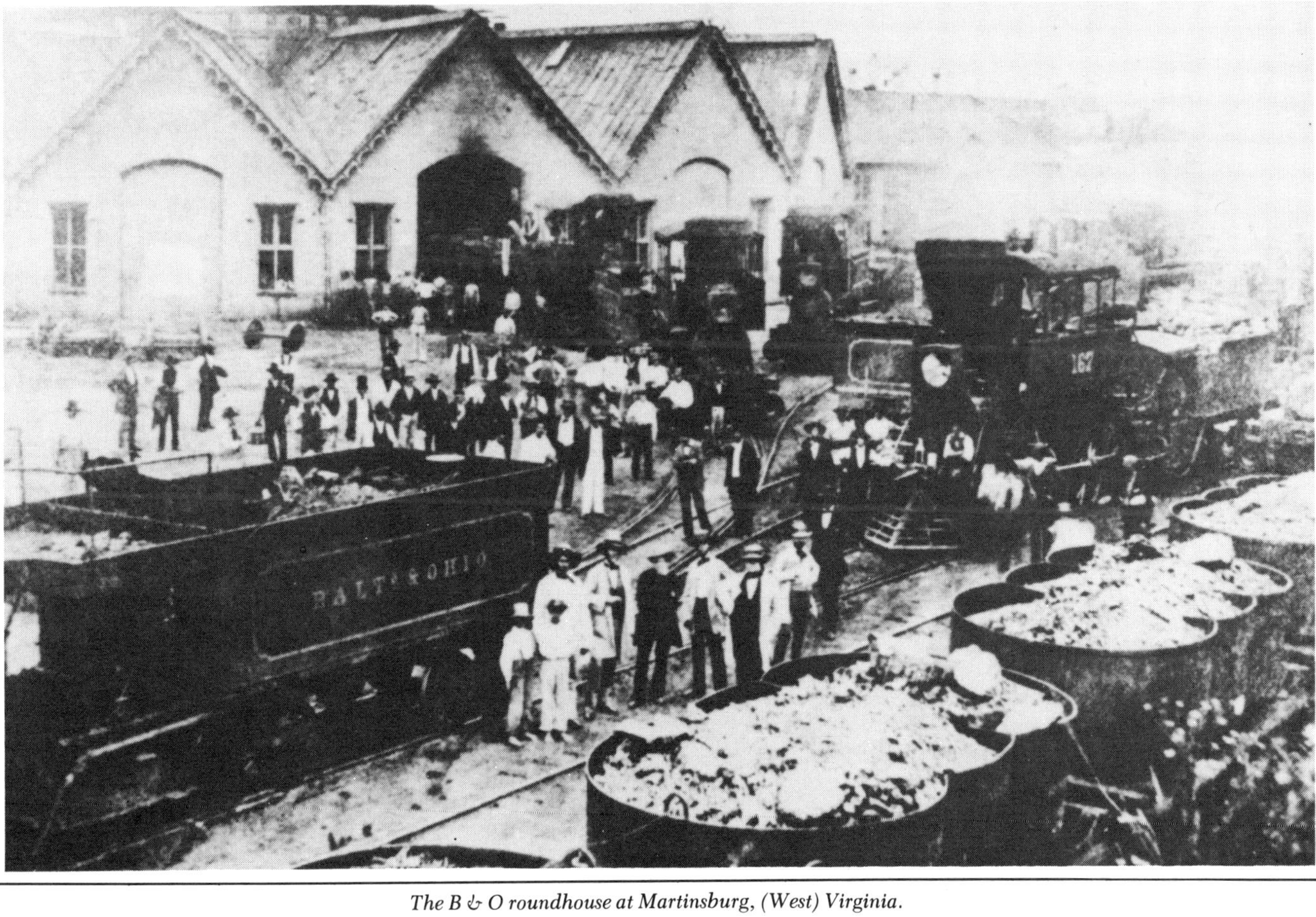

The B & O roundhouse at Martinsburg, (West) Virginia.

blankets for storage some place until needed next fall. Geo K. Covert and Adrian Shaffer, being unable to go further were left with the blankets.

In line at 7. A.M. and started towards Winchester a walk of two and half miles brought us to Darkesville where we stopped near another large spring and stream from it and rested. A five mile walk brought us to the Village of Bunker Hill. This is the most beautiful and best improved country I have ever seen.

While resting here and getting our Coffee, some one said this was the region of Va. where George Washington, then a youth, surveyed land for Lord Fairfax and where Wirt, the historian in his Life of G. W. inadvertently said that Washington "Cooked himself."

About the middle of the afternoon we halted in a nice open woodland pasture five miles from Winchester, where it is said Gen. Williams' brigade had a brisk skirmish with the enemy, and report says they had several brushes with the rebels between this and town. Received mail this afternoon.

Near Winchester, Va. Friday, Mar. 14, 1862. Last evening a short train passed into Winchester. This morning it went on to Charlestown. This is the line of railroad reaching from Wheeling W. Va. to Washington and Baltimore.

Our wagons constantly pass to and from Martinsburg as regular trains now reach that place.

At 2. p.m. were told to prepare to march. The 7. were soon on the move. One and half miles brought us to a clover field on the right of the road and near a spring branch where we pitched tents, the rest of the brigade are on the opposite side of the road, Some firing in front today. Drew Molasses for dinner.

Near Winchester, Va. Saturday Mar. 15, 1862. Yesterday afternoon we Hopewell and Franklin boys met several members of the 12th Ind. Inft.

Among them were Lew McLaughlin & John Webb of 12th, also Captain Wm Johnson and Wm Matthews of the 27th Ind. Matthews attended school at Hopewell Academy three years ago. Says his regt. were the first to enter Winchester. The 12 & 27, spent last winter in good Quarters just across the Potomac in Md. Another skirmish below town.

Near Winchester, Va. Mar. 16, 1862. Reveille at 6, called us from our beds at roll call were told to prepare for Company Inspection at ten A.M.

Winchester, Va. Mar. 17, 1862. This afternoon Comrade James M. Bone came into camp with seven recruits for Co. F, they were Amzi T. Demaree, R. B. Demaree & Wm C. Voris, from Shiloh. John W. Hathaway from Hopewell, and H. G. Fishback, Samuel Garrett and George Rains. They brought many small trinkets from our friends. Among the items were Letter paper, Envelopes, Stamps, dried peaches and Maple sugar.

Winchester, Va. Mar. 18, 1862. Were called at 2 a.m. and ordered to draw three days rations and to be ready to march as soon as possible, this caused a stir and much surmising.

We were ready and started at 5 a.m. Halted in Winchester at dawn of day, soon started again out on the Front Royal road through a very fine country. The Eight Ohio were in the lead. At Burnex Springs 15 Miles out we turned to the right on the road to Middletown six miles distant. When within three or four Miles of Middletown we heard the boom of artillery in the front, we quickened our step. Soon an orderly met us whereupon we slung Knapsacks and double quicked most of the way to Middletown the rebels were driven to Cedar Creek, we followed, they crossed and burned the bridge. When the troops that came on the Winchester & Strasburg Pike came we returned for our Knapsacks and came back and bivouaced near the Creek, having made near 25 Miles during the day.

On Cedar Creek Va. Wednesday, Mar. 19, 1862. A bridge was built over Cedar Creek and the Division crossed and advanced. The force that came on the Front Royal road yesterday to Burners Spring, consisting of the 8th Ohio, 7th Ind. and two companies of the 4. Ohio, under command of Col. Mason of 8. Ohio, followed as a reserve. Artillery was soon heard at the front. The enemy were driven from Strasburg and five or six miles beyond where they burned a bridge and checked our advance. Apparently very little hurt was done to either side to day. We fell back to Strasburg and bivouaced for the night.

Strasburg, Va. March, 20, 1862, Thursday. Commenced raining about dusk and continued through the night. The Division began early this morning to move back and Col. Mason's command was designated as rear guard. It was noon when we started, the distance to camp was 27 Miles. Strasburg is a small place old and dirty, but few stores and many Taverns each with its bar room and whisky. Is on the Turnpike and Alexandria and Staunton R.R. Middletown is but a village, one mile long and two

The streets of Winchester, Virginia.

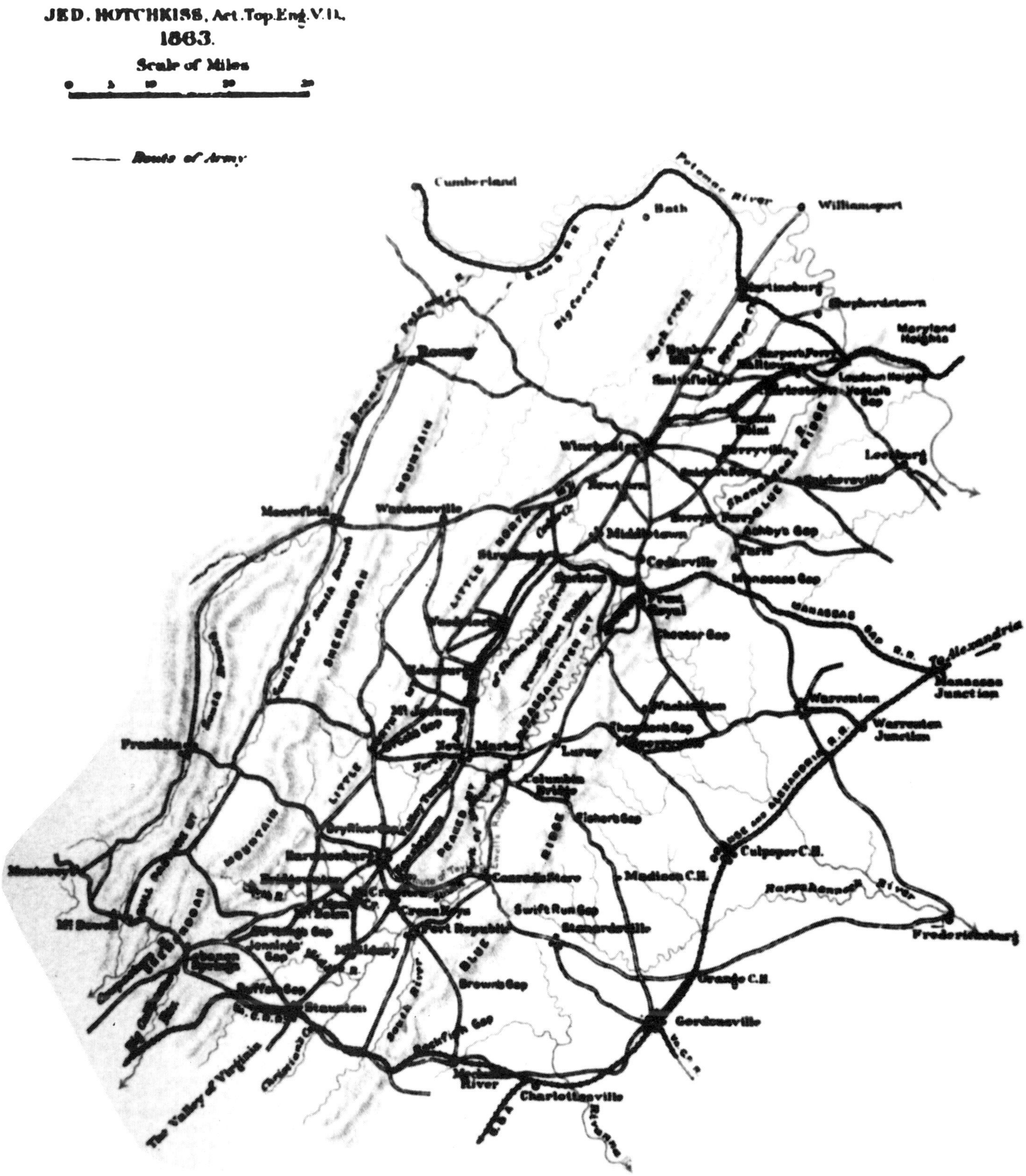

Virginia — from Moorefield to Fredericksburg and from Martinsburg to Staunton.

James Shields, commander of the Union forces at Kernstown.

houses wide, on either side the road and large garden space between each two. It rained all day but we trudged on and arrived in Camp at 9 p.m. wet, muddy, foot sore and worn to a frazzle.

Near Winchester, Va. Friday, Mar, 21, 1862. On arriving in camp last night we found Comrade J. M. Bone abed with Measels and comrade J. C. Henderson sick with fever, Comrade S. W. Vannuys is sick with cold to day. Snowed last night.

All quiet in camp, for we are all two tired to move about.

Saturday, March, 22, 1862. Comrades Bone and Henderson no better today. Find good news in papers from our Western Armies.

Report says that Gen. Banks is moving to Strasburg, also that we are under marching orders. Had Dress parade at 5. p.m. At the same time we heard heavy firing beyond Winchester. At dusk orders came to fall in, no time to get haversacks started at a double quick, troops along the line had gone, many reports met us; one that Stonewall Jackson was nearing Winchester, another that Gen. James Shields our division commander had been wounded. We moved to the edge of town, then about faced and marched back a mile and a half when we again about faced and moved to the edge of town and there bivouaced.

At Winchester, Va. Sunday, March, 23, 1862. The Third Brigade moved back near Camp where massed column was formed and Col. Tyler addressed us for a few

Erastus Tyler, commander of Billy's brigade.

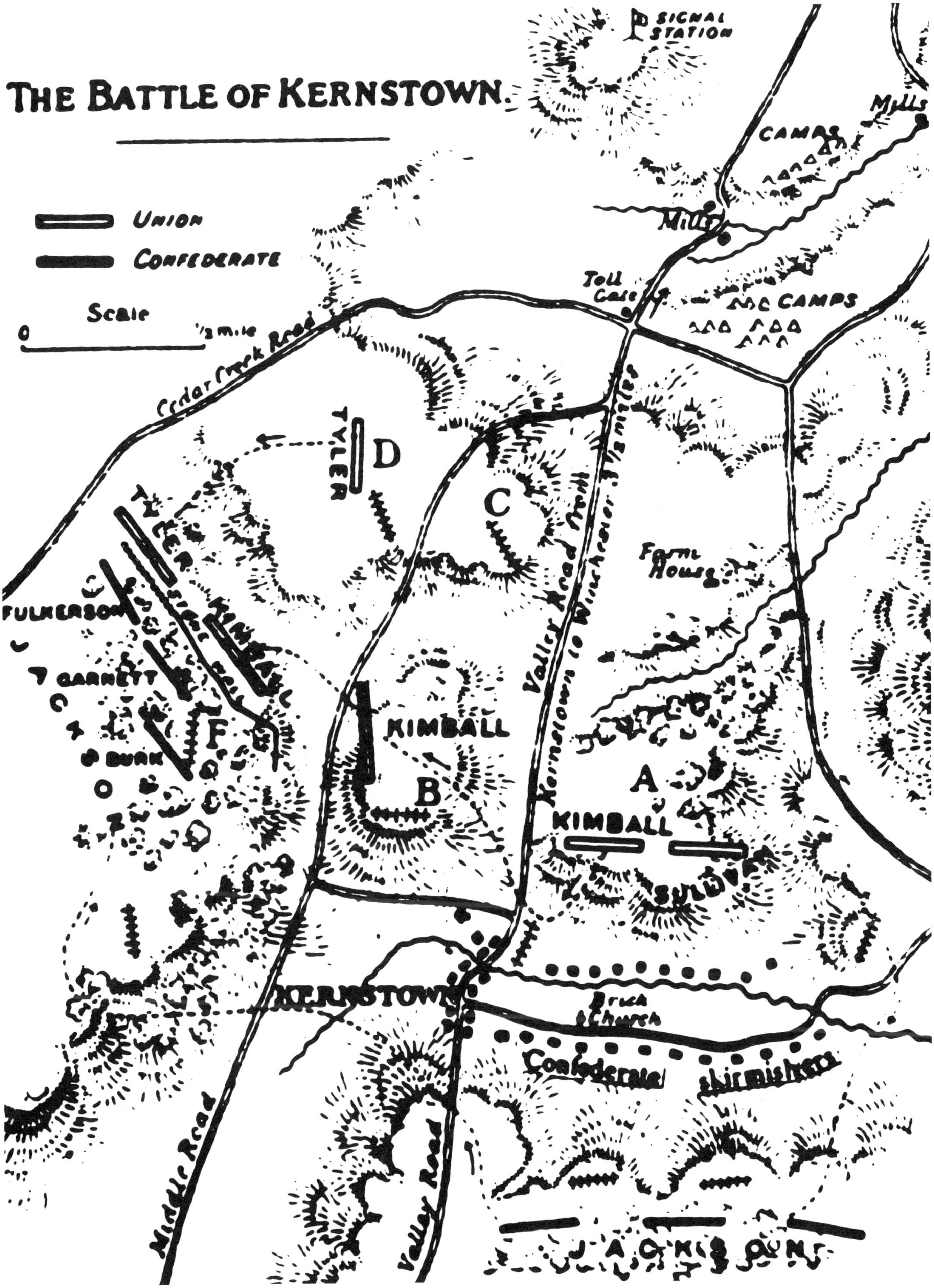

Tyler, including the 7th Indiana, attempted to turn the Confederate left.

minutes and ordered three days rations and sent us to camp. Rations were drawn and prepared as directed and we held ourselves ready to move on a moments notice.

An Incident. Comrade A. I. Canary and G. K. Covert, had quite a tussle over a picture of a Miss Wiley, a personal friend of each. Canary had carried the picture — a Deguara Type — since he entered the Service. Covert insisted that he was more entitled to possession of that picture because of his and Miss Wiley's friendship than Canary was, this Canary denied. A friendly scuffle followed, but Covert kept the picture and put it in the left breast pocket of his coat. *(See Subsequent Mention.)*

About One p.m. the 7. Ind. was called into line and started at once. The heavy firing in front quickened our step. The Third Brigade moved on thru Winchester and to Kernstown four miles below where Col. Nathan Kimball of the 14. Ind. Inft. in command of the Division, was fighting Gen. T. J. (Stonewall) Jackson, we moved onto a hill where Rebel shells began to fall among us.

The rebels made an effort to flank us on our right. The Third Brigade was sent to meet them. We had reached an open timber and were marching in Column by division when Artillery opened with Canister; and Infantry from behind a Stone Wall. We formed battle line and opened fire, the fight continued for some time they having the advantage in position, Col. Kimball sent the 13, & 14. Ind. to our help they went to our right and wheeling struck the enemy on their left flank and routed them from the Stone wall in our front.

Nathan Kimball, former Colonel of the 14th Indiana, was the Union commander on the field at Kernstown.

Now began their hasty retreat and our hurried pursuit which continued until dusk, perhaps four miles from the battlefield where lines were formed pickets placed and arrangements made for sleeping on our arms for the night. It was known that Lieut. Col. Cheek's horse had been shot in the beginning of the engagement disabling him somewhat, later that Major Shaw's horse had been shot and in falling had thrown Major against a tree hurt the Major badly, and still later that Adjutant Lostetter had been wounded in the Elbow.

It was known too that Corporal Daniel W. Prichard of Co. F. and several others of the Regiment had been killed; and that corp'l George Holmes, Amzi T. Demaree and Geo K. Covert, Co. F. and many others of the regt. had been severely wounded, while very many more had received slight wounds.

When we stopped pursuit at dusk, five beside myself were permitted to return to the battle field to help care for the wounded. On our way back we saw a number of rebel dead and others severely wounded, who had fallen on their retreat; at and near the Stone wall were quite a number dead and wounded, from one of the wounded we learned that the 5. Va. of Stonewall Jacksons old brigade had opposed us. Upon our arrival where we fought we found that our ambulance Corps had removed all our killed and wounded, but there were a number of rebel dead in the timber and we found several severely wounded rebels who had doubtless been overlooked by our ambulance force whom we collected and built a good fire to help keep them warm and to give a light that they might be cared for somewhat, when this was done my companions

Jeremiah Sullivan, former commander of the 13th Indiana, commanded the Second Brigade at Kernstown.

Harper's *captioned this one, "Searching for the Dead and Wounded."*

returned to the regiment and left me to keep the fire going and to assist the Confederates.

It was a long and trying night for me and worse for the suffering wounded. They called very frequently for water, two or three canteens furnished water and rails were plentiful. The groans of the wounded were constant and most piteous, often calling for Mother, wife or sister. One stalwart fellow sat up most of the time, he was shot through the mouth from side to side, many of his teeth were gone and tongue badly cut.

Shortly after day light an ambulance and several men came out from the Hospital searching for any wounded who might have been missed. I was relieved and started for the regiment.

Kernstown to Deer Creek, Va. Monday, Mar. 24, 1862. When relieved, I started to find the regt. It had started at day light. I went to the Staunton pike and soon overtook them. The enemy made several stands during the day but were soon driven from their positions and at night our division camped on the high ground North of Cedar Creek, while the rebels were among the hills on the south side.

We learned to day that the loss of the 7th Ind. in yesterdays battle was nine killed and thirteen severely wounded. Of Co. F. Daniel W. Prichard was the first one Killed; George Holmes, Geo. K. Covert and Amzi T. Demaree, Jesse Y. Demaree were wounded. *Holmes so severely that he was discharged Aug. 18, '62. because of disability from wounds. Jesse Y. Demaree was also severely wounded and because of his wounds was discharged on Aug. 23, 1862. Amzi T. Demaree was less severely wounded and in time was again with the regt. He had joined us as a recruit only six days before the battle. Geo. K. Covert came near getting a fatal shot. See how he escaped.*

A Sequence. After the scuffle between Canary and Covert, mentioned on the 23rd Covert had put the Deguereotype picture of Miss Wiley in his left breast coat pocket, between his New Testament and his body. The bullet went through the Testament and struck the picture and bent the plate, and was by it glanced from his body, but left a black & blue spot that was very tender for a month or more, evidently the picture helped to save his life. Neither Covert nor Canary married Miss Wiley after their return from the army and prison. Canary married a Miss Demaree, a cousin of Coverts and Covert married a Miss Lagrange.

Cedar Creek, Va. Tuesday, Mar. 25, 62. Our command began early to cross Cedar Creek and to advance. Soon the booming of Cannon was heard in our front. The enemy took position several times to day, but were soon routed and driven farther back. Near night they formed on the ridges just south of a small stream. After placing a strong picket line most of the division moved back and bivouaced in the vicinity of Fishers Hill south of Strasburg.

Fishers Hill Va. Wednesday, Mar. 26, 1862. Having a large fire of rails at our feet we rested well after our three days hard work.

A clear beautiful morning greeted us and it is quiet about camp as a Sabbath day.

Tents and camp equippage are reaching us and tents are being pitched, which indicates a rest for us.

Thomas Jonathon "Stonewall" Jackson.

The Start of Jackson's Valley Campaign

American historian and educator, Henry Steele Commanger, wrote: "Jackson's Valley campaign has long been regarded as one of the most brilliant in the history of modern warfare. . . . The grand strategy was Lee's, and to some extent, Joe Johnston's, but the tactics were Jackson's. . . . The Valley campaign, as he conducted it, was a military chess game; his objective not so much to defeat the enemy as to distract, confuse, check, and eventually checkmate them."[1]

For 11 weeks, beginning in late March 1862, Thomas Jonathon Jackson taunted Union army field commanders and the government administrators in Washington D. C. The primary purpose of the Confederate plan was to draw Union attention away from Richmond. Of major concern, the Confederates anticipated a large Union offensive toward Richmond in the Spring. However, if the Federal government became preoccupied with defending their own doorsteps there would be fewer men for a move on Richmond. It would be Confederate Major-General "Stonewall" Jackson, in the Shenandoah Valley, who would carry out the Confederate strategy.

It began near Winchester, Virginia in March 1862. Billy Davis and the Union troops under General Nathaniel B. Banks became Jackson's first target. Banks had moved his troops from Harpers Ferry and Martinsburg through Winchester on their way south. This, Jackson could not allow. He burned bridges in Banks' front and pushed one division back toward Winchester. He moved his own division of 3,300 men northward — in the face of three times his number at Kernstown — undaunted, he wanted to strike first.[2]

The Battle of Kernstown

The 7th Indiana was part of Erastus Barnard Tyler's Third Brigade, James Shields' Division, Nathaniel Banks' Fifth Corps of the Army of the Potomac. Four other regiments joined the Hoosiers in Tyler's Brigade: the 7th and 29th Ohio, 1st (West) Virginia and the 110th Pennsylvania.

By March 22 Major General Banks had moved three divisions out of Winchester. Shields, however, fell back to Winchester after meeting resistance from the rebel cavalry. There was skirmishing during the afternoon of the 22nd as Jackson's cavalry commander Turner Ashby moved closer to Winchester and engaged some of Shields' pickets. The small Southern cavalry force retired and Shields' men did not pursue. Shields did deploy his troops so as to resist further harassment. It was decided Tyler's Brigade (of Shields' division, including the 7th Indiana) should be held in reserve.[3]

Sunday morning, March 23, found Shields confident that there would not be a general engagement. Jackson, in fact, was some 14 miles away. However, Jackson still intended to strike Shields. He wanted to frighten Banks into recalling all of his forces. It was 1 p.m. when Jackson came north on the turnpike below Kernstown. Initially, he decided to wait until the next day to attack. (Jackson wished to keep the day holy and, furthermore, his men were fatigued.) Then, realizing the vulnerability of his own position, Jackson decided he could not wait.[4]

Colonel Kimball was commanding the Union forces and had deployed his infantry and artillery in excellent field positions. Of special advantage, Union artillery was placed on Pritchard's hill, squarely in Jackson's path — and a point from which Jackson's movements could be watched. Jackson directed his cavalry to continue skirmishing near the turnpike. This activity would hold the Union forces in place. Then, in an attempt to outflank the Union positions, Jackson sent infantry and artillery to Sand Ridge, two miles to the northwest. Once on Sand Ridge, the Confederates started shelling the Union positions.[5]

Colonel Tyler and his Third Brigade were ordered forward from their reserve position, six miles to the north. They were to proceed south toward Kernstown and then move to the west, striking the Rebels on Sand Ridge. The 7th Indiana, the 7th Ohio and one battery of artillery passed off the road into a narrow valley. As these men neared the far right, they formed into a solid column. And proceeded up and down two hills in full view of their enemy. The Rebels did not squander this opportunity.[6] The 23rd and 37th Virginia opened with a murderous fire from behind a low stone wall. The Union boys were thrown into confusion. Determined, they took cover and for the next two hours and forty minutes they traded ball and buckshot with the Confederates.[7] Six additional Union units were sent to help turn the Confederate left. Failing this, the Union fire was concentrated toward the center of the Rebel line.[8]

The Confederate line wavered. General Richard Garnett (the cousin of the Confederate general killed at Corrick's Ford) feared he was going to be overrun as the ammunition ran low. There were reserves on the way, but Garnett felt it prudent to withdraw his three regiments. Once Garnett's men started back, the line could not be held. A full retreat was underway. Jackson, from his position behind the lines, personally tried to block the retreat. It was too late.[9]

Billy related how he and the Federals pushed forward for four miles. The Battle of Kernstown would be Stonewall Jackson's only defeat although he did accomplish his purpose of alarming Corps Commander Banks and the officials in Washington.

The Confederates lost 80 killed, 342 wounded and 269 missing for total casualties of 691. (About 70 of the wounded were left on the field — some comforted by Billy Davis.)[10] Union General Shields' forces suffered losses totalling 590, 118 killed, 450 wounded and 22 captured or missing. Kernstown cost the 7th Indiana seven dead, 33 wounded and nine missing or captured.[11] This, as Billy said, was the 7th's first real battle.

Pritchard's Hill, a critical terrain feature at the battle of Kernstown, is to the left on the horizon. (Very dim.)

Jackson and his men passed this barn on their way to the battle, photograph circa 1880s.

The famous stone wall at Kernstown.

Ambulances waiting to go to the front.

END NOTES

(1) Henry Steele Commanger, Editor, *The Blue and the Gray* (Indianapolis, 1950); p. 148.

(2) James I. Robertson, Jr., *The Stonewall Brigade* (Baton Rouge, 1962) and Robert G. Tanner, *Stonewall in the Valley* (Garden City, 1976) are recent accounts of the 1862 Shenandoah Valley Campaign. For a biography of T. J. Jackson, see Lieutenant-Colonel G. F. R. Henderson, *Stonewall Jackson and the American Civil War* (Two volumes, London, 1899). Or, for a flattering account, see R. L. Dabney, *Life and Campaigns of Lieut.-Gen. Thomas J. Jackson* (New York, 1866).

(3) William Allan, *History of the Campaign of Gen. T. J. (Stonewall) Jackson in the Shenandoah Valley of Virginia* (Reprint, Dayton, 1987); p. 46. This same military history can also be found in J. William Jones, et. al., Editors, *Southern Historical Society Papers*, (52 volumes, first published 1920; reprinted New York, 1977); v. 43, pp. 111-294. Hereafter cited as *Jackson in the Valley*.

(4) Tanner, *Stonewall in the Valley;* pp. 118-119.

(5) Allan, *Jackson in the Valley;* pp. 49-50.

(6) *ORs, series I, v. XII, part 1, pp. 375-377. (General Tyler's official report.)*

(7) Thomson, *Seventh Indiana;* pp. 86-87.

(8) Tanner, *Stonewall in the Valley;* pp. 123-124.

(9) Robertson, *The Stonewall Brigade;* pp. 73-74.

(10) Allan, *Jackson in the Valley;* p. 53.

(11) *ORs*, series I, v. XII, part 1, pp. 346-347. Orville Thomson, the regimental historian, wrote the 7th Indiana suffered its worst losses while marching in column toward Sand Ridge.

Richard Garnett would be arrested and relieved of command by Jackson for pulling back from the stone wall.

PICTURE CREDITS

—110—Courtesy, Allegany County (Maryland) Historical Society.

—111—Courtesy, USAMHI.

—111—Courtesy, B & O Railroad Museum, Baltimore.

—112—Both courtesy, USAMHI.

—113— *Atlas to Accompany the Official Records of the Union and Confederate Armies.*

—114—Courtesy, The Louis A. Warren Lincoln Library and Museum.

—114—Miller's *Photographic History.*

—115—Map. *Battles and Leaders.*

—116—Both courtesy, USAMHI.

—117—*Harper's Pictorial History of the Civil War.*

—118—Courtesy, USAMHI.

—120—Both, same.

—121—Same.

—121—Miller's *Photographic History.*

—122—Courtesy, USAMHI.

CHAPTER 9 A VERY RICH AND WELL IMPROVED VALLEY

Fishers Hill, Va. Thursday, Mar. 27, 1862. Another beautiful day. The rest of our tents and baggage came at noon and tents were being pitched when orders came to bundle up for a move, the regt. was soon in line and started. 29. Ohio with us. We soon learned that it was for picket duty and not to move camp. Went three or four miles toward Woodstock. Three companies of each regt were sent out on skirmish line. The rebels fired three shots at them, no casualties.

At dusk the reserve were moved back about one mile.

March, 28, 1862, Friday. Some incident in our Cavalry caused an alarm, but it soon subsided. At noon the regiment started back, stopped at Second Brigade Headquarters, while there the rebels shelled the woods which we left at noon. Reached our own brigade camp an hour by sun, and found tents had been pitched by the Convalescents. Small mail today.

March 29, 62. Saturday. All quiet in Camp to day. Are many reports about the battle of the 23rd. The Baltimore papers give full reports of the engagement. It furnishes interesting reading for us. That being our first real battle. Straw was obtained from near by stacks and our tents thickly carpeted with it, and a supply of rails secured for fires. After prayers we retired.

Sabbath, March, 30, 62. Commenced raining late yesterday afternoon and rained very hard most of the night.

This morning eight from each Co. were detailed to go work on a bridge across the North branch of Shenandoah river, about three miles from camp.

Gen. Williams Brigade was camped near the bridge. Gen. N. P. Banks visited the bridge while we were at work and greeted all of us, he has a keen black eye. Reached camp about Eight p.m. The Mess prayer Meeting was being held. Had rained all day.

Had just got to bed when orders came for Co's E & F to go on picket. Those on duty to day were excused. It was still raining. Boys had drawn three days rations late this afternoon.

Nathaniel Banks, Commander of V Corps.

The Shenandoah Valley — Strasburg, Virginia and the Massanutten Mountains.

The Valley Turnpike.

Fishers Hill, Va. Monday, Mar. 31, 1862. This morning our pickets came in very much vexed out of humor, having wandered in the woods in the darkness until Midnight without finding those whom they were to relieve. Cleared off and became a beautiful day. Many of us used the day to do our washing. After supper orders came to be ready to march at a moments notice, was soon countermanded. North Branch of Shenandoah is in flood from yesterday's rain.

Fishers Hill Va. Tuesday, April, 1, 1862. Were called early to prepare to march at 7. A.M. Breakfast was soon over and we were ready on time. Near 8. A.M. Col. Mason with two or three regiments started west. We soon started along the Mount Jackson road, taking our time. All the Infantry, Artillery and Cavalry seem to be moving, the latter in front.

Ashby's rebel Cavalry were met and driven back several times. When in two or three miles of Woodstock we saw a large smoke ahead, which later proved to be rebel camps burning. Woodstock is a neat village. Some of the ladies cheered us. Some distance from Woodstock, we engaged the enemy again. Saw several rebel camps destroyed, were mostly brush bivouacs.

Rebels had tried to destroy a partly built bridge over a small creek. Just before sundown we stopped in a timber for the night.

Wednesday, Apr. 2, 62. Early this morning the ball opened, by the firing of several Cannon. Rained some last night, and is still threatening. Skirmished frequently with the enemy as we advanced slowly. Rained again this afternoon. Provisions were brought up and issued this p.m. The 7. was ordered at sundown to guard a battery, went about three miles, passed thru the village of Edenburg. Saw a large R.R. bridge destroyed with fire by the rebels as they retreated. The battery was in a timber, we went to the right and prepared for the night. Comrade R. B. Demaree came in from Winchester, and reported J. Y. Demaree and James M. Bone as improving. They hope to get a furlough home soon.

Thursday, April 3, 1862. Up early again this morning and breakfast over, we were ready for any emergency. We expected some shots from the enemy this morning but they did not come. The 29. Ohio, came out and relieved us and we returned to camp.

This forenoon some of the boys were chasing a Rabbit. The Colonel was looking on & turning to some one wondered what the boys would do with it if caught. Some one standing by said, "guess they will swear it to support the Constitution and let it go like our officers do the rebels when we get them." Some skirmishing this afternoon.

Friday, April, 4, 62. I was not well last night. Wm Mitchell of the 14. Ind. spent last night with us. He reports having recently been out as a spy and in the enemy's camp and on one occasion came very near being caught.

Some cannonading and skirmishing today. Captains and some companies got their tents and knapsacks this afternoon.

Saturday, April, 5, 1862. Rained last night and some again today. Had inspection of Arms this afternoon.

Sunday, April 6, 1862. At bed time took the tooth ache and suffered until one p.m, when I was prevailed upon to take a chew of Tobacco, which made me very sick and while it eased the tooth it prostrated my nervous system. Slept some before Morning but I got up with ear ache.

Packed up and moved near a Mile to a Pine grove which we trimmed and policed. Tents came and were pitched.

Late this afternoon a Library of Seventy Volumes reached us, a gift to Company "F" from our friends of the Franklin, Ind. Presbyterian Church. They are Publications of the Presbyterian Board of Philadelphia.

Monday, Apr. 7, 62. Near Edenburg, Va. This morning Lieut. Jeffery, asked me to take charge of the Library. The books were all numbered, and the names of all the members of Company "F," written in a New Pocket Memoranda and record kept by noting No. of book taken opposite the comrades names. Most of them were soon out.

There were then Ninety four members in the Co. but some were at home on furlough and others in hospitals.

On leaving the vicinity of New Market Va. on May 12, for Fredericksburg, Va, there being no longer transportation for the box and books they were distributed generally among the Members of Company F, and subsequently were exchanged among the boys without record.

There is reason to believe that several were taken by comrades to hospitals and that one or more copies were taken by comrades into Confederate prisons.

After June 14, 1862, the record book was used for Daily Memoranda, with the Library record unchanged, and is now Oct. 21, 1915, in my possession.

Commenced snowing about noon.

Report says that Gen McClellan has landed at Fortress Monroe and engaged the enemy on the Peninsula.

Tuesday, April, 8, 1862. Still snowing and raining. At roll call this Morning orders were given for Co. F. to prepare for picket with one day's ration. Soon started on

Alpheus Williams, a Union army division commander in the Valley Campaign.

our muddy walk. Missed road and added a five mile tramp to the post which proved to be the one we held some days ago. Soon put up our Poncho tents and made fires. Snowed or rained all day. Our mail came late.

Wednesday, April 9, 1862. Snowed all night. Col. Buckley came quite early in the forenoon with the 29. Ohio, and relieved us and we returned to camp. Drizzled sleet and snow till noon, when it commenced snowing hard. Heard that Gen. McClellan had had a hard fight on the Peninsula and had captured one Gen'l, and many prisoners.

Thursday, April, 10, 62. The sun shone all day but it was so cold that but little snow melted. All who could do so stayed close about camp. Report says there has been a big engagement at Pittsburg Landing, Tenn. and that Island No. 10, in the Mississippi river has been captured.

Friday, April 11, 62. Are conflicting reports in camp about the late battles in the west. At Dress parade Col. told us that Gen'l Hallock had been attacked at Pittsburg Landing, Tenn and that the rebels had been whipped and Gen'l Johnston killed and that Gen. Bearugard had an arm blown off,(?) and a lot of prisoners taken, and that Island No. 10 was taken with the Gen'l and his command, also that Gen. Lew Wallace of Ind. had been killed.

Late this evening news came that the Merrimac an Armored rebel war vessell had been sunk with all its crew. After prayers we retired.

Saturday, April, 12, 62. News of the sinking of the Merrimac and the taking of Norfolk, Va. confirmed.

This is a beautiful day. About three p.m. orders came to roll up our blankets and prepare what rations we had. Soon the order was countermanded and we were told to get our guns and get into line. We went near a mile where the brigade was formed. All the Division was in sight. Soon cheering was heard, then came Gen. Shields in a buggy, his arm in a sling, he was loudly cheered as he passed each regiment and brigade. At Dress parade a member of this regiment was reprimanded, he having been Court Martialed.

To day the boys of our Mess subscribed for three Daily papers — Viz. — The "New York Herald," The "Philadelphia Enquirer", and The "Baltimore Clipper." We are able to get these papers at a cost of .90 c. per week. Rumor says our Paymaster is coming this way soon, we hope it is so.

Camp Tyler Va. Sunday April, 13, 1862. Yesterday we were told that to day would be observed by Gen'l Shields Division as a day of Thanksgiving to Almighty God for the success of our several armies the last few days.

At 10.30 we marched to the Parade grounds of the 7. Ohio. The Chaplain of the 7 Ohio presided and lead. Genl N. P. Banks, and Staff were present. It is one year today since the fall of Fort Sumter. What a tense and stirring year.

Camp Tyler, Va. April, 14, 62. Monday. Rained some last night. About 8. am, orders were given for us to prepare by One p.m. to march, with two days rations and blankets, by ten A.M. all were ready to take arms. At three

Henry Halleck — falsely rumored as having been attacked at Pittsburg Landing (or (Shiloh) — actually it was U. S. Grant who was attacked.

Lew Wallace of Indiana was rumored as killed in action.

p.m. the rebels threw some shells across the creek into the camp of the 27. Ind. No damage is reported.

At 3.30, we were ordered out for Inspection, we returned to camp and stacked arms still expecting to march soon. At night we still listened for orders. It has been a day of suspense. Mail came very late. I received a letter from my friend J. L. Jones.

Camp Tyler, Va. Tuesday, April, 15, 62. Raining some this morning. Got orders to go out on picket, but that was countermanded and we signed the Pay rolls, expect payment tomorrow. I bought a copy of the New York Illustrated News and Harpers Weekly containing pictures of Genl James Shields and other prominent Military men, news of Gen. McClellan at York Town, Va. and some particulars at Pittsburg Landing. President Lincoln issued his call for 75,000 troops for three months, one year ago to day.

Camp Tyler, Va. Wednesday, April, 16, 62. A clear beautiful Morning. Sharp Cannonading at 7. a.m. At noon heard that one Company of Col. Ashbys rebel cavalry had been captured.

Near four p.m. we were called into line to receive pay for four months, $52.00. — $13.00 per. month.

At Sundown marching orders came. Two days rations were drawn at dusk. Wrote letter to father and sent $30.00. with it by comrade John Forgay.

At ten p.m. made our beds and after a Prayer Meeting Service layed down to sleep expecting to be called at two a.m. to march.

Camp Tyler Va. Thursday, Apr. 17, 62. At 20 minutes of 3. a.m. we were called and at 3. A.M, we started, passed through Edenburg crossed Stoney Creek, went one mile and halted.

At day break Gen. Shields and staff and guard passed to the front. After sunup Gen. Banks and Staff and orderlies also went to the front. Some heavy cannonading this Afternoon but the enemy were driven back.

Rebels burned a small bridge but we crossed on a railroad bridge. At Hawkinstown a very small village we saw several large smokes ahead. Near Mount Jackson three new buildings were seen, on getting nearer hospital flags were seen on them. When within one mile of Mount Jackson, we came to a large building near the R.R. near which was a new grave yard in which were forty or fifty fresh mounds, we supposed the persons buried there had been killed at Winchester on March 23 or had died from wounds or disease. On reaching Mount Jackson we found that one smoke was from burning cars and lumber and the other was a bridge. Stopped for dinner near the burning cars. Started again about two p.m. found Mount Jackson to be a small place with four or five New buildings. Crossed a small stream on the remnant of a burnt bridge, and filed out behind a hill, soon advanced and crossed North Fork of Shenandoah river on a bridge that our Cavalry had saved, the material for the fire was ready for the match.

After crossing the river our Brigade filed to the right and formed column by division and advanced across the level valley near two miles to a rising ground and rested for

Irvin McDowell and George McClellan, early Union army commanders in the Civil War — neither lasted.

a short time, from this point I saw more growing wheat than I ever saw before from one point of view.

Was occasional cannonading during the Afternoon. We advanced to within sight of New Market and at dusk filed into a meadow and bivouaced for the night. I enlisted one year ago to day.

Friday, April 18, 1862. Slept well last night. After having despatched our Coffee, Hardtack and Bacon, the Regiment was ordered out as we thot for picket. About the center of New Market we filed to the right onto a very Muddy clay to the river thence up the river three miles to a Grist Mill and Saw Mill, where we halted, Co. K was sent out on picket, the regt. filed left in to an orchard and stacked Arms. Company C went out on a scout but soon returned. It threatened rain very much and the regiment being with out tents sought shelter, Several Cos, went into the Mill and some into barns. Co. F went in to a Cooper shop and adjoining rooms in which were three beds. No person was found near, and from appearances the occupants had left in a hurry.

Two Federal Army Blankets one Knapsack and three Canteens were found. Winchester, with a date was found on one of them.

From a near by barn we got Straw for beds. Two persons were captured to day.

Belle Plains Mills, Va. Saturday, 19, 62. Did not rain last night, this Morning Col. Gavin ordered us back to the orchard and a proper camp was formed.

Colonel ordered Co. drill in the forenoon and Regt. drill in the afternoon.

When the Cos. returned from drill there was a fisticuff fight in Co. G, the contestants were sent to the guard house.

Commenced to rain at noon and we went to our Shelters again. The Grist Mill is run by water from a very large Spring and flows through a large Meadow, and the Saw Mill by water from the river furnished through a race from a Stone dam.

In the Mill is a lot of flour and bran and several hundred bushels of wheat, said to have been put here by near by farmers for the use of the rebel army, evidenced by the amount of hauling that has been done from this place.

We are now given a ration of flour from the Mill, which we prepared as flapjacks, short cake or biscuits, or have Citizens bake for us. Good expert Millers were found in the regiment who were at once detailed to run the Mill and teams were put to hauling in wheat from the surrounding country, and flour is now furnished to the rest of our Army in this vicinity. By foraging we get beef, pork and bacon and other things — verily we are living on the fat of the land.

Belle Planes Mills, Va. Sunday, Apr. 20, 62. This is a very rich and well improved Valley. Good apple and peach orchards on every farm. The wheat is promising and Meadows and clover fields are taking on the green rapidly. Peach trees are in full bloom and all nature seems to be gladdened by the coming of Spring and the Federal Army. Rained all day.

Monday, April, 21, 62. Commenced raining at noon and rained almost constantly the remainder of the day. Very little of interest about camp to-day.

Tuesday, April, 22, 1862. Company F were ordered out on picket and went two or three miles and some distance from the river. Very quiet on the picket line to day. Last Night some one tried to burn the flouring Mill but the fire was discovered and put out.

Belle Plains Mills, Va. Wednesday, Apr. 23, 62. Our picket post was in a barn, at night twelve men were sent out a half mile or More in advance where we stopped in a small Cabinet shop, with two guards out all the while.

At Nine a.m. this morning we were relieved and returned to camp and found the regiment pitching tents in a Meadow near the Mill. Dress parade at 5. p.m. Tattoo at 8.30 and Taps at 9. p.m.

Thursday, Apr. 24, 62. Roll call and Co. drill before breakfast. Commenced early in forenoon to snow, and snowed hard till noon, then began to rain and kept it up till night.

Most of us are kept close in camp and many of Co. F are enjoying the books our friends of the Presbyterian church of Franklin sent us recently. No news of importance to day.

Friday, Apr. 25, 1862. I was detailed on camp guard. Ten from each Company were detailed for picket. Rained hard last night, and has drizzled frequently today.

Belle Plaines Mills Va. April. 26, 62. Have drawn flour the last few days most of which the Citizens bake for us. I went to day near one mile to get bread baked for our Mess. Regimental drill at two p.m. and Dress parade at 5 p.m.

Report says that Gen. Hallock attacked Gen. Beauregard and was defeated. It is reported that Gen. McClellan, has taken York Town, Va. Gen. Banks of our department entered Harrisonburg today.

Sunday, Apr. 27, 62. Some frost last night but there is heavy fog to day. Had Company Inspection at 9. a.m. and regimental drill and Dress parade in the afternoon.

Monday, April, 28, 62. Company drill at 10. a.m. and regimental drill from two to four p.m. and Dress parade at the usual hour. At Dress parade our col. said that the Federal troops had taken New Orleans, La.

Tuesday, Apr. 29, 62. Raining this morning. I am on regimental guard again to day. Drill in the Afternoon. Report says that Gen'l McClellan is still fighting at York Town. The Quartermaster still issues flour to us, most of which we get the citizens to bake.

Wednesday, April, 30, 62. Inspection and Muster for pay today. Is cloudy and looks much like rain.

The Chaplain of the 13th Ind. Inft. Rev. Mr Cotton preached to us this afternoon, a very good sermon, good advice and fine illustrations. He was pastor of the Franklin Ind. Methodist Episcopal church a few years ago.

Camp Belle Plains Mills, Va. Thursday, May 1, 1862. Last evening Capt. Samuel Lambertson received a leave of Absence and started for home at ten p.m. We had no time to write letters to send with him.

Yesterday I received a letter from home and one from Cousin James S. Thomas of Andrain Co, Mo. Answered both to day.

We had a fine regimental drill this Afternoon. Commenced raining at Dress parade.

Friday May 2, 62. Rained hard last night. I am one of the detail from Co. F for picket. We are two or three miles from camp. I am acting as Corporal. Has been a beautiful day.

The Countersign came at dusk. I at once took it to the other posts.

Saturday, May, 3, 62. I was up at 3. a.m. and on guard. Hard chopping of wood at 4. a.m. which I supposed to be in camp. About an hour by sun a Cavalryman came and told us to hurry to camp, as the regiment had orders to March at 8. a.m. We reached camp in time, the regiment formed line and followed a road that led to the Pike a few miles south of New Market.

The day was very warm, and having to carry our knapsacks we went slow and made about ten miles and camped within Six miles of Harrisonburg.

Camp Near Harrison Cave, Rockingham Co. Va, Sunday, May, 4, 62. This morning we rolled our blankets and the regiment moved to a woods near by and pitched our tents. A very pretty place to camp.

We now get our Daily Papers again. At dusk we were ordered to be ready to march on a moments warning.

Several of the boys went some distance to Harrison's Cave, they describe it as being magnificent in scenery. This is a fine fertile and well improved Valley.

Monday, May, 5, 62. Last night we drew one days rations and cooked them at once.

Were awakened at 4. A.M. and prepared to march, with blankets on knapsacks. Had breakfast Early and started at sunup, baggage train in front, we started back towards New Market and marched seven or eight miles where the Division formed in a strong defensive position with the Third Brigade on the left of the road and went into bivouac for the night. Comrade Lewis W. Richardson came to us from home.

Tuesday May, 6, 62. Officers staked off our Camp early and we pitched our tents. I then wrote two letters. Our Cavalry had a brush with the rebel Cavalry and lost an Adjutant and seven men taken prisoners.

The papers state that York Town has been evacuated. And that our forces have captured Baton Rouge La. and rumor says that Corinth Miss. has been evacuated by the Confederates.

There is much enthusiasm in camp.

Wednesday, May, 7, 62. Nothing about camp of more interest than Company and regimental drill and Dress parade until our Daily papers came.

Evacuation of York Town confirmed.

Particulars of bombardment and surrender of Fort Macon, and much other cheering news.

We were inspected by one of Gen Shields aids de camp. We are under very rigid camp orders now. This camp is in Rockingham Co. Va. in a beautiful and highly cultivated and productive valley. Small mail today. Much loud cheering in some of the other regiments this Afternoon.

Thursday, May, 8, 1862. Report has the Stars and Stripes floating over Richmond, Va. We think the report with out foundation, in fact.

Rumor says that we are to march soon. Some say Via of Strasburg. Others say we will cross the Massennuten Mountain and go Via Luray to Front Royal.

Friday, May, 9, 62. I was called early to go with eight others to Plains Mills to carry Wagon Master _____ Tucker to New Market, a distance of full three miles. He was shot in the right breast last Sunday night, by a picket, when crossing the river below the mill and had to be left at a farm house near the ford, on the opposite side of the river. We waded the river, found him improving, We placed him on blankets on stretcher and waded the river again, and carried him through the hot sun over a rough muddy road. Sheltered somewhat by an umbrella, four of us carried at a time. He was much fatigued by the tedious trip. He started in an Ambulance to Strasburg.

On returning to camp found that all the tents but those of Regimental Officers and Captains had been struck, rolled and were gone. Comrade Campbell Thompson received his discharge and started home. The sick and those not able for a long march were sent to Strasburg.

Saturday, May, 10, 1862. For several days we have had much evidence that we were to move soon.

This morning orders came to draw three days rations and to be ready to march at Six A.M. tomorrow morning. I made every thing ready in the afternoon, then went on Cattle guard, and when off duty slept at a mill door. On coming into camp, I found that the order had been countermanded. Received news of the defeat of the Rebels at Williamsburg, Va.

Sunday, May, 11, 62. There are many surmises and guesses as to why the order was countermanded.

From the papers of the 9th inst we learn the particulars of the taking of Williamsburg, and get the official account of the fall of New Orleans, and other movements of our Armies.

Had Company Inspection by one of Gen'l Shields aids at 9. a.m.

Late in the afternoon Co. F was sent out three or four miles on the Pike on picket and the several out posts placed. At dusk Lieut. Jeffery and I visited the posts to give them the countersign. Saw a Citizen who told us that Col. Ashby's horse was shot as he passed through New Market on April 18.

On Picket Rockingham Co. Va. fifteen miles North of Harrisonburg. Monday, May, 12, 1862. At one a.m. we were called up to return to camp. The out posts were called in at once and we started, On reaching camp we found that the regt. had been gone near two hours. We stopped and made coffee.

At 3. A.M. we started to follow the regiment which we understood had orders to report at a point two miles beyond New Market.

At Sun up we were in New Market, where we learned that the regt. had gone toward Strasburg as Wagon train guard.

From our daily papers we learn that Gen. Franklin and Gen. Sedgewick had engaged the rebels at West Point on York river and at Williamsburg, that General Burnside was moving up Roanoke river, N.C. that Gen. McDowell, had crossed the Rappahannock river and now occupied Fredericksburg that Sewells Point had been taken and that our Gun Boats were starting up James River.

We overtook the regt. at Stoney Creek, moved about two miles farther and camped for the night. Co F having marched twenty eight miles or more.

North of New Market, Va May, 13, 62. Words came last night that the Merrimac had been sunk and Norfolk Va. taken. Yesterday was a very hard day on all of us being very warm and the roads dusty.

Indications are that all our troops are leaving the valley. Shields division to cross Mountains and go via Luray to Front Royal and perhaps East, Gen. Banks via Strasburg and North.

We started at day break, soon overtook Gen. Williams division, and as they monopolized the Pike, we went to the R.R. track till we passed them, then the pike to the creek near Strasburg and stopped for dinner.

Rumor says that Col. Ashby and twelve or fifteen of his men have been captured, we think it doubtful. Dinner over we started and went by a short cut and did not pass through Strasburg.

There are a great many troops and much baggage etc. etc. in and around Strasburg.

Lieut. Jeffery being unable to march any longer went to the Ambulance. Reached Cedar Creek and found that the bridge had been rebuilt by the Federals. Otherwise things appeared much as they were on the 19 of March. We crossed and went into camp, pitched our bivouacs, then went bathing. Comrade Henderson took a hook and line and caught four small fish. The Papers have taken Richmond again. Have official confirmation of the taking of Norfolk and Portsmouth and the blowing up of the "Virginia" (old Merrimac.)

Camp on "Cedar Creek" twenty miles South of Winchester, Va. Wednesday, May, 14, 62. Commenced raining at ten o'clock last night and was raining when we were called, and when we started at day break. At Middletown we turned to the right, taking the Burner Springs road over which we marched at Double quick the 18. of last March, in an effort to catch Col. Ashby and his Cavalry. At Bruners Springs we turned to the right on the Winchester and Front Royal Pike, going near four miles we came to the North Fork of the Shenandoah river and found that the bridge had been burned last March by Stonewall Jackson on his retreat from Winchester.

After waiting a few minutes Col. Gavin dismounted and started to wade. The regiment followed, for we were already wet from the days rain, the water was waist deep and swift.

A short walk on the railroad brought us to the South Branch of the Shenandoah which we crossed on the New R.R. bridge, the other having been burned by the rebels. It was very long and was near one hundred feet above the water. The R.R. had been rebuilt to this point and they were now rebuilding the North branch bridge to Strasburg, the same that I was assisting on as one of the detail on March 30, rebels had destroyed it again. Just above the

Cedar Creek, Virginia.

The terrain near Front Royal, Virginia — a battle was fought here on May 23, 1862.

R.R. bridge was a large flouring mill. Followed the Railroad one mile to Front Royal, a village of three or four hundred people and the County seat of Warren Co. Went about one mile beyond town and stopped. Has rained all day; bivouacs were soon up and straw obtained from a near by stack for beds. We are told that Gen. Shields Division is all in this vicinity.

Thursday, May, 15. One mile east of Front Royal, Va. Most of the boys speak of having rested well last night. Were up and Coffee drank when orders came to prepare to march. The Third Brigade soon started South East, going up a Small stream which we are told is "Happy Creek," on this creek are several Flouring Mills.

Scenery very fine, farm houses rather small, passed one house where some young ladies greet us by waving of handerchiefs. Roads very rough, on reaching the top of the Blue Ridge were ordered to load our muskets, just then Gen. Sullivan came up and surveyed the hills through his field glass.

Report says that a squad of the enemies Cavalry were seen this forenoon, four of them came near capturing the Major of the 1st W. Va. After dinner we moved a few miles and camped for the night on a Swift stream near a Mill. Made bivouacs of rails and covered them with our gum blankets. No Straw to be had for beds. Three beeves were killed for this brigade. Rained all day.

South East of Front Royal, Va. Friday, May, 16, 62. Yesterday and last night were rather trying on the Third Brigade, marching through the day in the rain and being with out tents last night and it still raining this morning.

Col. Cheek is at home on Leave, and Doctor New has care of his horse and buggy, late yesterday after noon the horse ran away and broke the buggy to pieces.

It was late in the afternoon when we started across a hilly country over rough muddy roads. Four miles brought us to Flint Hill a small village, in a well cultivated district, and two miles further brought us a Pike. Soon came to a Plantation of several hundred acres and a large Mansion and slave quarters near. One mile more and we reached a timber where we found rails and water in abundance when we stopped for dinner. Soon we were told to build bivouacs as we would likely spend the night here. The Rebels have camped here recently. Report says that the rebs surrounded a company of our Cavalry but the 110 Penn. regt. helped them out. Six rebel saddles were emptied and two prisoners were taken. Rained some this afternoon.

Fauquier Co. Va. Saturday May, 17, 1862. Slept well last night. Pickets are in sight of each other, consequently some firing last night.

Ordered up at 4. A.M. with orders to move at 5. Gen'l ______ Sullivan now in command of this Third Brigade. Our regt did not start until our Brigade were on the road towards Warrentown.

Some little sunshine this Morning. We have crossed the Blue Ridge and are on the head waters of the Rappahannock River. The scenery is fine but the Soil appears poor. Passed thru the Village of Amissville. Are many sacafrac and Persimon bushes.

The bridge over the Hageman river having been burned; we were oblige to go one mile above to a deep ford near a large Mill and wade across. At two p.m. we were eight mile from Warrenton. Country is growing better. Reached Warrenton at 7. p.m. The place has much wealth and a show of Aristocracy. Are many Negros here. Are several good Hotels. This is a real Southern place. The First and Second Brigades are in camp near us.

Near Warrenton Va. Sunday, May, 18, 62. Last evening we camped about one mile from Warrenton, no rain yesterday or last night, is clear to day, and we are enjoying a days rest after a week of hard marching.

At 9. AM, drew two days rations and were ordered to prepare to march on call, it is intimated that there is a hard march ahead of us. Some think we are on our way to the coast. No Mail or papers since we left Front Royal.

Near Warrenton, Va. Monday, May, 19, 62. We were called early and by 7. A.M. the Third Brigade were on the move going East four miles brought us to a stream difficult for wagons to cross where we waited some time, while here we heard as we supposed the report of cannon. After

Warrenton, Virginia (above and below) — Billy said, "This place has much wealth and a show of Aristocracy."

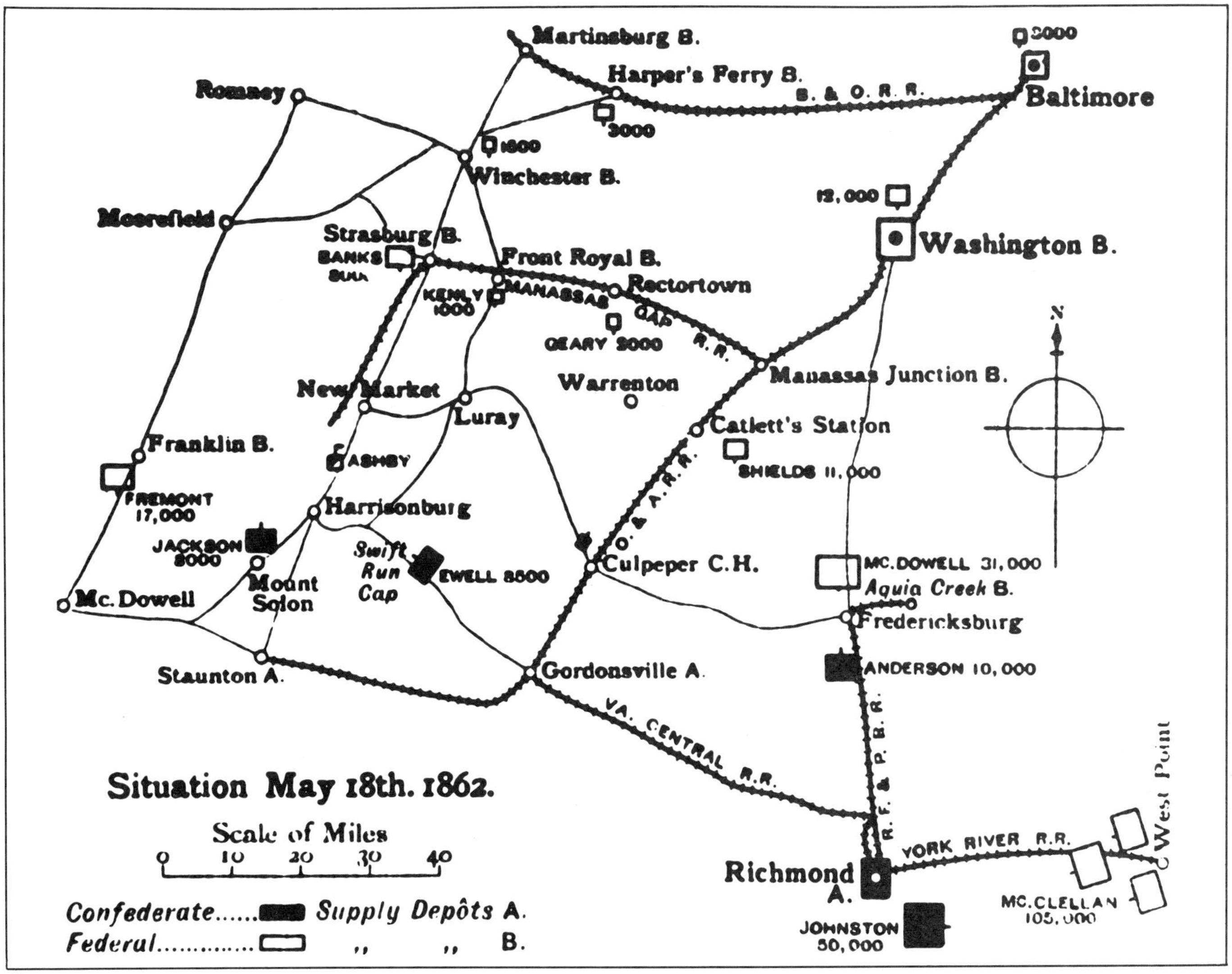

Note that Shields' 11,000 troops (including the 7th Indiana) are at Catlett's Station. They had left New Market on May 13 and had passed through Strasburg and Front Royal on their way to Fredericksburg.

crossing the creek we trudged on across fields worn out and thrown to the conifers years ago, judging from the appearance.

The land is very poor, if ever good it had been worn out in growing Tobacco.

About Eight miles from Warrenton came to the camp of Gen'l Duryea's brigade of Zouaves camped on high ground, their camp was in excellent order and had been well policed.

Some distance from Gen. Duryea's camp we came to a small stream and the Alexandria and Orange Railroad at Catletts Station; here we met Captain Lambertson who had just returned from a Leave of absence home; he brought letters and many small useful articles for Members of Co. F. Soon pitched our bivouacs and dispatched our Supper and Coffee.

Catletts Station Va. Tuesday, May, 20, 1862. Late last p.m. James M. Bone, John H. Vannuys, Ben. G. Trout, Jack Tucker and James M. Hay, Comrades of Co. F. came into camp from home, they were given a hearty welcome. They too brought us letters, paper etc. etc.

Had orders early to Wash by noon and prepare for Inspection of Arms at 3. p.m. Many went bathing. Drew two days rations. I wrote a letter home. No news of importance in the papers.

Catlett Station Va. Wednesday, May, 21, 62. Rained hard last night and washed Capt. Lambertson out of his bivouac and he had to pitch it on higher ground.

Were called early again to make ready to march at day break. The First Brigade lead out and the Second followed; but it was ten a.m. when we struck the road. The wagon trains being just ahead of us we moved slow over a very poor Country, mostly through fields and across washed out gullies. Late in the afternoon, then fast till 11. o'clock p.m.

On road to Falmouth, Va. Thursday, May, 22, 62. Last night it was 11. p.m. when the last wagons went into Park. Soon found wood for fire, then made coffee with water from a muddy pool, and laid down to sleep with out blankets and slept very well considering the situation. Up at day break a hastily prepared breakfast was soon over and we were ready for the road. We made fifteen miles yesterday, near half of it after dark.

Started early this morning; passed the Second Brigade. Roads some better than yesterday and the country better than for the last few days. Much of the land was formerly cultivated but has for years been turned out as waste and useless.

Very little Wheat, Oats or Rye and that little cant yield much per acre. No corn planted yet and but here and there a few acres broken. Rebels used this road when retreating from Manassas.

About three in the afternoon came in sight of Falmouth, a small town on the left bank of the Rappahannock river about one mile above Fredericksburg on the right bank of the river.

Falmouth is on the low bottom lands, has a number of business Stores and more Groceries or "grog shops," the latter doing a thriving business. Came by a circuitous road of near two miles to higher ground almost opposite Fredericksburg, where we pitched our bivouacs. All of Gen. Shields division is in camp in this near vicinity. Gen. Irwins Corps is in camp near here and back to Acquia Creek on the Potomac river, and Gen. McDowells headquarters is in a large Mansion half a mile away, the owner of the property is said to be an officer in the rebel army.

Opposite Fredericksburg, Va. Friday, May 23, 1862. This is a beautiful morning, with fine scenery in every direction. The R.R. Train came in early from Aquia Creek, and brought President A. Lincoln and E. M. Stanton, Secretary of War.

Gen'l McDowell and staff met them at the Station and took them to his Headquarters.

All of Gen. McDowells troops were reviewed by the President and Secretary, and the First and Second Brigades of Gen'l Shields division.

Our Brigade, the Third was not reviewed. We wonder why not. All the troops cheered Mr Lincoln, very heartily. The fact that Mr Lincoln is a very awkward horseman did lessen the Soldiers admiration for him as a man and as president.

The President and Secy. left on the train at dusk for Washington.

Our camp is full of rumors. Many of us went bathing in the Rappahannock river, then visited the R.R. Bridge, the Pontoon Bridge and the one in course of construction. Excellent facilities for crossing.

Opposite Fredericksburg, Va. Saturday May, 24, 62. Commenced raining early last night and rained all night, having only our bivouacs our bedding and clothing is all wet. Was about clear at Sunup but soon began to rain again. Some Companies of the 7th drew other guns today. There are indications that some changes are being made in the formation of this division. Wrote a letter to my brother. Is quite cool to day.

Opposite Fredericksburg, Va. May, 25, '62. Sunday. Last afternoon new guns came for our Regt. We were called at Midnight to go and exchange our old guns for new ones. Were given the Remodeled Springfield Smooth bore Muskets.

Report says that Gen. Banks had been driven back near to Winchester. The opinion of many is that we will go at once back to the Strasburg Valley.

Went early in the forenoon and got our new Cartridge boxes and accouterments and forty rounds of fixed ammunition — one ball and three buck shot. We also drew

This brick home, Chatham, was 91 years old when McDowell headquartered here in May 1862.

"Opposite Fredericksburg."

new Poncho Tents, and learned that a Fourth Brigade has been formed in this division composed of the First W. Va. Seventh Ind. Eighty Fourth Penn. One hundred and tenth Penn. and Sixty Second Ohio, under command of Col. S. S. Carroll now a Brigadier.

There were several very loud explosions in Fredericksburg about 10. A.M. At the same time Gen. McDowells troops on the other side of the river were seen crossing to this side. Hurried preparation are apparent every where, and all Gen. McDowells Corps are in motion.

There is much confusion in many camps and many rumors as to what it all means.

By noon the First and Second Brigades of this division formed and stacked arms; they moved out early in the afternoon. The Third Brigade soon followed them. Shortly after two p.m. the Fourth Brigade formed line and started about 3. p.m. We marched very slow and until two p.m. at the place where we halted for dinner on the 22nd. We heard this afternoon that Gen. Hallock had been defeated.

Monday, May, 26, 62. This morning finds us eight miles N. W. of Falmouth. We started early. Report says that Gen. Banks has fallen back to Winchester and that Stonewall Jackson with a large force is in close pursuit. No reliable news to day but many rumors.

Darkness again settled about us before we reached our camping place. On coming a mile or two of Catlett Station we saw large lights ahead which proved to be the Third Brigade in camp. Reached the station at ten p.m. and found great confusion. Commissary Stores being shipped by car. Drew two days rations and at 12. M. laid down to sleep have made 18 or 20 miles.

Catlett Station Va. Tuesday, May, 27, 1862. Up early again. Started at Seven A.M. but instead of going to Manassas Junction as we expected we went West about one mile to a large opening where Gen. Duryea's brigade were encamped on the 19th inst. here we were told to put up our Poncho's. All the 4 brigades are here, but we know nothing of the whereabouts of the rest of Shields division. No news this afternoon.

Wednesday, May, 28, 62. Our camp is one mile west of Catlett Station. I went to the creek to do some washing. Orders to prepare for Inspection at ten A.M. It was raining at ten o'clock, rained almost an hour. At 11. A.M. the Col. came calling "fall in for Inspection," and just a little way behind him came the Major, giving the order to get ready to march immediately.

All were soon ready, dinner followed, and we started at two p.m. the 7th Ind. in lead of the brigade. Eight miles across the fields brought us to the Alexandria pike, and three miles more to the Manassas Railroad at Hay Market, where we found a good road, and three miles more found us on a little stream where we halted for the night at eight p.m. having made fourteen miles since two in the afternoon.

Coffee was soon made, and supper over we soon pitched our bivouacs, and being tired were soon abed.

Thursday, May, 29, 1862. Started early at the rear of the Brigade, a few miles brought us to Thoroughfare Gap in Carter Mountains through which the R.R. and wagon roads pass, where some cars and a Pork Packing Establishment had been burned and the Railroad tracks torn up by the Rebels.

Trudging on over the hills we reached Rectortown at three p.m. where we found all of the Division in Camp. Col. Gavin said "pitch your bivouacs." That was soon done. Supper was eaten by 4.30. About five p.m. orders came to prepare to march. "Take only your gum blankets."

Two days rations were dealt out and all our baggage was piled up and those not able to march were left with it. We had already made fifteen miles.

Rectortown Va. Friday May, 30, 62. We started at seven last night, did not go far till we stopped, moved up twice and stopped; in two hours we had made near one mile. Laid down and slept until one a.m. then moved on over rough roads slipping often.

After sunup we stopped for Coffee; then moved to the front of the brigade to a timber to sleep an hour if we chose, the Col. said.

Between eight and nine in the forenoon, passed over some fine Country, ridges and Valleys, rich and well cultivated. Near a Station on the R.R. saw the residence of Col. Ashby, of the rebel army. At noon we stopped for dinner in Manassas Gap of the Blue Ridge.

A good dinner over and an hours rest ended, a heavy rain we went to the road again, now slippery on the hill sides, for it rained all afternoon. About five p.m. we reached Front Royal.

The Depot, some cars and a shop had been burned by the retreating rebels. A man was said to have been burned in the Shop, a Negro who had died with Small Pox a few days before.

Report says there are several cases of Smallpox in town.

The advance of our division reached here at noon. Our Cavalry made a charge and routed the rebel Cavalry; took near two hundred prisoners, saved two Locomotives and the R.R. bridge. We lost seven or eight men, all Cavalrymen one a Captain.

Col. J. F. Cheek overtook us here. When arms were stacked we all went in search of boards for Shelter from the rain as we had only our gum blankets for shelter.

Front Royal Va. Saturday, May, 31, 62. Rained very hard last night, with much heavy thunder. We all got wet.

Up to noon all was quiet, except reports, many and confusing.

About one p.m. the Fourth Brigade was ordered into line, took the road toward Winchester, crossed both Shenandoah's on bridges built by Gen. Banks, both ends of the R.R. bridge burned by the rebels. Passed the hills on North branch from which our two batteries shelled the Pike for two or three miles as we advanced.

Saw the horses killed in yesterdays Skirmish.

Soon the crack of an occasional Musket was heard in front, then came shells whistling over our heads and struck back of us.

The advance regiments threw out a line of skirmishers, right and left, the Artillery took position and we loaded our Muskets. Several shells came near us but no one of the 7. was hurt.

The rebels were soon routed and we advanced two miles beyond Burner Springs, but saw nothing more of them. The skirmish was about four in the afternoon — casualties, one Lieut. killed and one private wounded in the left hand, both of 1st W. Va. about six p.m. we started back and arrived in camp at dusk.

About the time we reached camp it began and rained hard for an hour, several boys went to the Mill for shelter and sleep. After supper we went to bed and hoped for a good nights rest and sleep, but were soon called to draw a half days rations.

John Fremont, Union Commander of the (Allegheny) Mountain Department.

Catlett's Station — Billy marched through here going east on May 21 — and then marched through going west on May 27.

CHAPTER NINE BACKGROUND

Why All The Marching?

The Battle of Kernstown on March 23 was the first of five battles in the Shenandoah Valley Campaign of 1862. Although each battle was significant and different, it was the campaign which achieved military uniqueness. T. J. "Stonewall" Jackson generated so much chaos that Federal army decision makers were confounded for 11 weeks. Billy's record of marching up, down, out, and back in the valley is an indication of the Union reaction.

After Kernstown, Union Major General Nathaniel Banks did not pursue Jackson. He chose to wait for reinforcements. Banks, the ex-governor of Massachusetts, with two divisions, moved to Strasburg on March 25 and then (again) waited for supplies. On April 1, caution was also being exercised in Washington. General George McClellan started moving troops out of the Capital in preparation for a Spring offensive toward Richmond. President Lincoln, however, feared McClellan was not leaving enough troops to protect Washington and countermanded part of McClellan's orders. Lincoln and McClellan never did agree on what constituted "protection." And McClellan was blameworthy for double counting. The dispute was settled when 30,000 of General Irvin McDowell's men were withheld from McClellan's "On to Richmond" campaign.(1)

In the Valley, Banks continued to nudge Jackson, and by April 20, one division of Federal troops was as far south as Harrisonburg. The other division with ex-senator James Shields in command was near New Market. (This was Billy's unit.) Shields' superior, Corps Commander Banks, had wired Washington indicating Jackson had abandoned the Shenandoah Valley.(2) Actually, Jackson had just moved to the other side of the Massanutten Mountains, in the Luray Valley. Banks had to decide whether to push southward and risk having his supply line cut. Or, take the offensive and go after Jackson and probably fight him on the side of a mountain. Or, he could sit still. Banks chose to sit.

Jackson refitted and strengthened his force to approximately 6,000 men. On April 28 he asked General Lee for 5,000 additional troops. This Lee could not do but a suggestion was made that Jackson might combine forces with Generals Edward Johnson and Richard Ewell. Johnson was in the Allegheny Mountains and Ewell was east of the Blue Ridge. The proposed reorganization would provide Jackson with an army of 17,000. The top command would consist of three West Point trained professionals — Johnson, Ewell and Jackson. Jackson would render the overall direction.

Johnson, however, could not move to join with anyone — he had an immediate problem. There was a Federal

Richard Ewell

Edward Johnson

Two of Jackson's subordinates.

force of 6,000 in his front, soon to be reinforced with another 9,000. Plus, Union General Banks was still in his rear at Staunton.(3)

Jackson, who was thought to be slipping eastward to Richmond, secretly boarded trains and headed west to support Johnson. Leaving the trains at Staunton, Jackson's men continued westward on foot. They combined forces with Johnson and, together, started into the Alleghenies after Major General John Fremont. Fremont was another Union Army political general, having been the Republican candidate for the presidency in 1856.

On May 8, Jackson's total force of 9,000 clashed with 6,000 of Fremont's soldiers near the village of McDowell. Jackson's men had marched 92 miles in four days. (This effort contributed to the designation "foot cavalry.") Fremont's men had hustled too, making 34 miles in 23 hours. Jackson found the high ground first but the undaunted and out-numbered Yankees mounted several attacks. Jackson won the field although his forces suffered more casualties than their enemy. The Union troops fell back to Franklin, Virginia and Jackson headed for the Shenandoah Valley. Jed Hotchkiss, Jackson's topographical engineer, sealed Fremont in the Allegheny Mountains by obstructing the passes into the Valley.(4)

It was mid-May and the guessing games continued. While Jackson rested his troops south of Harrisonburg, Ewell waited on the other side of the Massanuttens with 8,500 men. The situation appeared calm. President Lincoln, in his new role of General in Chief, ordered General Shields to march out of the Valley with 10,000 men (including Billy Davis). Shields was to join General McDowell at Fredericksburg. Shields would be positioned in readiness for a movement to the Richmond area. Once there, Shields could assist in General McClellan's major campaign against the Confederate capital. Banks remained in the Shenandoah Valley.

Jackson with his new 17,000-man "Valley Army," coiled at the southern end of the Massanuttens. Banks was at the northern end in two camps — 7,000 men at Strasburg and 1,000 at Front Royal. On May 21, Jackson started north in two columns. At New Market, Jackson crossed his column of men eastward over the Massanuttens to combine with the other column (Ewell's). This movement was screened from Union General Banks' (larger and fortified) force at Strasburg. The Confederates overpowered and routed the 1,000 Union troops at Front Royal on May 23.(5) Banks then decided to evacuate his position at Strasburg and head northward.

A chase began as Banks scurried for Winchester where he hoped to establish a stronger defensive position. However, Banks fell back so fast that some of his troops did not stop until they crossed the Potomac.

Banks did get 6,400 men in line at Winchester by 2 a.m. on May 25. At 5 a.m. after a two-hour rest, Jackson moved on Winchester. By 9 a.m., Jackson had turned Banks' flanks and the Battle of Winchester was over. From Front Royal to the Potomac, Banks lost one-third of his army. Of the 3,500 casualties, 3,000 had been captured. Also lost were cannons, small arms, supplies and a toe-hold in the Valley. It cost Jackson 400 killed and wounded.(6)

Bewildered, the Washington officials proceeded to Fredericksburg to consult with the field commanders. (This is where the boys of the 7th Indiana saw Lincoln on horseback.) A plan was devised in which Jackson would be trapped as he fell back into the Valley. At the time, Jackson's main body was farther north near Harpers Ferry. Union General Fremont was to depart the Alleghenies and march eastward to Strasburg. Shields and another Union division at Fredericksburg would not be sent to Richmond after all. Rather, they about-faced and marched westward toward Strasburg. Banks was to regroup his troops along the Potomac River and apply pressure on Jackson from the north. Three pursuing Union armies of 50,000 would pinch (and bag) Jackson at Strasburg. Washington would be safe![7]

Jackson soon realized that the Union troops were on the move — and converging on him. He, too, started to move. On the evening of May 30, he reached Winchester. Many of his troops (and 2,300 prisoners) were strung out all the way to Halltown, near Harpers Ferry. The situation was precarious for Jackson. Shields was 12 miles east of Strasburg, Fremont 20 miles to the west. Jackson, after a 25-mile march, was still 18 miles north with the tail of his army 43 miles distant. As it turned out, it was not much of a contest. With only a skirmish, Jackson held off Shields and Fremont and moved his men, prisoners and wagons through Strasburg — unmolested. He had moved his army 48 miles in two days.[8]

General Shields' explanation of why he did not move more quickly on Strasburg was threefold: first, he waited for another Union division to close up on his rear; secondly, he had received information which persuaded him to divert his line of march to the north toward Winchester; and last, he did not have cavalry.[9] Strangely, the rumors which reached Billy Davis implied the Southerners had been stampeded — little did the boys in the ranks understand that their leaders had lost a grand opportunity.

Shields turned around and proceeded south along the east side of the Massanuttens through the Luray Valley. On the west side of the Massanuttens, Fremont trailed Jackson's army into the Shenandoah Valley. Jackson had escaped a trap but there would be no peace of mind — he still would have to contend with two Union armies on two fronts.

END NOTES

(1) T. Harry Williams, *Lincoln and his Generals* (New York, 1952); pp. 75-79.

(2) Tanner, *Stonewall in the Valley;* p. 160. Shields had been a senator in three states. He is best remembered as the man who challenged Abraham Lincoln to a duel.

(3) Allan, *Jackson in the Valley;* pp. 66-69.

(4) Jedediah Hotchkiss (Archie P. McDonald, Editor); *Make Me a Map Of the Valley* (Dallas, 1981); pp. 39-44. Fremont was not at the Battle of McDowell. The Union troops were led by two of Fremont's subordinates, Brigadier Generals Robert Milroy from Indiana and Robert Schenck of Ohio. Neither Milroy nor Schenck was considered to be "military" by profession. Milroy, however, when age 24, had enrolled at a Norwich, Vermont military academy — and graduated in 1843.

(5) Tanner, pp. 207-211. It was here that the 1st Maryland of the Confederate army fought the 1st Maryland of the Federal army.

(6) Allan, pp. 115-118.

(7) Tanner, p. 264, 275.

(8) Allan, p. 132.

(9) *Ibid.;* p. 134-135. General Irvin McDowell's report to the Committee on the Conduct of the War. Also, *ORs*, series I, v, XII, part 1, p. 683.

Jedidiah Hotchkiss, Jackson's mapmaker.

PICTURE CREDITS

—123—Courtesy, The Louis A. Warren Lincoln Library and Museum.

—124—Both, courtesy, USAMHI.

—125—Miller's *Photographic History.*

—126—Courtesy, The Louis A. Warren Lincoln Library and Museum.

—127—Both, Miller's *Photographic History.*

—130—Courtesy, USAMHI.

—131—Both, *Harper's Pictorial History of the Civil War.*

—132—Courtesy, Library of Congress.

—132—Courtesy, USAMHI.

—133—Map. *Stonewall Jackson and the American Civil War* by Lieutenant-Colonel G. F. R. Henderson.

—134—Miller's *Photographic History.*

—135—Same.

—136—Courtesy, The Louis A. Warren Lincoln Library and Museum.

—137—Miller's *Photographic History.*

—138—Both, *Generals of the Confederate States Army 1861-1865.*

—139—Miller's *Photographic History.*

CHAPTER 10 HE COMMENDED OUR COURAGE AND PERSEVERANCE

Front Royal, Va. Sunday, June, 1, 1862. Gen. Rickets brigade of Gen'l Ords division of Gen'l McDowells Corps came in, from his troops we learn that Gen. McDowell and most of his Corps were now in this vicinity.

We are all wet from last nights rain. At ten a.m. heavy cannonading was heard in direction of Cedar Mountain and Strasburg.

At noon the boys left at Rectortown with our knapsacks and other baggage came in and reported the wagons a few miles back. The Railroad will be rebuilt to this place to day.

Had just finished eating our dinners when Orders came to fall in line. At one p.m. we, at the head of the line moved to the top of the hill near the South Branch, where we found one brigade of McDowells Corps in position, rested a while then about faced and marched into town, turned to the right and started out on the road toward Luray. The road was close to the river for several miles, then led into the hills, we walked at a rapid pace, soon a thunder and rain storm came up, we trudged on through the mud and camped at dark having made eleven miles from Front Royal. After the rain it was very slavish walking and many of the boys gave out.

Eleven Miles South of Front Royal Va. Warren Co. Monday, June 2, 1862. Rained hard again last night. At 4. a.m. we were called to prepare to march, as our wagons came up last night we now rolled our blankets for carrying across our shoulders and at 6.30 at the head of the brigade again. The clouds soon cleared a way and it became very warm. We walked rapidly notwithstanding the slick roads. Many men of the regiment were compelled to drop out and rest.

From ten A.M. till near noon heavy cannonading was again heard in direction of Strasburg. When within about four miles of Luray came to a clear stream and stopped for dinner. While in camp the 13. Ind. of Second brigade came up and camped near us. At 2.30 we started again. Passed through Luray, found it a neat thriving town — County seat of Page Co. Good stores and residences and other indications of more than usual wealth. The ladies seen were aristocratic in bearing as though they were of the "F. F. V." class.

Are six pieces of Artillery now with us, followed the Pike out of town, but as that turned to the right and crossed the river in direction New Market in the other Valley and as the bridge had been burned we turned left up the valley over clay roads and gone but two miles when a heavy rain broke upon us. We sought shelter in the timber, but most of us got quite wet, then moved near a mile to a Dunker Church and camped in the Grove got straw for beds and drew one days rations. Had made seventeen miles to day.

Tuesday, June, 3, 1862. South of Luray Thirteen Miles at a Dunker Church. Rained very hard last night. I rolled out of the bivouac and got wet.

About 8. a.m. to fall in to march to the river four miles, went slow and stopped frequently, reached the river at noon and found the bridge burned and river much swollen. Pitched our little tents in a near by timber and made our selves as comfortable as possible. Some rebels were seen on opposite side of the river.

Gen. Fremont is said to be approaching the other valley from some point in West Va.

About 8. p.m. orders came to prepare to march. Take only Gum blankets said Col. Gavin. It was raining at the time. Col. said he would get us excused if possible, but soon returned and said Col. Carroll said he could not do so as he wanted the 7. Ind. to go because of the work to be done. Colonel said that he would dismount and walk at the head of the regt. and that his horse would be at the rear for the most needy to ride.

Company F had thirty six men present in line. Col. said we must make seventeen miles before day break, if possible. It was 9 p.m. when we started. The Col. at the front afoot.

Wednesday, June 4, 62, South of Luray, Va. near line of Page and Rockingham Co. Before we started last night we were told that we must talk only in a whisper and keep

Colonel Samuel Sprigg Carroll, Billy's brigade commander.

very quiet as the enemy were patrolling the opposite bank of the river.

Day light found us but seven or eight miles from our last camp. It had been a fearful night. Constant rain and very dark. The road either muddy and slippery or stony and rough, sometimes in the low bottom, near or on the brink of the swollen river, then over small stony hills and across many small rapid streams.

We were not permitted to strike a match for Cigar or pipe or to see the face of a watch. As Fire flies were numerous, when we wanted to learn the time of night some one would catch a Lightning bug and hold at the face of a watch and wait until it would turn on the light, and thus we knew the time of night with out artificial light or noise.

At day break stopped for breakfast. It was raining hard, in order to make our coffee we held gum blankets over our fires and then we had to do much fanning. The road had been so rough or slippery that we often fell consequently most of us were very muddy. After day light we got along better, soon came to an Iron Furnace and Foundry, where we were told that it was yet six miles to the bridge we were trying to reach. Had not gone far when we saw by the burned timbers floating on the swollen stream that bridge had been destroyed.

One mile further brought us to a Mountain stream that we could not cross. Col. said we could go into a barn and some old houses out of the rain. Near by was a mill from which we got some wheat flour and Corn meal from which we made Pancakes (Flapjacks) and hasty pudding.

We have enjoyed something of a feast while we waited. About three in the afternoon the teams and stragglers began to come up. Pitched our bivouacs in an orchard. Have had no news from any part of the country since we left Front Royal. Has rained all day.

Thursday, June 5, 62. In camp on South bank of South Branch Shenandoah river near Swift Run Gap in Blue Ridge. Clouds cleared away last night. I slept well notwithstanding that my clothes were wet when I laid down. This morning a detail was made from the regiment to build a bridge across the creek, this was done by noon and we crossed. A four miles march brought us to a rise of ground near the still smoking bridge where we camped.

Foraging parties were sent out who brought in an abundance of corn for the horses and bacon and fresh beef for us, we have no salt.

Several rebels were seen across the river today.

Citizens who visit our camp say they are "Union," and that there are seventy five or more in the mountains of this vicinity who talk of joining the federal army. Say they had a fight with a band of guerrillas a short time ago. Several of our boys not in yet. I am on camp guard.

Friday, June, 6, 62. Camp between Big Top Gap and South Branch. Did not rain last night.

There is much excitement in camp caused by heavy cannonading in the other valley in direction of Harrisonburg. Perhaps Banks and Fremont forces are engaging "Stonewall" Jackson.

Major B. C. Shaw and Captain Samuel Banta have resigned and started home to day.

Saturday, June, 7, 62. Same camp as yesterday, fifteen or sixteen miles north of Port Republic. Clear and warm. At noon came orders to prepare to march at five p.m. Left our knapsacks taking only our blankets. Lieut Jeffery came to us and was left in command of the post.

When we started we followed the road up the river, two or three miles brought us to a guide board marked "To Port Republic, 14 miles."

We walked on about five miles through swamps. When we came to an opening and stopped for the night in a barn where we found plenty of wheat and straw.

Sabbath, June, 8, 1862. Eight or Nine Miles North of Port Republic, Va. We were called at 2. a.m. had our Coffee and started at 4. A.M. About five miles brought us up with our Cavalry, here we loaded our Muskets. It was just Six A.M. Were soon on the march again. Waded several small streams and marshes, all the while through the timber.

Going at a quick step we soon came in sight of Port Republic. Looking across the river we could see Jackson's wagon train. A few minutes our artillery opened fire; at once their infantry Artillery and Cavalry, were seen maneuvering.

Very soon their Artillery opened on ours and as we were on open fields in plain view of the rebels and under a hot fire, we moved at a double quick.

The Cavalry and two of our guns went to the town and bridge; two of our guns went with us to a rise of ground one fourth to half mile from the village near a

A typical ford on the South Fork of the Shenandoah — when the water is at its normal level.

Port Republic from the ridges overlooking the village. At the time of this photograph an iron bridge had been constructed over the North River not far from the site of the old wooden (Civil War era) bridge.

farm house and other buildings and in plain View from the ridges on the opposite side of the river.

The Confederates continued to shell us from three batteries and opened on our little force at the bridge in the village; before the bridge could be fired a rebel force from up the river rushed down and dispersed our squad of cavalry and captured our two guns. As we were in plain view and easy range of three batteries upon the ridges on the opposite side of the river that were pouring a galling fire of shot and shell into our ranks, and as we were alone and unable to do any thing; the order was given to fall back, which we did in double quick and in very good order.

When passing from the field onto the road several shells struck some piles of rails and the splinters and pieces hit a number of the regiment.

Just after reaching the road we saw to our left one of the guns that had been with us on the hill, mired in mud and water, the men and horses were gone; farther up the road we found the other piece abandoned and the pole broken. As we were still under fire of the enemy's eighteen guns, no effort was made to rescue either of the pieces.

About one and half miles back from our advanced position near the bridge we found shelter behind a hill where we halted to rest.

We had been resting but a short time when Col. Daum Chief of Artillery on Gen'l Shields staff came to us and at once went forward to look after the two guns left on the way, he soon returned and asked for fifteen volunteers to go back after the two pieces.

Comrade John C. Henderson and myself of Co. F, comrade T. J. Clark, Co. I, comrades Jas. M. Lambertson, N. Williams, William Merrill, William Ripkin, and A. J. Connelly, of Co. K, stepped to the front and started back with Col. Daum.

As soon as we were in view the Confederates opened fire upon us from three batteries on other side of the river. We went on a rapid double quick to the gun in the swamp where we found a Lieut. and one or two others; as the horses mired down in the water, a prolong was fastened to the piece to which the horses were attached on dry ground, while we eight men from the left wing of the Seventh Ind. waded in and lifted, pulled and pushed thus assisting the horses and after several efforts were able to extricate the caisson and piece, and to get them to the road. Twenty or thirty minutes were required for this although it seemed longer, for we were under fire of the eighteen guns with solid shot and shell whistling or bursting all about us and blinding us with the water. Nor did they cease until we were out of range, and yet no one was injured in any way.

So far the Seventh Indiana had been alone in support of our artillery and Cavalry, we now moved back near three miles where we met the rest of the Fourth Brigade, then about faced and moved forward to a good position and waited until the Third Brigade came up, then went back through the woods near to the bridge and halted.

While laying here comrade James M. Bone came to us, said that he had been struck by a piece of rail, that when he had sufficiently recovered he crept to the timber hoping to avoid capture.

Samuel V. List wrote that the calm would last only until daylight — he was correct.

About sundown we returned to our position on the road, made coffee, gathered leaves and prepared to rest for the night. It had been a strenuous day for the Seventh. Comrades Joseph Graham, Leo Morgan, E. Forsyth, C. Reynolds and James M. Bone of Co. F had been slightly wounded, and many of the regiment had been wounded, some severely and many were missing.

The following sentence is found in the Diary of a private of the Seventh regiment. — Samuel V. List, Company "F," entry made on evening of 8th.

"We felt confident that the calm would last only until day-light, and that the day would cut down like withering grass many who were now in health and vigor. We thought of the kind familiar faces far away, and the dear hearts which were ignorant of our awful danger, but which never forget to pray for us; unrestrained tears fell over many a brown cheek, but we looked to high heaven for protection and fell a sleep on our arms."

Port Republic, Va. June 9, 1862. Were called early, Coffee was made and at seven we were called into line; our batteries on the left took position. Soon the enemy opened fire and we responded.

Three pieces were sent to the right into a wheatfield and the Seventh Ind. was sent as support to the wheatfield fence and near the river bank, soon the 29 Ohio came to our help. Cannonading was going on all the while, and musketry was heard on our left. Just then a body of the enemy's cavalry advanced across the wheat in our immediate front, and we fell back and halted in a corn field, and formed a hollow square prepared to receive the cavalry, but at the fence they passed to the rear and a heavy infantry line took its place along the fence, the Seventh deployed, then commenced the Musketry on the right, and for perhaps an hour both parties stood under a galling fire of Musketry and canister although they out numbered us greatly.

Now our center and right advanced and drove the enemy's center and left back to the farther side of the wheat field, and captured one of the guns and many prisoners. In the wheat field we could see the effect of the grape and canister from our guns and from the ball and three buckshot from our smooth bore muskets; the ground was strewn with their dead and wounded and with guns, cartridge boxes, knapsacks, clothing haversacks and canteens. From the wounded we learned that the regiments in our front had been the Fifth Va. and the "Louisiana Tigers". (Seventh Louisiana)

The Seventh Ind. until the advance had been in an open corn field, the musketry and canister had greatly thinned our ranks. One Captain Solomon Waterman, of Co. C. had been killed and many had been wounded, some severely, others slightly, and Col. Gavin's horse was shot five times and he dismounted.

When the enemy's left gave way and we advanced the rebel right having been heavily reenforced attacked our left and forced it back. Then commenced our retreat. Before advancing we had shot away most of our ammunition and had sent back for a supply, we soon met this and filled our cartridge boxes.

Shortly after we started there was some confusion among the wounded and teamsters, but it was quieted. We had not gone far when the enemy began to shell us, this they did with sad effect, then came their Cavalry in a charge on the rear, a mild panic ensued for a few moments but coming to a small opening our lines were reformed.

The cavalry as a body came no further, and we moved off the field in good order. Soon their artillery opened out

A hollow square as executed on a drill field.

Joseph Thoburn commanded the 1st (West) Virginia Infantry.

again but shot too high, but endangered our heads from falling branches.

The First Va. and the Seventh Ind. covered the retreat, squads of rebel cavalry made frequent charges, when we turned and fired they would wheel and run.

The road was very bad making our retreat slow on account of artillery, ambulances and wagons. Several pieces were left on the field the horses having been killed, many of our comrades are missing, some we know were captured.

Company F marched from the field with ten beside Captain Lambertson; they were Corp. Frank J. Pusey, carrying the colors, the next were B. & J. Dragoo, next B. & L. Richardson, next John C. Henderson and myself, Corporal Saml V. List and Wm Gordon and corporal James H. McIlvain. Others of the boys (mostly wounded) joined us before we met the other two brigades of Genl Shields division and when we halted for the night twelve miles from the battle field there were twenty three of Co. F in line, several of them wounded. After resting for some time we moved back to Naked creek and camped for the night. Our camp was small.

Of Co. F, Henry F. Swarr was killed, shot in the head, 2nd Lieut. James A. Holmes, bullet through the wrist. Sergeant Abner Hardin, in shoulder and captured, Corp. L. P. Garr, in chest, Richard V. Ditmars, ankle broken, John H. Fisher in knee, S. Garrett, in the side, Joseph Graham, in shoulder, and John C. Henderson, Leo Morgan, C. Reynolds, E. Forsyth, Jacob Stevens and Isaac Watkins, slightly. James M. Bone, H. Fishback, Austin D. Springer, Orderly David Holmes, T. T. Knowlton, Sergeant D. B. Branch, J. H. Vannuys, B. G. Trout and Robert Carter, missing. Other Co's of the regt. doubtless suffered as heavily as we did. The First Va. and 29 Ohio suffered severely, and the 84 and 110 Penn. perhaps suffered as much or more.

Twelve Miles from Port Republic Va. Tuesday, June 10, 1862.

An incident showing the two sides of human nature.

In our march through swamps and over foot hills late on the afternoon of the 7, we passed a small but neat log house. At the gate in front were two young ladies with whom comrades Johnson and Hay stopped for a brief chat. The ladies were bitter rebels and knew us to be federal. In the conversation they said they hoped their army would whip our army and that we would every one be killed.

Yesterday Afternoon, when on our retreat and nearing the same house, Hay (F. M.) and Johnson (Jno. M.) were wondering how they could pass with out being seen by their new friends of two days before; when to their great surprise they saw them at the gate each with a bucket of water from the Spring, which they were passing out to the tired soldiers as they passed. Johnson and Hay stopped for another talk, and expressed their agreeable surprise at the changed attitude and conduct of the ladies, and asked the cause for it. Whereupon the elder of the two said, "We have a brother in Jackson's army; I said to sister, if brother was in the battle and was wounded as some of these men

Thomas Munford was Jackson's new cavalry commander — his men pursued the retreating Union troops.

are, or is as tired as all these men are, wouldn't it be nice if some Union folks would give him water to drink, and we agreed to stand at the gate with buckets of water and try to be as kind to the Yankees as we hoped some body would be to our brother, and that is why we are here." Johnson and Hay accepted a refreshing drink from their gourds, and thanked them; as did many weary comrades that warm afternoon.

Up early, Coffee hastily made and as hurriedly disposed of. Just at day break it commenced and rained until two in the afternoon. Soon after breakfast was over we were called into line and at once moved off toward Luray. Roads were very muddy and badly cut up by wagons, ambulances and artillery, so that many teams stalled, thus making our progress slow. Stopped at noon for Coffee, then moved on to Columbia bridge and went into camp for the night, all very much fatigued.

Wednesday, June 11, 62. Our bivouacs came late last evening and were pitched, consequently we were slow in getting up this morning. Started by Eight in the forenoon and walked quite leisurely, and by noon came in sight of Luray. At the edge of town we met Lieut. Jeffery and many of the sick and wounded of the regiment from whom we received a hearty greeting. Passed through town and near two miles out on the Sperryville pike.

Near Luray, Va. Thursday, June 12, 62. Yesterday afternoon our knapsacks came, and, as several of our comrades are yet missing, we took care of their belongings.

I wrote a letter last evening to acquaint the home folks of my good fortune in the battle, and of my welfare since.

Charles Candy commanded the 66th Ohio at the coaling.

Charles Winder, commander of the Stonewall Brigade.

Many such letters have been, and are being written. Lieut. J. A. Holmes, who was wounded in the right arm during the battle, started home this afternoon on Leave of Absence.

This afternoon at the request of Col. Philip Daum Chief of Artillery, the eight of our regiment who assisted to rescue the two guns on the 8th went to report our names, Co. and regiment. After a very pleasant meeting with Col. Daum and part of his Staff, at his headquarters, during which he commended our courage and perseverance; wishing us much good fortune he bade us good bye.

I then went to the different Federal Hospitals and enquired for sick or wounded comrades and was told they had all gone to Front Royal. After helping sweep a Hospital, I returned to camp. A small mail came yesterday afternoon, but nothing for me. All the teams have gone to Front Royal.

It is thought we will move as soon as they return. No news of importance today.

Billy Is A Civil War Hero

At Port Republic, Virginia on June 8, 1862, Thomas Jonathon Jackson experienced one of the more dramatic moments of his military career. The same was true for Billy Davis.

After Jackson slipped the trap at Strasburg on June 1, he burned three bridges on the South Fork to keep the divided Union troops from consolidating. He spared one bridge — at Port Republic. If he were to join Lee's Army at Richmond, he needed the bridge at Port Republic.(1) From the Union perspective, if Jackson was going to march on Washington, as President Lincoln and Secretary of War Stanton feared, he must come out of the Valley at Port Republic. Both sides understood the importance of Port Republic, even if for differing reasons. Union General Shields moved his command toward Port Republic on the east side of the Massanuttens while Fremont followed Jackson on the macadamized Valley Pike. The armies of Fremont and Shields had a unique opportunity if only they could box up Jackson before he crossed at Port Republic. They failed. Jackson and his staff made their headquarters in Port Republic on June 7.

Confederate General Ewell was left behind at Cross Keys to watch for Fremont. Jackson would attend to Shields at Port Republic, if necessary. Cross Keys was some four miles north of Port Republic on the other side of the river. Displaying much confidence, Jackson separated his troops from their supply train, and his own headquarters. So on June 7 Jackson's headquarters and supply trains were over the bridge, into Port Republic. His 16,000 troops, however, had still not crossed.(2) And as Billy recorded it, two brigades of Yankees were camped only eight miles away.

On the Sabbath morning of the 8th, Jackson was at Dr. Kemper's house on the western outskirts of town. Although Sunday was a special day for Stonewall Jackson, he slept until eight o'clock. A cavalry patrol reported the advance of some Union cavalry on the east bank of the South Fork but failed to report just how fast they were advancing. Jackson sent word to Ewell not to provoke Union General Fremont. He intended to make the day holy.(3)

Then, suddenly, about 150 Union cavalrymen of the 1st (West) Virginia unit crossed a ford and rode west toward Dr. Kemper's house. Jackson was on the porch and heard the first Union artillery shell explode. He saw his own cavalry guard scattering through the streets. Quickly, two pieces of Confederate artillery were brought into the yard. Jackson and his staff raced toward the bridge and the Confederate camps on the east bank. The two pieces of rebel artillery at the Kemper house opened on the Union

Dr. Kemper's house — Stonewall Jackson's headquarters.

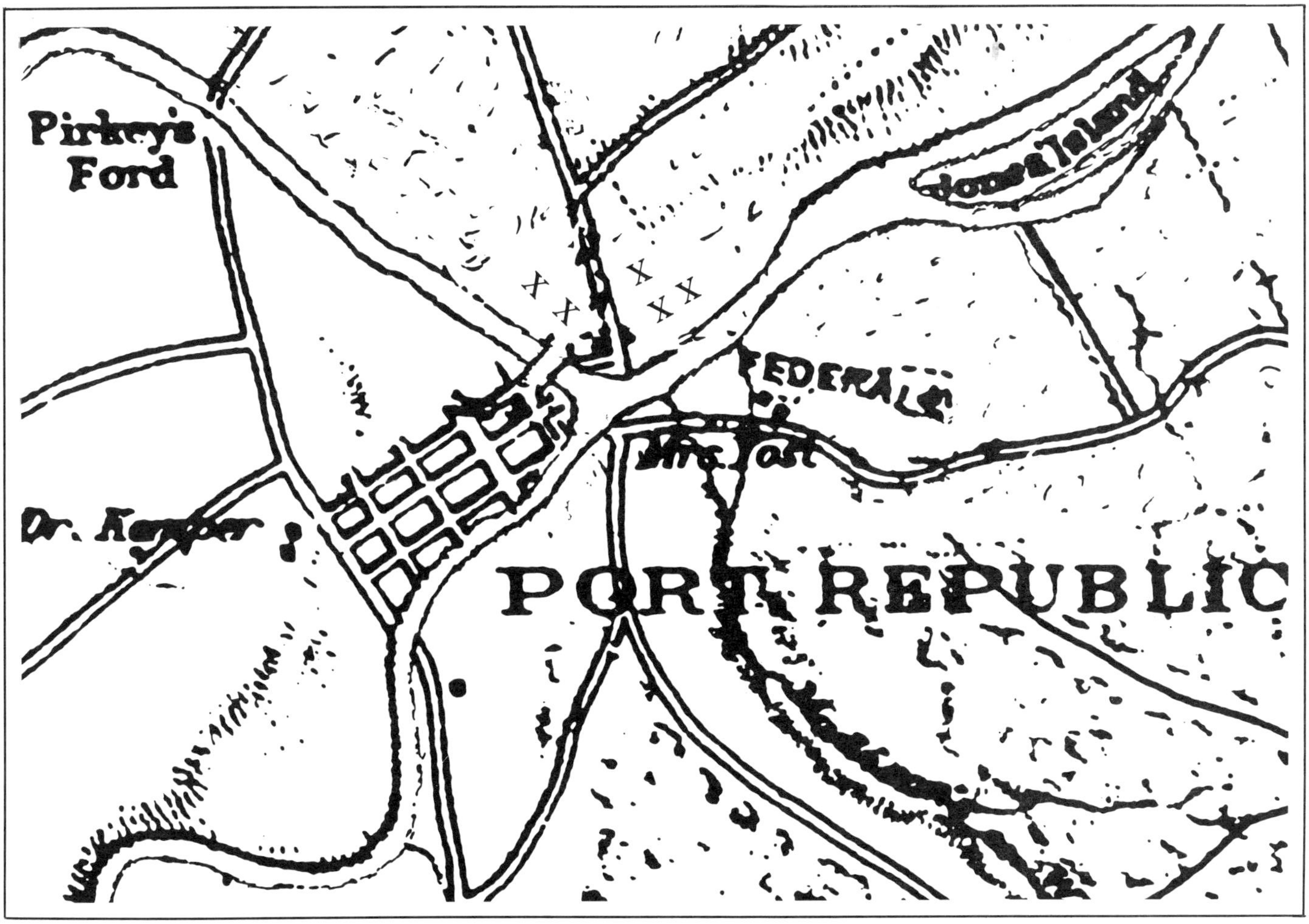

An enlarged and touched up map of the Port Republic area — Xs mark the Confederate camps and artillery positions.

cavalry as Jackson made his way safely across the bridge. Two of his staff were captured but Jackson escaped. A small skirmish took place around Jackson's headquarters but the Federal cavalry was repelled and the Confederate wagon trains were safe.[4]

Jackson, after his escape, stood on the ridges overlooking Port Republic where he took charge of the Southern cannons. Two Union cannons were now on the west end of the covered bridge. The 37th Virginia Infantry was sent down to the east end to drive them off. The Union cannons responded — point blank. Two sides of the bridge collapsed. When the smoke cleared, the bridge flooring was still intact and the Virginians pushed across and captured the Union cannons. Temporarily all was safe for the Confederates.[5] Then Jackson heard cannonading from the direction of Cross Keys. This presented a major problem. However, General Ewell at Cross Keys would have to contend with Fremont on his own. Jackson had a more immediate problem at Port Republic.[6]

The situation had been desperate for Billy Davis too. While all the action seemed to be going on in town, he was on the south side of the South Fork about ½ mile distant. Billy was helping provide support for two guns on a knoll near Mrs. Yost's house. The 18 Confederate guns on the ridges across the river "overlooked" the Union's two-gun emplacement on the knoll. The position could not be held and the two pieces were abandoned.

Billy described how the 7th fell back — out of range of those 18 guns on the ridges. Then Colonel Phillip Daum, Chief of the Union Artillery, asked for volunteers to go back and retrieve the two cannons. After the battle, Daum reported the situation as he remembered it: "I went to the next infantry regiment, which I found about one-half mile to the rear, and succeeded in procuring the assistance of eight volunteers of the 7th Indiana Regiment. With these brave fellows. . .I was lucky enough to bring the piece to the road,. . .under concentrated fire of eighteen of the enemy's guns. Pursuing the road in retreat with the. . . secured gun, I found. . .another piece of the same battery also abandoned, the pole being broken. . .I mended the pole and had the piece brought to the rear by infantry." Daum goes on to list the "names of a few brave officers and men who deserve to be rewarded for their personal valor." Among the named was William Davis, Company F, 7th Indiana.[7] It is reasonable to believe Billy never forgot June 8, 1862 — and he probably quietly reveled in the recognition received in the *Official Records*.[8]

Billy wrote that June 8 had been a strenuous day for the 7th Indiana. Indeed, the Brigade Commander reported the 7th lost eight killed and 27 wounded.[9] Later, historians would record the drama and tragedy of June 8 as only a footnote to the renowned Battle of Port Republic.

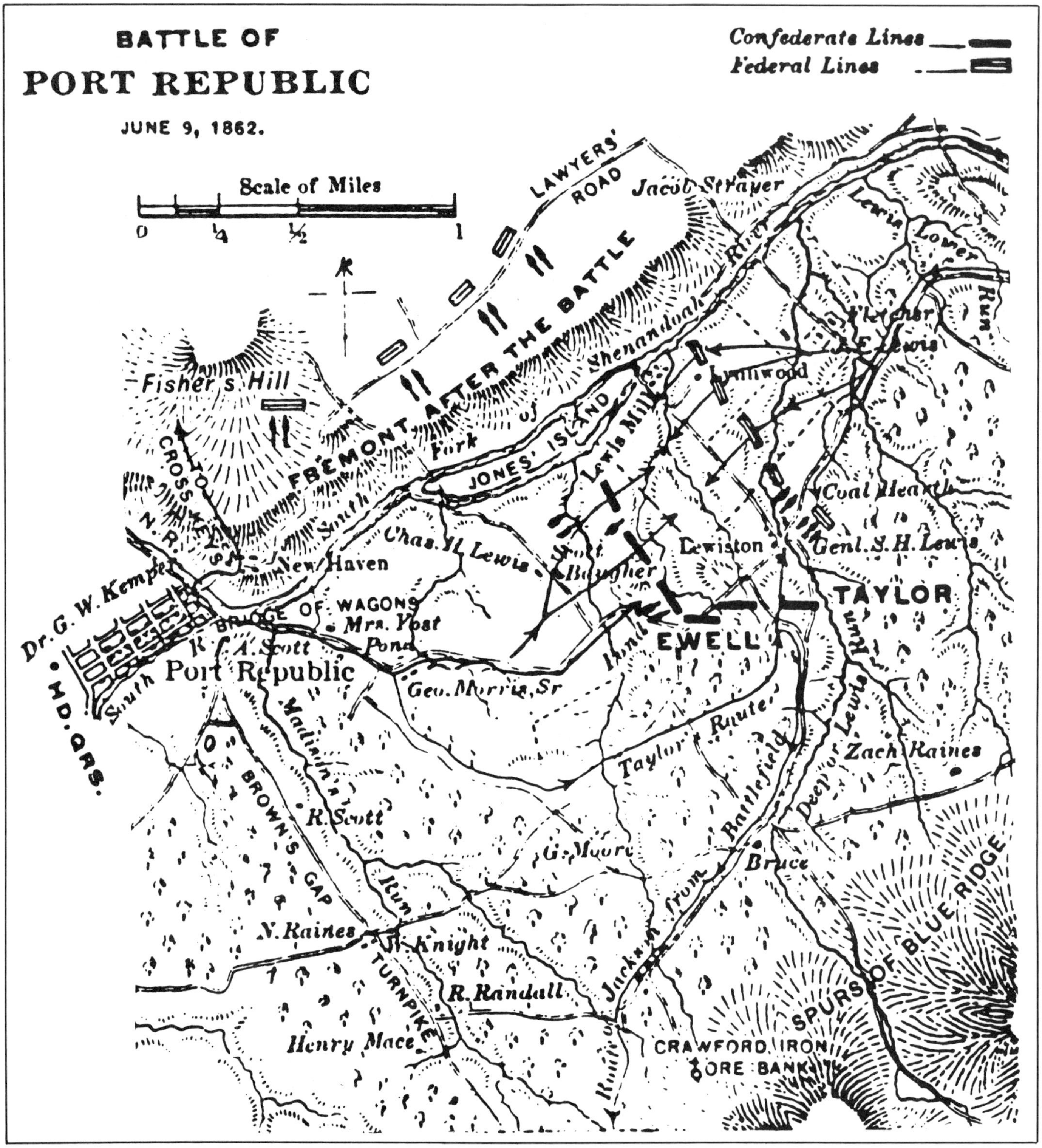

Jed Hotchkiss' classic map of the Battle of Port Republic. Note the Union line stretched from Lynnwood on the north to the coal hearth (or the coaling) on the south.

The Battle of Port Republic

Just to the east of Port Republic and the spot where Billy performed his heroics was the ground destined to become the Port Republic battle site. The major landmarks were a large home known as Lynnwood, near the South Fork of the Shenandoah, and a large hill, actually a spur of the Blue Ridge, where charcoal was produced. The hill was referred to as "the coaling" or the coal hearth. To outline the battlefield, a triangle could be formed with Port Republic, the coaling, and Lynnwood on the three points. Inside the triangle was a large field, knee high in wheat. Another farm field east of the wheatfield, surrounding the Lynnwood property, was planted in corn. What Billy saw and recorded in his diary occurred just west of Lynnwood.

Samuel List was right when he wrote in his diary on the night of June 8 that the calm would last only until daylight.[10] Jackson had put together an audacious plan.

Lynnwood at the turn of the century.

The coaling site — Union artillery was placed half way up the left side — infantry provided support from behind the guns.

From the coaling looking about 1,000 yards distant to the South Fork — in June 1862, an open field knee-high in wheat — this was the battlefield.

He would first attack (and defeat) the Union army south and east of Port Republic by 10 a.m., then reverse his army, cross two swollen rivers, and attack (and defeat) Fremont to the north at Cross Keys. This was his plan! Sandie Pendleton, a member of Jackson's staff, mumbled "Jackson is crazy again." A contemporary author of the Valley Campaign wrote: "Military history before and since offers no parallel."(11)

It all began at about 3:45 a.m. Jackson moved his men westward over the bridge into Port Republic and then across the ford to the south. Because of the high water, Jackson had a bridge of wagons constructed at the ford.(12)

At daylight, the 2nd and 4th Virginia Infantry regiments and two pieces of artillery started toward the coaling. The 5th and 27th Virginia with support of the 2nd Virginia Cavalry and two pieces of the Rockbridge Artillery moved through the wheatfield along the south bank of the South Fork.(13) On the Union side, the Third and Fourth Brigades from Shields' Division were encamped northeast of the coaling. General Shields, with two more brigades, was at Luray, some 30 miles to the north.(14)

Billy Davis' Brigade Commander, Sprigg Carroll, urged a withdrawal from their position but was overruled by the field commander, Brigadier-General Erastus Tyler. (Colonel Carroll's official report of subsequent events offered little detail.) Carroll recorded that two cannons and the 7th Indiana were sent into the wheatfield. Then the 7th fell back, were reinforced, and the right wing (including the 7th) drove the Confederates through the wheatfield.(15)

Corporal John V. Hadley of Company B, 7th Indiana Infantry, in later years offered more detail: "We took our position at 8 A.M. & at 9 we heard a tremendous yell arise in our fron[t]. Following it [we] saw rais up over a hill a rebel brigade & with flying colors & prancing steeds [of the 2nd Virginia Cavalry]. . .Within 200 yards of us they poured a volley into our ranks when we without delay returned the compliment which brought them to a halt."

Hadley, in the same letter to his girl friend, reasoned it had been a "place to try mens soulds." "We were in an open field without a stump or bush to shelter us from bullets. We stood & fired 80 rounds."(16)

Colonel James Gavin, the 7th's commanding officer, was out front, on foot, displaying courage and sharing the risks. His horse had collapsed after taking five shots.(17) This stand-up fight featured some of the South's finest fighting units — two guns from the Rockbridge Artillery, the 5th and 27th Virginia from the Stonewall Brigade and the famed "Louisiana Tigers."

Jackson's first attack on the Union left had been repulsed. The coaling was a formidable parcel of land — particularly when defended with six cannons. Jackson, outgunned and outmanned, seemed to be enraptured with the fighting as he told General Taylor it was "delightful excitement." Some of the subordinates thought it looked more like another Kernstown.(18) Whatever the emotions, Jackson realized the seriousness of the situation — he had underestimated the tenacity of Shield's two brigades of less than 3,000 men. He ordered Major-General Richard Ewell, with two more Confederate brigades, to slip away

The battlefield at Cross Keys.

from Union General Fremont's front at Cross Keys and hurry to Port Republic.

A small engagement had been fought at Cross Keys the day before and the lines were still drawn up as if there would be more fighting. The anticipated second day of fighting never happened. Thus Jackson was able to leave a small force in Fremont's front and siphon off the major portion of his forces and move them to Port Republic.[19]

Jackson initially attacked piecemeal at Port Republic with only four infantry regiments of about 850 men and four pieces of artillery. The high ground at the coaling had been the focal point — later, it served as a door hinge as the Union right wing swung forward. The right (which included Billy Davis and John Hadley) moved through the wheatfield and it appeared the Confederates might be driven back into Port Republic. ". . .Col Gavin dashed in front & commanded us to charge bayonetts," Hadley remembered. "Off every man started with an unearthly yell on the double quick. It was too much for the guilty rebels. Their line began to stagger & when within 40 yards of them they broke & ran with all speed. . .Their officers with drawn swords tried in vain to rally them. . .We chased for half mile & left them running."[20] Jackson's plan for a defeat of Shields by 10 a.m. was discarded. But all was not lost — the Confederate commander did have more brigades on the way.

The reinforcements were slow in arriving as there was confusion in the village of Port Republic. The bridge of wagons had collapsed and troops were backed up, waiting to cross at the ford. When fresh troops finally made it to the field, Jackson immediately fed them into the contest.[21]

The balance of power was definitely shifting to the Confederates. And in terms of military brainpower, the Confederates had been ahead from the start. For the South, Jackson, Ewell and Taylor were on the field — all had or would reach the rank of Lieutenant-General. For the North it would be Brigadier-General Erastus Barnard Tyler and Colonel Samuel Sprigg Carroll — nothing extraordinary.

When the Federal right wing pushed the Confederates back through the wheatfield, they exposed their left flank to the Confederate position near the coaling.[22]

At about 11 a.m. Taylor slammed into the coaling (again) with three regiments of Louisianans. He was joined by Ewell and two regiments of Virginians. Colonel James Walker arrived at the opportune time and struck with two more regiments of Virginians and the 12th Georgia.[23]

Defending the seven guns on the coaling were only three blue-jacketed regiments. It was a tenacious struggle for the coaling. Charge and counter-charge occurred. Possession of the guns passed back and forth. At one point, the Louisianans, in an attempt to thwart the re-taking of the cannons by the Midwesterners, slit the throats of the artillery horses. One participant later wrote that the blood of men and beast almost flowed in a stream.[24] The cannons, when secured by the rebels, were quickly turned to enfilade the Yankee regiments in the wheatfield. The Confederates now possessed a sweeping field of fire.

Harry Hays would be wounded leading the Louisiana Tigers.

Henry Kyd Douglas, youngest member of Jackson's staff.

The rebels continued to flood the field with lead and men. Three fresh infantry regiments advanced into the wheatfield. Hadley wrote "they began to come at us by acres. We saw their numbers — thought it wise to retreat & beat off."(25) The Union right wing started to disintegrate. Jackson, once again, had prevailed with (superior) numbers — this time, however, it took a little longer to get the numbers together.(26)

The remainder of Jackson's forces safely crossed the river and the bridge at Port Republic was burned. Jackson moved his Army off to the south and east on (what would be) his way to Richmond. The Valley Army and the Shenandoah Campaign of 1862 would be no more.

But what a Campaign. No one would dispute Jackson's strategic success. In 48 days his 17,000 "foot cavalry" had marched 650 miles, an average of 13½ miles a day for seven weeks. He defeated three separate Union armies. He fought five battles. He inflicted twice the casualties he received. He captured 3,500 prisoners. He seized supplies. And most importantly, he immobilized 60,000 to 70,000 Union troops. The mighty "Stonewall" had achieved immortality.(27)

Regardless of the strategic success, Jackson would be criticized for his tactical performance at Port Republic. He had engaged 6,000 men against a force of 3,000 or less. The losses were approximately the same on both sides — about 1,000 men each. This had been Jackson's severest casualty loss of the Campaign and, certainly, he did not handle his army as a single force.(28) It was written he was too careless, too bold, too ambitious. Henry Kyd Douglas, a Jackson staff officer and an ardent supporter, said, "The fact is, Jackson went into the fight impetuously . . . ." And then added that even Jackson was disappointed.(29) Perhaps Jackson was correct when he said, "He who does not see the hand of God in this is blind, sir, blind."(30)

Then, too, the personal courage and sacrifice of the Union troops was a factor. The 7th Indiana went to Port Republic with 350 men; 17 were killed on the field, 134 were wounded and 29 came up missing — 51 percent casualties.(31)

Billy Davis would be commended for his courage and perseverance at Port Republic. More importantly, he could write a letter on June 11 "to acquaint the home folks of my good fortune in the battle."

END NOTES

(1) Allan, *Jackson in the Valley;* pp. 138-139.

(2) Robertson, *The Stonewall Brigade;* p. 105.

(3) Tanner, *Stonewall in the Valley;* p. 288.

(4) Allan, p. 149-150. And *ORs*; Series I, v. XII, pp. 698-699. This is Colonel Carroll's report. The two captured Jackson staff officers were Captain Edward Willis and Colonel Stapleton Crutchfield, Jackson's Chief of Artillery. Each would escape.

(5) *Ibid.*

(6) Tanner, p. 293.

(7) *ORs*, Series I, v. XII, pp. 698-699, for Daum's report.

(8) For Billy Davis, at least in later years, it was "a day in the sun." His journals contained many little clippings, poems, notes, a picture of

Lincoln — things he must have cherished. One item was a typewritten carbon copy of a report first printed in the *Official Records* — the bible of Civil War history. The report is that of Colonel Daum, the Chief of Artillery, who had asked for volunteers to retrieve the two guns. Orville Thomson wrote that Colonel Daum promised each of those courageous men a commission when he got to Washington. Thomson then added sarcastically, "It has been a long weary wait."

(9) *ORs*, Series I, v. XII, p. 699.

(10) Samuel List made it all the way to Petersburg only to be mortally wounded on June 18, 1864. He was among the first to be buried in Arlington National Cemetery. At one time Billy had access to (and quoted) the diaries of Samuel V. List, Samuel W. Vannuys and John C. Henderson.

(11) Both quotes from Tanner, pp. 296-297.

(12) *Ibid.*; p. 298 and 296.

(13) *Ibid.*; p. 298. Also Robertson, *The Stonewall Brigade*, p. 108.

(14) Allan, p. 159.

(15) *ORs*, Series I, v. XII, p. 699.

(16) James I. Robertson, Jr., Editor, "An Indiana Soldier in Love and War: The Civil War Letters of John V. Hadley," *Indiana Magazine of History* (Indianapolis, September 1962); v. LIX, n. 3, p. 213.

(17) Merrill and Company, Editors, *The Soldier of Indiana;* p. 466. Samuel List's diary is also quoted here. No reference to the diary's author other than "a private in the Seventh regiment."

(18) Richard Taylor, *Destruction and Reconstruction* (New York, 1879); p. 74. Robertson, *The Stonewall Brigade*, p. 111.

(19) Allan, *ibid.*; p. 161.

(20) Robertson, ". . .Hadley," p. 213.

(21) Tanner, pp. 299-305. Robertson, *Stonewall* . . .,; pp. 108-111.

(22) Allan, p. 160.

(23) Tanner, pp. 304-305.

(24) Terry L. Jones, *Lee's Tigers* (Baton Rouge, 1987); p. 89. Scholars and students have been fascinated with the fighting on the coaling; however, 71 percent of the Union casualties and approximately 73 percent of the Confederate casualties occurred in the wheatfield. These calculations based on "Returns of Casualties" found in *ORs*.

(25) Robertson, ". . .Hadley," p. 213.

(26) Tanner, pp. 306-310.

(27) There are many quantitative summaries of Jackson's accomplishments in the Shenandoah Valley. The numbers (usually) vary from source to source. The data used here are based on the following sources: Tanner and Robertson,; also E. B. Long's *The Civil War Day by Day Almanac;* Mark M. Boatner III, *The Civil War Dictionary;* Patricia L. Faust, Editor, *Historical Times Illustrated History of the Civil War.* Also a pamphlet by Edward T. Downer, *Stonewall Jackson's Shenandoah Valley Campaign 1862.*

(28) Tanner, p. 307

(29) Henry Kyd Douglas; *I Rode With Stonewall* (St. Simons Island, 1979); p. 96.

(30) *Ibid.*; p. 97. (Statement made to General Ewell.)

(31) *ORs*, Series I, v. XII, pp. 690, 699.

An ambrotype found on the Port Republic battlefield between the body of a Confederate soldier and the body of a Union soldier.

PICTURE CREDITS

—141—Courtesy, USAMHI.

—142—Same.

—143—Same.

—144—Courtesy, Johnson County (Indiana) Historical Society.

—145—Miller's *Photographic History.*

—146—Courtesy, USAMHI.

—147—Both, same.

—148—Courtesy, The Society of Port Republic Preservationists, Mrs. Anita Cummins.

—149—Map. *Battles and Leaders.*

—150—Same.

—151—Courtesy, The Society of Port Republic Preservationist.

—151—Courtesy, *Blue and Gray Magazine.*

—152—Courtesy, USAMHI.

—153—Same.

—154—Both, Miller's *Photographic History.*

—155—The Museum of the Confederacy.

EPILOGUE

Billy Davis walked safely off several more battlefields. Later in 1862 he was at Cedar Mountain, Second Bull Run, Antietam and Fredericksburg. In 1863 he was promoted from the ranks to Second Lieutenant and was with the 7th at Chancellorsville, Gettysburg and Mine Run. Then came the first battle of 1864 and the Wilderness. During the fighting at the Widow Tapp's farm on May 6, he was permanently crippled as Cutler's Union Brigade faced Hood's old Texas Brigade. Billy was wounded in the right thigh, four inches below the hip joint. As he lay suffering on the ground, he was wounded twice more as the armies fought back and forth over his body. Now wounded in both thighs, Lieutenant Davis lay for hours until picked up by the Confederates. Officially listed as "missing in action," Billy was alive — a prisoner in a Lynchburg, Virginia hospital. On June 19 he escaped. He was recaptured and then given a release. This time Billy made it all the way to Hopewell. Arriving home on July 4, 1864, he found his family in mourning for him. They thought he was among the dead.

After his discharge on September 20, 1864, Billy opened a small merchandising business in Franklin, Indiana. In 1869, he sold out and as the Davis generations before him, moved westward to help establish a new Presbyterian community on the frontier. In 1831 the frontier had been Indiana, in 1869 the frontier was Kansas. With John Vannuys, a childhood friend who had also served in the 7th Indiana Infantry, he built a business house on the south side of the square in Iola. Here the new partners sold clothing, boots, shoes and operated a tailoring business.

On May 16, 1872, William Davis married 24-year-old Candace Grimes. She too had been born in Indiana. A daughter, Mary Louisa, was born to William and Candace Davis on January 25, 1874, but lived only until September 28. In 1875 William gave up the business and performed

The Stars and Stripes flying over a battered Fort Wagner. (Miller's Photographic History.)

The McCook Post, Number 51 at Iola, Kansas in 1906. William Davis is probably somewhere in this photograph. (Courtesy, The Allen County Historical Society.)

missionary work as he travelled through Kansas and the Indian Territory. Elected Clerk of the District Court in 1878, he served that function for four years. Then he farmed for three years on land he had acquired at Carlyle, Kansas, some five miles north of Iola. On October 10, 1882, another child, Grace, was born. That same year William became a charter member and the first chaplain of the McCook Post, Number 51 of the Grand Army of the Republic (GAR). Then in 1890, William returned to his Sabbath School Missionary work for the Presbytery. In 11 years, serving in the Indian Territory, he organized 147 Sunday Schools, made 22,953 "visits" and traveled 51,166 miles. Seeking less strenuous work in 1902, William found work in the Iola area as a rural mail carrier. He had built a house on East Street in Iola in the late 1890s, but he kept the farm.

As a result of his Civil War experiences, Billy wore one built-up shoe and in 1906 he stumbled and broke his hip. It may have been at about that time he started transferring his diary entries to his journals. It is known that as late as 1916 he was working on his journals, although the strength of his handwriting had noticeably deteriorated. Then in the Spring of 1922, he suffered a heart attack which left him an invalid. He and Candace went to daughter Grace's home in Muskogee, Oklahoma. Grace had married a schoolmate from Iola High School, John Fred Brett, who had become a prominent Muskogee attorney.

Billy held on until 4 a.m. on November 21, 1922 — 84 years, 10 months and nine days. The *Iola Register* declared on its front page that William Davis had been "a Christian, a soldier and a gentleman if there ever was one."

Billy's old clothing store had been in the left side of the white building. (Courtesy, The Allen County Historical Society.)

The body of William Davis would have been brought down this wide Iola street on its way to the cemetery. (Courtesy, The Allen County Historical Society.)

APPENDIX A

ROSTER OF COMPANY F, 7TH INDIANA (THREE YEARS SERVICE)

This section provides an alphabetical list of the men who served in Company F, 7th Indiana Volunteer Infantry Regiment (three years service). Billy Davis' journal is the primary source for the information concerning each of the members. Two other sources were used when they contained additional and/or conflicting data. The source of information, in each case, will be indicated by:

(BD) for a notation from the Billy Davis journal.

(AG) for a notation from the *Report of the Adjutant General of the State of Indiana.*

(OT) for a notation from the *Narrative of the Service of the Seventh Indiana Infantry in the War for the Union,* "Roster of Companies," by Orville Thomson.

If the soldier's image appears in the Appendix B photographs a star or stars will precede the name:

★ Refer to First Platoon photograph, Appendix B.

★ ★ Refer to Second Platoon photograph, Appendix B.

Each man's date of muster was September 13, 1861, unless noted with the word "Recruit." The recruits were mustered into service, individually and irregularly, throughout the war. Unless noted otherwise, each man's residence was Johnson County, Indiana, according to the *Report of the Adjutant General of the State of Indiana.*

ROSTER

Adams, Elisha; Died of disease at Franklin, Indiana, June 30, 1862. (BD)

Adams, Milford D.; Taken prisoner, Catlett's Station, Virginia, August 22, 1862. Discharged for disability January 15, 1863. (BD)

Alexander, William J.; Recruit, July 21, 1862. Transferred to Veteran Reserve Corps, October 30, 1863. (BD) Marion County resident. (AG)

Allison, William G.; Had severe attack of rheumatism at Big Levels, Hampshire County, Virginia, February 9, 1862. Again, in the winter of 1863 and summer and winter of 1864. Clerk in Inspector General's Office. Mustered out September 20, 1864 at end of enlistment. (BD)

★ ★ Banta, Isaac; Officers' cook much of time. Mustered out September 20, 1864 at end of enlistment. (BD)

★ ★ Bone, James M.; Taken prisoner at Port Republic, Virginia, June 9, 1862. Promoted Corporal, August 31, 1863. Mustered out September 20, 1864 at end of enlistment. (BD) Wounded Port Republic. (OT)

Brady, James; Discharged January 5, 1863 for disability. (BD)

Branch, Dudley B.; 4th Sergeant. Promoted 1st Sergeant November 1, 1862. Transferred to Invalid Corps, January 16, 1864. (BD) Transferred Veterans Reserve Corps, January 25, 1864. (AG) Mustered out September 20, 1864. (OT)

★ Brown, James M.; Mustered out September 20, 1864 at end of enlistment. (BD)

★ ★ Brown, Shadrack C.; Taken prisoner at Catlett's Station, Virginia, August 22, 1862. Wounded in Wilderness, Virginia, May 6, 1864. Lost right arm. Mustered out September 20, 1864 at end of enlistment. (BD) Shadrac. (AG) Shadric. (OT)

Burk, Thomas; Recruit, July 21, 1862. Wounded at Union, Virginia, November 2, 1862. Discharged February 18, 1863. (BD) Burke. Discharged February 18, 1863, wounds. (AG) Discharged February 19, 1863, wounds. (OT)

★ Byers, William L.; Killed or captured in Wilderness, Virginia, May 5, 1864. (BD) Byres. Captured Wilderness. (AG) Byres. Captured Wilderness, died Arma [sic.]. (OT)

★ ★ Canary, Abraham I.; Captured in Wilderness, Virginia, May 5, 1864. In Andersonville, Georgia and Florence, South Carolina. Exchanged. Spent ______ months in Federal Hospital. Mustered out April 4, 1865. (BD)

★ ★ Carter, Robert J.; Promoted Corporal January 6, 1862. Mustered out September 20, 1864 at end of enlistment. (BD)

Coughran, Abraham; Transferred to Invalid Corps, August 20, 1863. (BD) Cochran. (AG) Cockran. Mustered out September 20, 1864. (OT)

★ ★ Covert, George K.; Hospital at Grafton, (West) Virginia. Struck by a bullet in the breast at Winchester, Virginia, March 23, 1862. Life saved by young lady's picture. Promoted Corporal August 31, 1863. Captured in Wilderness, Virginia, May 5, 1864. In Andersonville, Georgia and Florence, South Carolina. Exchanged __. __ months in Federal Hospital. Discharged March 17, 1865. (BD)

★ Daniels, Martin V.; 3rd Sergeant. Promoted 1st Sergeant January 16, 1864. Killed at North Anna River, Virginia, May 25, 1864. (BD)

★ Davis, William; Took up colors twice when bearer was killed. Promoted 1st Sergeant December 16, 1862 [sic.]. 2nd Lieutenant November 1, 1862 [sic.]. Wounded at the Wilderness, Virginia, May 6, 1864. Taken prisoner. Escaped from Lynchburg, Virginia, June 10, 1864. Reached Federal lines on June 18 and home on July 4, 1864. Promoted 1st Lieutenant June 19, 1864. Mustered out September 20, 1864 at end of enlistment. (BD) Appointed Sergeant May 1862; promoted to 2nd Lieutenant November 1, 1862; to 1st Lieutenant June 19, 1864. (OT) [Note Billy indicated he was promoted to 1st Sergeant on December 16, 1862 and promoted to 2nd Lieutenant on November 1, 1862 — six weeks earlier? His military records indicate he was promoted to 1st Sergeant on October 26, 1862 and 2nd Lieutenant on November 31, 1862 — not November 1 as Billy recorded. This adds confusion as there is not a November 31.]

Carver — Typical of Civil War hospitals in Washington D. C. area. (Miller's **Photographic History.**)

Dawson, William H.; 4th Corporal. Reduced to the ranks. Mustered out September 20, 1864 at end of enlistment. (BD)

Decoursey, Joel; Died at Cumberland, Maryland (disease) January 13, 1862. (BD) Decourcy. (OT)

Decoursey, Miles; Discharged for disability January 3, 1863. Died. (BD) Decourcy. (OT)

★ ★ Demaree, Amzi; Recruit, February 23, 1862. Captured in the Wilderness May 5, 1864. Was in Andersonville, Georgia until about September, 1864, was taken to Florence, South Carolina where he died about November 15, 1864. (BD) Recruit, March 11, 1863. Name transferred to 20th Indiana Infantry Regiment. (AG) Amos. Died in rebel prison. (OT)

★ ★ Demaree, Brack; Identified in Second Platoon photograph but no other information for a Brack Demaree. Possibly Robert B. was known as Brack.

Demaree, George W.; Recruit, August ____, 1862. Was injured about the hip joint by gun carriage at Bull Run, August 30, 1862 and crippled for life. Discharged April 11, 1863. (BD) Date of muster, August 21, 1862. (AG)

Demaree, Jesse Y.; Wounded at Winchester, Virginia, March 23, 1862. Discharged August 23, 1862. (BD) Discharged August 23, 1862, wounds. (AG) Discharged wounds April 23, 1862. (OT)

Demaree, Robert B.; Recruit, February 23, 1862. Transferred to 20th Indiana Infantry Regiment, September ____, 1864. (BD) Recruit March 11, 1862. (AG) Died of wounds, December 22, 1864. (OT)

Ditmars, Richard V.; Wounded at Port Republic, Virginia, June 9, 1862. Discharged September 30, 1862. (BD) Discharged, disability. (AG)

Dragoo, Belteshazer; Killed at North Anna, May 25, 1864. (BD)

★ ★ Dragoo, John; Mustered out September 20, 1864 at end of enlistment. (BD)

★ ★ Dunlap, James R.; Went to Cumberland Hospital February 8, 1862. Wounded in Wilderness May 5, 1864. Mustered out September 20, 1864 at end of enlistment. (BD)

★ Dunlap, Joseph M.; Recruit, July 28, 1862. Transferred to 20th Indiana Infantry Regiment, September ____, 1864. Promoted 2nd Lieutenant on 20th. Discharged at close of war. (BD)

Dunlap, William L.; Appointed Wagoner. Mustered out September 20, 1864 at end of enlistment. (BD)

★ ★ Evans, Robert; Recruit, August 11, 1862. Wounded on North Anna River, Virginia, May 23, 1864. His wounding was the result of a comrade's nervousness. Died in hospital at or near Washington, July 6, 1864. Buried at Arlington. (BD)

Robert Evans. (Courtesy, Craig Dunn.)

Feathergill, James; 1st Corporal. Died December 19, 1861 of disease, Beverley, (West) Virginia. (BD)

★ Fishback, Harvey G.; Recruit, February 23, 1862. Wounded in Wilderness, Virginia, May 5, 1864. Transferred to 20th Indiana Infantry Regiment, September ____, 1864. Discharged. (BD) Mustered out May 25, 1865. (OT)

Fishback, Thomas H.; Taken prisoner at Manassas, Virginia, August 30, 1862. Mustered out September 20, 1864 at end of enlistment. (BD)

Fisher, Adolphus; Recruit, July 22, 1862. Died at Fredericksburg, Virginia, December 27, 1862. (BD) Date of muster, July 21, 1862. (AG) Died, December 17, 1862. (AG and OT)

★ ★ Fisher, James M.; Promoted Corporal January 4, 1863. Wounded at North Anna. Died in hospital near Washington, July 3, 1864. Buried at Arlington, Virginia. (BD)

Fisher, John H.; Wounded at Port Republic, June 9, 1862. Wounded at Wilderness, May 6, 1864. Lost right arm. Mustered out September 20, 1864 at end of enlistment. (BD)

Fisher, Thomas H.; Promoted Corporal July ____, 1862. Wounded at Bull Run, Virginia, August 30, 1862. Died in Carver Hospital near Washington, September 17, 1862. Buried at Alexandria, Virginia. (BD)

Forgeay, John; Discharged for disability, May 22, 1862. (BD)

Forsyth, Elkanah; Recruit, February 4, 1862. Transferred to 5th U. S. Artillery. (BD)

Garr, Lawrence P.; 8th Corporal. Wounded at Port Republic, Virginia, June 9, 1862. Discharged October 6, 1862. (BD) Discharged October 6, 1862, wounds. (AG and OT)

Garrett, Samuel; Recruit, February 23, 1862. Transferred to Veterans Reserve Corps, January 16, 1864. (BD) Mustered in March 11, 1862. (AG) Mustered out March 11, 1865. (OT)

★ ★ Good, Francis M.; Wounded May 6, 1864. Died in hospital at Fredericksburg, Virginia, July 16, 1864. Buried in National Cemetery, Fredericksburg, Virginia. (BD) Died Alexandria. (AG)

Gordon, William; Wounded August 9, 1862. Mustered out September 20, 1864 at end of enlistment. (BD)

★ Graham, Joseph; Mustered out September 20, 1864. (BD) Wounded, Port Republic. (OT)

★ Green, William D.; Recruit, August 5, 1862. In Drum Corps. Transferred to 20th Indiana Infantry Regiment, September ____, 1864. Discharged. (BD)

Griffin, John; Discharged for disability May 10, 1862. (BD) Both Greffeth and Griffets. (AG)

Hall, Jonathon T.; Recruit, August 3, 1862. Discharged March 11, 1863 for disability. (BD) Hill. (AG and OT) Date of muster, July 16, 1862. (AG)

★ ★ Hamlet, William H.; Captured May 1864 in Wilderness, Virginia. In Andersonville, Georgia and Florence, South Carolina. Enlisted in Confederate Army. Captured by Federals. Colonel Grover got him released. (BD) Enlisted in rebel army while prisoner. (AG)

Hard, Henry C.; Recruit, July 16, 1862. Discharged January 4, 1863 for disability. (BD) Date of muster, September 13, 1861. Discharged January 4, 1863 for disability. (AG) Discharged January 4, 1863, reentered U. S. Cavalry. (OT)

★ ★ Hardin, Abner; 5th Sergeant. Wounded and prisoner, Port Republic, Virginia, June 9, 1862. Promoted 1st Sergeant June 26, 1864. Mustered out September 20, 1864, end of service. (BD)

The Camp Morton site in later years. (Courtesy, Indiana State Library.)

★ ★ Hathaway, John W.; Recruit, February 23, 1862. Wounded in the Wilderness, Virginia, May 6, 1864. Transferred to 20th Indiana Infantry Regiment, September ____, 1864. Discharged. (BD) Date of muster, March 11, 1862. (AG) Mustered out February 22, 1865. (OT)

★ Hay, Francis M.; Captured Yellow House August 19, 1864. (AG) Captured August 19, 1864, escaped October 5, recaptured October 20, mustered out December 10, 1864. (OT)

★ Hay, James M.; Captured Yellow House August 19, 1864. (AG) Captured August 19, 1864, escaped October 5, recaptured October 20, mustered out December 10, 1864. (OT)

Henderson, John C.; Slightly wounded in several battles but never left the field. Sick with fever and in hospital during the Gettysburg Campaign. Mustered out September 20, 1864 at close of enlistment. (BD) Appointed Corporal. (AG)

Hendricks, Alban; Died of disease at Cumberland, Maryland, February 11, 1862. (BD) Hendrix. (AG and OT)

★ Herriott, Ephraim M.; Promoted Corporal ____, Sergeant ____. Carried flag in Wilderness Campaign. Mustered out September 20, 1864 at end of enlistment. (BD) Wounded. (OT)

Hill, Jonathon; See Hall, Jonathon.

Hill, Thomas; Detailed as cook. Died of disease at Franklin, Indiana January 14, 1862. (BD)

★ ★ Holmes, David; Orderly Sergeant. Promoted 2nd Lieutenant October 26, 1862, 1st Lieutenant November 1, 1862. Killed at Petersburg June 18, 1864. (BD) Promoted 2nd Lieutenant December 24, 1861. (AG)

Holmes, George; 6th Corporal. Wounded at Winchester, Virginia, March 23, 1862. Discharged August 18, 1862. (BD) Discharged August 18, 1862; wounds. (AG)

Holmes, James A.; 2nd Sergeant. Promoted 2nd Lieutenant January 6, 1862. Wounded in right wrist at Port Republic June 9, 1862. Resigned October 25, 1862. (BD) Holes. Promoted 2nd Lieutenant December 24, 1861. (AG) Resigned October 15, 1862. (OT)

★ Jeffery, Thomas A.; 2nd Lieutenant. Promoted 1st Lieutenant January 6, 1862. Captain November 1, 1862 and discharged September 20, 1864. (BD) Date of commission September 1, 1861. Promoted 1st Lieutenant December 24, 1861. (AG) Wounded, Petersburg. (OT)

Some "boys" from the 7th Indiana on Culps Hill at Gettysburg, July 3, 1913 — the 50th anniversary of the battle. Ephraim Herriott is standing to the immediate left of the 7th's monument. (Courtesy, Max Herriott.)

★ Johnson, John M.; Joined regiment at Cincinnati, Ohio September 15, 1861, was but 16 years old. Was on every march and in every battle, and yet never wounded. Was promoted Corporal October 6, 1862 and Sergeant ____. Mustered out September 20, 1864 at expiration of enlistment. (BD) Date of muster; September 13, 1861. (AG)

★ ★ Johnston, Oscar W.; Recruit, July 16, 1862. Transferred to 20th Indiana Infantry Regiment. Discharged. (BD) Johnson. (AG and OT) Unaccounted for. (OT)

Jones, Bazil G.; Recruit, December 31, 1863. Volunteered as one of a "Forlorn hope" in Wilderness Campaign, to go burn bridges and destroy railroad. Was not heard from again. Name transferred to 20th Indiana Infantry Regiment. (BD) Captured June 22, 1864. (AG) Mustered out, June 19, 1865. (OT)

Jones, Marion; Recruit, July 14, 1862. Transferred to Veterans Reserve Corps. Mustered out July 14, 1865. (BD)

Jones, Nelson; Discharged September 5, 1861, disability. (BD) Discharged, no date. (OT)

Kelley, William, M.; Discharged for disability September 18, 1862. (BD)

★ ★ Knowlton, Theopholus T.; Killed at Spotsylvania Court House May 10, 1864. (BD) Theophilus. (AG and OT)

Lambertson, Samuel; Captain. Resigned October 31, 1862. (BD) Date of commission September 1, 1861. (AG)

Langston, Sylvester; Recruit December 31, 1863. Killed in Wilderness, Virginia, May 5, 1864. (BD)

List, Peter D.; Recruit, November 24, 1863. Killed in Wilderness, Virginia, May 5, 1864. (BD) Date of muster, December 2, 1863. Captured Wilderness. Transferred to 20th Indiana Infantry Regiment. (AG) Captured, Died in rebel prison. (OT)

★ List, Samuel; Company Clerk. Promoted Corporal February 28, 1862 and Sergeant January 16, 1864. Slightly wounded on head and on right leg at Spotsylvania Court House May 12, 1864. Not severe enough to go to hospital. Fatally wounded before Petersburg, Virginia June 18, 1864. Died of wounds July 2, 1864. Buried at Arlington. (BD) Died at Washington. (AG)

Lowe, David B.; Killed in the Wilderness May 5, 1864. (BD) Low. (AG and OT)

★ ★ Lowe, Lawrence; Wagoner. Discharged for disability May 22, 1862. (BD)

Marquis, George A.; Discharged for disability January 20, 1863. (BD) Wounded. Mustered out with regiment. (OT) Marion County resident. (AG)

Marquis, James G.; Killed in the Wilderness May 5, 1864. (BD) Marion County resident. (AG)

Massey, Hiram; Wounded at Petersburg June 20, 1864. Mustered out September 20, 1864 at end of enlistment. (BD)

McGee, Isaac M.; Recruit, July 28, 1862. Took the regimental flag at 2nd Bull Run, August 30th, 1862. Slightly wounded by a piece of shell at Antietam, Maryland, September 17, 1862. Killed by bursting shell at Union, Virginia, November 2, 1862. (BD)

McIlvain, James H.; Promoted Corporal January 6, 1862. Transferred to Veterans Reserve Corps January 16, 1864. (BD)

McIlvain, Panter; Discharged because of disability December 19, 1862. (BD) Pantor. (OT)

Miller, William C. T.; Recruit July 28, 1862. Discharged August 24, 1863 for disability. (BD) Discharged August 2, 1863. (OT)

Morgan, Leo H.; In hospital some. Mustered out September 20, 1864 at end of enlistment. (BD)

★ Mullikin, Huron P.; Wounded at Mine Run, Virginia November 30, 1863. Mustered out September 20, 1864. (BD)

Mullikin, Joseph; 3rd Corporal. Died of disease at Cumberland, Maryland, February 27, 1862. (BD)

★ Norton, James H.; [Not sure which James Norton is pictured in First Platoon photograph.] Captured at Yellow House, Virginia, September ____, 1864. Escaped by dropping into brush in darkness. Took guidon from sleeping Rebel. Mustered out September 20, 1864 at close of enlistment. (BD)

★ Norton, James P.; [Not sure which James Norton is pictured in First Platoon photograph.] Date of muster, July 20, 1862. Discharged June 15, 1864 for disability. (AG) Discharged June 15, 1864. (OT) Not listed in BD, see Larner Bracher Norton below.

★ ★ Norton, Larner Bracher; Recruit, July 20, 1862. Discharged June 15, 1864 on account of disability. (BD) Not listed in AG or OT, see James P. Norton above.

★ Norton, William T.; Mustered out September 20, 1864 at end of enlistment. (BD)

★ ★ Overstreet, Gabriel M.; In hospital at Cumberland, Maryland with fever December 1861. Drove Division ammunition wagon in Wilderness Campaign. Mustered out September 20, 1864. (BD) Wounded (OT)

Paugh, Millikin; Discharged for disability July 20, 1862. (BD) Paw. (AG and OT) Discharged July 30, 1862. (OT)

Payton, John W.; Recruit, December 1, 1862. Wounded in Wilderness, Virginia, May 5 or 6, 1864. Died from wounds. May ____, 1864. (BD) Date of muster, December 2, 1862. (AG) Peyton. (OT) Died of wounds, May 18, 1864. (AG and OT)

★ Phillips, George; Mustered out September 20, 1864 at end of enlistment. (BD)

Prichard, Daniel W.; 5th Corporal. Killed at Winchester, Virginia, March 23, 1862. (BD) First man killed at Winchester. (OT)

Pusey, Frank J.; Fifer. Promoted Corporal, January 6, 1862, Sergeant November 1, 1862. Mustered out September 20, 1864 at expiration of enlistment. (BD)

Rains, George; Recruit, February 23, 1862. Discharged May 22, 1862. Disability. (BD)

★ Ransdell, John C.; Recruit, August 6, 1862. Captured at Yellow House, Virginia, August 19, 1864. Taken to Salisbury, N. C. Was sick in prison. After the fall of Confederacy, spent several months in Federal hospitals and was discharged August 11, 1865. Name was transferred to 20th Indiana Infantry Regiment, September ____, 1864. He was sick for more than a year and has never fully recovered. (BD) Randall. (AG and OT) Mustered out July 11, 1865. (AG)

★ Reynolds, Columbus; Mustered out September 20, 1864 at end of enlistment. (BD) Wounded. (OT)

Reynolds, William J.; Recruit, August 16, 1862. Thumb shot off at South Mountain, Maryland, September 14, 1862. Discharged because of wounds, February 9, 1863. (BD)

★ Richardson, Bluford; Wounded at Union, Virginia, November 2, 1862. Mustered out September 20, 1864 at end of enlistment. (BD)

★ Richardson, Lewis; Promoted Corporal July ____, 1863. Killed in Wilderness, Virginia, May 5, 1864. (BD)

★ Richardson, Nelson; Recruit, August 11, 1862. Captured in Wilderness, Virginia, May 5, 1864. In Andersonville prison until last of September 1864 along with A. I. Canary, George K. Covert, Robert Sloan, Amzi T. Demaree and others. In Florence, South Carolina until fall of Richmond, Virginia. Was very sick with fever while in Florence and spent month and half in Federal hospital before able to return home. Was mustered out May 25, 1865. (BD) Date of muster, August 18, 1862. (AG)

Robbins, Abner; Mustered out September 20, 1864 at end of enlistment. (BD) Peter Robbins, but no Abner. (AG and OT)

Sanders, Peter; Discharged at Indianapolis, Indiana, September 12, 1861. (BD) Saunders. Died at Indianapolis September 12, 1861. (AG) Saunders. Died, September 10, 1861. (OT)

★ ★ Shaffer, Adrian; Promoted Corporal January 16, 1864. Mustered out September 20, 1864 at close of enlistment. (BD) Adrun. Date of muster November 1, 1862. Transferred to 20th Regiment. (AG)

Shepherd, Charles A.; Recruit, November 16, 1863. Wounded in Wilderness, Virginia, May 6, 1864. Bullet passed through right groin and broke left thigh near the hip joint. Laid three hours between the firing lines in a fierce battle and was struck by a second ball which broke his left ankle. The enemy passed over him three times on forenoon of May 7. He was taken back two miles to Confederate field hospital. On May 8, his wounds were dressed and his limb splinted. He died of wounds May 13, 1864. (BD) Date of muster, November 17, 1863. (AG) Sheppard. Died in rebel prison. (AG and OT)

Shutters, David; Discharged on account of disability, May 10, 1862. (BD)

Shutters, John; Wounded at Gettysburg July 3, 1863 and Mine Run, Virginia, November 30, 1863. Mustered out September 20, 1864 at expiration of enlistment. (BD)

Simpson, David; Mustered out September 20, 1864 at end of enlistment. (BD)

Sims, James G.; Transferred to Veterans Reserve Corps August 20, 1863. (BD) Mustered out September 26, 1864. (OT)

Sinnett, James; Recruit, August 8, 1862. Discharged for disability. (BD) Date of muster, September 13, 1861. Discharged January 29, 1862, disability. (AG) [No correlation of dates and events.]

★ Sloan, Robert; Was very much troubled by rheumatism. Wounded August 9, 1862. Captured at Wilderness, Virginia, May 5, 1864. Taken to Andersonville, Georgia until late September 1864, was then taken to Florence, South Carolina where he died about November 1, 1864 of dropsy and scurvy. (BD) Died Andersonville prison. (OT)

★ Smith, Adolphus H.; 2nd Corporal. Promoted Sergeant January 5, 1862. Captured August 22, 1862. Escaped. Wounded. Mustered out September 20, 1864, close of enlistment. (BD) Adelphus. Wounded, Wilderness (OT)

Smith, George; 1st Lieutenant. Died of disease at Franklin, Indiana, December 24, 1861. (BD) Date of Commission September 1, 1861. (AG)

Snedicker, William H.; Died of fever at Elk Water, (West) Virginia, November 14, 1861. (BD)

★ Springer, Austin D.; Drummer. Taken prisoner at Port Republic, Virginia, June 9, 1862. Escaped July 16, 1862 and reached regiment August 4, 1862. Transferred to Regimental Band June 1, 1864. Mustered out September 20, 1864, end of enlistment. Reenlisted ____ 1865. Mustered out at end of war. (BD)

Stevens, Jacob; Hit by bullet at Port Republic June 9, 1862. Transferred to Veterans Reserve Corps. (BD) Stephens. (AG) Mustered out September 20, 1864. (OT)

Surface, John M.; Recruit, November 27, 1863. Wounded in Wilderness, Virginia, May 6, 1864. Transferred to 20th Indiana Infantry Regiment, September ____, 1864. (BD) Date of muster, December 2, 1863. (AG) Mustered out as Corporal, July 12, 1865. (OT)

Surface, William J.; Wounded at Slaughter Mountain August 9, 1862. Discharged March 30, 1863. (BD) Discharged, wounds. (AG and OT)

Swarr, Henry F.; Killed at Port Republic, Virginia, June 9, 1862. (BD)

Taylor, Pierson T.; 7th Corporal. Reduced to ranks. Mustered out September 20, 1864, end of enlistment. (BD)

Thomas, Lewis W.; Discharged November 3, 1862 on account of disability. (BD)

Thompson, James C.; Discharged May 22, 1862 on account of disability. (BD) Not listed in OT.

★★ Thompson, William E.; Reenlisted as Veteran for three years at Culpeper, Virginia, January 1, 1864. Killed at Petersburg, Virginia, June 23, 1864. (BD)

★ Tinkle, William W.; Recruit, July 14, 1862. Transferred to 20th Indiana Infantry Regiment, ____, 1864. (BD) Mustered out May 31, 1865. (OT)

Totten, Eugene L.; Recruit, December 11, 1863. Transferred to 20th Indiana Infantry Regiment, September ____, 1864. (BD) Date of muster, December 14, 1864. (AG) Appointed Corporal. Mustered out July 12, 1865. (OT)

Trout, Benjamin G.; Taken prisoner at Yellow House, Virginia, September ____, 1864. Escaped by dropping into brush in darkness. On way out took opera glass from sleeping Rebel officer. Mustered out September 20, 1864 at end of enlistment. (BD)

★★ Tucker, Andrew J.; Wounded at Petersburg, Virginia, July 29, 1864. Died at Portsmouth Grove, Rhode Island, September 24, 1864. (BD) Jackson Tucker. (AG and OT)

Vannarsdall, Cornelius B.; Discharged December 18, 1862 on account of disability. (BD) Vanarsdall. (AG) Varnarsdal. (OT)

Vannuys, John H.; Subject to rheumatism. Wounded at Petersburg, Virginia, June 18, 1864. Mustered out September 20, 1864 at end of enlistment. (BD)

Vannuys, Samuel W.; Promoted Corporal July ____, 1863. Appointed 1st Lieutenant in 4th U. S. Colored Troops August 4, 1863. Was promoted Captain and Chief of Staff of Brigadier General ________ and was killed when leading a charge on a fort on north side of James River near Richmond. (BD) Transferred, 4th U. S. Infantry. (AG) Transferred to 2nd U. S. Infantry. (OT)

Voorhies, Daniel L.; Recruit, December 4, 1863. Died of disease at Alexandria, Virginia, August 1, 1864. (BD)

★ Voris, William D. Recruit, February 23, 1862. Wounded at Fredericksburg, Virginia, December ____, 1862. Transferred to 20th Indiana Infantry Regiment, September ____, 1864. (BD) Mustered out February 23, 1865. (OT)

Watkins, Isaac N.; Transferred to Battery G, 5th U. S. Artillery. (BD) Transferred to 3rd U. S. Artillery. (AG and OT) Mustered out September 27, 1864. (OT)

Witt, Samuel; Discharged June 4, 1862 on account of disability. (BD) Wit. (AG and OT)

★ Woodruff, Jaob A.; Frequently in hospital, sick. Mustered out September 20, 1864 at end of enlistment. (BD)

Young, William G.; Wounded at Slaughter Mountain, Virginia, August 9, 1862. Lost foot. Captured at Culpeper, Virginia, August ____, 1862. Exchanged. Discharged November 27, 1862. (BD)

APPENDIX B

These two photographs were taken on September 19, 1862 near Pony Mountain, Culpeper County, Virginia. Captain Thomas A. Jeffery presented prints to the surviving members at a reunion held on September 13, 1912 at Franklin, Indiana. Photographs courtesy of the Johnson County Historical Society.

First Platoon.

Kneeling, left to right:
Samuel V. List, John C. Ransdell, Columbus Reynolds, James M. Hay, William W. Tinkle, Jaob A. Woodruff, Francis M. Hay, James M. Brown, William D. Voris, William T. Norton, and Lewis Richardson.

Standing, left to right:
Austin D. Springer, William D. Green (for reference, Green was six foot two inches tall), Joseph M. Dunlap, Thomas A. Jeffery, Martin V. Daniels, Ephraim M. Herriott, Huron P. Mullikin, George Phillips, Robert Sloan, William H. Byers, Harvey G. Fishback, James H. Norton or James P. Norton,* Nelson Richardson, Joseph Graham, Bluford Richardson, John M. Johnson, Adolphus H. Smith, and William Davis.

*There was a James H. and a James P. Norton in the 7th Indiana Infantry; the one in the picture is identified only as "James," with no middle initial.

PHOTOGRAPHS OF COMPANY F, 7TH INDIANA

Second Platoon.

Kneeling, left to right:
James M. Fisher, Abraham I. Canary, Shadrac C. Brown, Amzi Demaree, Robert J. Carter, John Dragoo, William E. Thompson, Theopholus T. Knowlton, Adrian Shaffer, Andrew J. Tucker, and Francis M. Good.

Standing, left to right:
David Holmes, James M. Bone, Oscar W. Johnston, John W. Hathaway, Robert Evans, James R. Dunlap, Gabriel M. Overstreet, Isaac Banta, David B. Lowe, Brack Demaree (possibly this was Robert B. Demaree), William H. Hamlet, Larner Bracher Norton, George K. Covert and Abner Hardin.

From *The Evening Star*, Franklin, Indiana, Sept. 13, 1912.

Old Comrades

The members of Co. F, Seventh Indiana Regiment, enjoyed one of the happiest reunions in their history today when they met with Comrade and Mrs. J. M. Brown at their home in East Franklin and spent the day. The attendance was probably the largest of any recent reunion of this company and was doubly enjoyable on account of a number of old comrades from a distance being present, and also this day being the seventieth birthday anniversary of the host.

Major Merit C. Welch commanded the 7th Indiana at the Wilderness.

Major Welch at age 85. (Photographs from **Indiana at Antietam***)*

Before dinner as the guests mingled and exchanged greetings, Major M. C. Welch of Greensburg, in behalf of the company, presented Comrade Brown a rocking chair as a token of love from the "boys." The captain of the company, T. A. Jeffery, of Indianapolis was also present and he had prepared as a surprise for each member a reproduction of a picture of Co. F taken in October, of 1863, near Rappahannock. He also presented each a large photograph of himself taken in his uniform from a picture taken during the war. It is needless to say the pictures were highly appreciated and much interest was taken in comparing the young soldier lads in the picture with the gray haired veterans of today.

The company with wives and friends at noon sat at one long table in the yard, and after the invocation by Rev. W. E. Edgin partook of a dinner that is rarely excelled. After the appetites of all had been satisfied to the utmost, Comrade R. V. Ditmars, president of the company, called for impromptu speeches and the boys lived over again their experiences of the war. Among the honored guests present from a distance, some of whom had not met since '63 were J. M. Johnson of St. Louis, Mo., who is now general traffic manager of the Missouri Pacific railroad; Major M. C. Welch of Greensburg; Capt. T. A. Jeffery of Indianapolis; James McIlvan of Illinois; Wm. Davis of Iola, Kansas; John Shutters of Greenwood; Mr. and Mrs. F. M. Hay and Mr. and Mrs. A. H. Smith of Indianapolis; E. M. Herriott of Greencastle; J. M. Surface of Kansas City, Mo., all members of Co. F, and Peter Carnine of Emporia, Kansas; William Montgomery of Chattanooga, Tenn. Members of the company present from the county, and wives were: Mr. and Mrs. John Henderson of Hopewell; Mr. and Mrs. H. P. Mullikin, Mr. and Mrs. R. P. Hamilton and daughter, Miss Roxie, Mr. and Mrs. W. S. Young and daughter, Mrs. Thomas House, Mr. and Mrs. J. M. Dunlap, Mr. and Mrs. R. V. Ditmars and guest, Miss Bella Bruce from Brooklyn, N. Y.; Mr. and Mrs. Adrian Shafer, Abner Hardin, Mr. and Mrs. Peter McGhee of Greenwood. Other guests were Mr. and Mrs. P. M. Brown, Dr. and Mrs. W. T. Scott, Louis Rothbaust, Rev. and Mrs. Edgin, Garner Wood of Shelbyville; Mrs. Guy Grant of Rensselaer; Mrs. Lydia Brown, Mrs. Angie Voris of Indianapolis; Mrs. Elizabeth Gribbin, Mrs. Mary Garrison of Indianapolis; Mrs. Ellen Lagrange, Mrs. Laura VonTalge, Misses Lavinia Mullikin, Mae Beeson and Mary Cross, and Mrs. Edgil Herriott.

Company F went out from Indiana in 1861, and returned in '64. Among the noted battles of the civil war in which it participated were Winchester, Bull Run, Antietam, Fredericksburg, Chancellorsville, Gettysburg, Wilderness, and Spotsylvania. Major Welch who was present today is the only field officer of the regiment living. He was with the company in every battle with the exception of South Mountain, and came out without a scratch. Capt. Jeffery recalled today that as Company F was passing through Cincinnati on its way to the front he was accosted by a young lad, fifteen years old, who begged to be taken in as a new recruit. Although not of the required age he was allowed to fill a vacancy, and after three years' service, upon the return of the company told the boys he did not want to return to his home, as he could not part with them. He came to Franklin and made this his home until 1873. The young soldier was John M. Johnson, now of St. Louis, and vice-president of the Missouri Pacific railroad, who today was an honored guest. At the close of the war he came to Franklin where he, assisted by some friends, purchased a dray and engaged in draying for a time, and later became an agent for the Big Four station here. By his trustworthiness and ambition he rose step by step, until he today is manager of 7,000 miles of railway. Comrade J. M. Dunlap recalls that he succeeded Mr. Johnson as agent of the station in '73. It was a source of great pleasure to meet with old friends again, and many were the war tales related.

Mr. and Mrs. Brown received a constant stream of callers this afternoon, and the day proved one of the happiest of their lives. Mr. Brown was the recipient of a number of beautiful flowers from friends who in this way expressed their congratulations upon his anniversary.

Old Comrades. (Courtesy USAMHI.)

APPENDIX C

OBITUARY

From the *Iola Daily Register*, November 24, 1922

Wm. Davis at Rest

An Allen County Pioneer, a Brave Soldier, a Good Citizen, Gone to His Reward

William Davis, oldest son of John Davis and Mary F. McGee Davis, was born in Johnson County, Indiana, January 12, 1838, his ancestors being of Welsh and Scotch-Irish extraction. The families of both his father and mother were among the Colonial settlers in America and men of his race and name had served in the Revolutionary armies and in the War of 1812. As a young man Mr. Davis had the advantage of excellent schools although reared on a farm at a time when the sons of farmers were not apt to be well educated.

Soon after coming to his majority President Lincoln issued his first call for 75,000 troops to suppress the rebellion in South Carolina. Mr. Davis responded to this call enlisting as a private in Company H, 7th Indiana Volunteer Infantry. As the first five Indiana regiments had served in the Mexican War, the State began numbering its Civil War regiments with the 6th; so the 7th was the second regiment raised in the State for service in the Civil War. This regiment got into action almost immediately, participating in some of the very first battles of the war. Mr. Davis was discharged at the end of his three months term of enlistment, but immediately re-enlisted, this time becoming a member of Co. F, of the same old Seventh. Two of his comrades in that Company have been his neighbors in Allen County for more than fifty years, John H. Vannuys and James Dunlap, who both survive him — and who both mourn him as a brother.

The regiment in which Mr. Davis served saw continuous and severe service during the whole of the war, being engaged in such deadly battles as Chantilly, South Mountain, 2nd Bull Run, Fredericksburg, the Chancellorsville and Gettysburg campaigns, and the long drawn and furious fights of the Wilderness. In all these battles William Davis played the part of a dashing and gallant soldier. At Port Republic, for example, a piece of Federal artillery was deserted dangerously near the Confederate advance, and Mr. Davis was one of eight men who volunteered to recover it, bringing it safely into the Union lines under fire of 18 guns. At 2nd Bull Run the color bearer was shot down and Davis caught the flag and carried it till a new detail was made. Again at Union he caught the flag under similar circumstances and was its bearer for the regiment until his promotion to orderly after the battle of Fredericksburg. In February 1863, he was commissioned a Second Lieutenant. On the second day of the Battle of The Wilderness he was wounded and lay for hours between the lines, receiving as he lay on the ground a second wound, wounds from which he suffered all the rest of his life but of which he never complained, regarding them always as a decoration. In this wounded condition he was captured and lay for a time in the Wilderness hospital then in the Lynchburg hospital for the convalescent, a prisoner. While still far from recovered he slipped away from the Rebel Lines, June 19, 1864, and in company with a comrade, managed to make his way through innumerable dangers and enduring great pain and hardship, to the Union lines near Lynchburg. Just before reaching the Union army he was recaptured by a squad of Rebel raiders, but being probably in too much of a hurry to encumber themselves with a sick man they merely robbed him and let him go. He was invalided and reached home July 4th to find his family in mourning for him, as he had been reported among the dead after the Wilderness fight. His wounds making it impossible for him to resume active service as a soldier he was discharged at the end of his three years' enlistment in September 1864.

When his health had been sufficiently recovered he engaged in the merchandising business in his old county seat town of Franklin, Indiana. He closed out his business in 1869 in order to come to Kansas and entered into a business with his old friend and comrade, John Vannuys, who had located in Iola some two years previously. The two friends built a business house on the south side of the square, now occupied by Leffler Jeweler Company, where they sold clothing, boots and shoes, and did a tailoring business. At the end of three years Mr. Vannuys withdrew from the firm in order to enter the Northrup Bank, and in about another year, in 1875, Mr. Davis, finding the close confinement detrimental to his health, disposed of the stock. For the next three years he served as a coleporteur under the Presbyterian Board, traveling through Kansas and into the Indian Territory. In 1878 he was elected clerk of the District Court, an office he filled with high efficiency for four years. He then went onto his Carlyle farm where he remained for three years. In January 1890 he again took up work under the Presbyterian Board, this time as a Sunday School Missionary in Oklahoma. For nearly thirteen busy, faithful, fruitful years he engaged in this work and in that time organizing nearly 200 Sunday Schools, many of which have grown into strong and flourishing churches.

With advancing years Mr. Davis found the work of a missionary too strenuous for his strength and in 1902 he gave it up and returned to Iola where for two years he was in the service of the Government as a rural mail carrier. While engaged in this work his team one day ran away, throwing him out of the wagon one wheel of which struck him in the face, breaking his jaw. It was several months before he entirely recovered from this injury, and he never again engaged in any consecutive and active employment, living quietly at his home in Iola and looking after the farm at Carlyle, the old Dr. Covert farm, which he continued to own. In 1906 an accidental fall resulted in a broken hip which confined him to his room weary months but from which, in spite of his age, he ultimately recovered sufficiently to be able to walk with the aid of a cane.

Mr. Davis was a man of slender build, probably never weighing above 150 pounds and he was far from robust in health. But he came of a long-lived race and his indomitable pluck and strong will seemed somehow to supply the place of physical strength. In spite therefore, of his battle wounds and of his accidental injuries, he maintained a fair degree of activity until about six months ago when he suffered an attack of heart failure which reduced him to invalidism. With his wife he went to the home of his daughter, Mrs. Grace Davis Brett, in Muskogee, Oklahoma, where with the tender care of his wife and daughter and the latter's husband, his last days were made very comfortable and serene and happy. The end came Tuesday morning, November 21, 1922.

Mr. Davis was married at Brownsville, Nebraska, May 16, 1872, to Miss Candace Grimes, by whom and by his daughter, Mrs. Grace Brett, their only child, he is survived.

The body was brought to Iola on Thursday where at three o'clock in the afternoon funeral services were held in the Presbyterian church. A profusion of flowers covered the pulpit platform, mute testimony of the love of friends and their appreciation of the beautiful life he lived. The casket was covered with the Flag he loved so well and seated in a body in the middle of the church were 30 of his comrades of the Old War. Upon the conclusion of the touching and appropriate tribute and discourse of the Pastor, Rev. H. G. Mathis, D. D., the Union Veterans under the direction of J. E. Henderson conducted the ritual service of the Grand Army of the Republic for the dead. Most of those present in the church followed the remains to the cemetery where as the day declined the body was laid to rest.

* * *

It would take many columns to relate in detail the story of this long and busy and fruitful life and to pay adequate tribute to the character, the public service and the private virtues of the man who lived it. William Davis was a remarkable man.

First of all he was a Christian. For 52 years and six months he was an Elder in the First Presbyterian Church of Iola, and for a period of 14 years and three months he was clerk of the Session. Most of his life he was a Sunday School teacher. For 16 years he was a Colporteur and Missionary. And every day of his life he exemplified the faith he lived. The writer of this has lived in the same town with William Davis for nearly 50 years and he never has heard so much as a whisper of a suspicion against his integrity. He was truthful and honest and upright. If any disagreement ever arose between him and another he was always willing to go more than his share of the way to overcome it. He had by nature a quick temper and he was a virile man, holding convictions strongly and expressing them fearlessly. But as a Christian he "ruled his spirit" so that he rarely gave offense. And he never lost the respect of those who knew him well nor was any ever heard to say that he fell short in his daily walk and conversation, of the "high calling" which he professed. First of all he was a Christian.

Second: he was a soldier. It has already been shown that he was one of the 75,000 who responded to the first call of Abraham Lincoln, 75,000 men to a war that was to last four years and to call three million men to the colors! We have already seen how promptly he re-enlisted when it was seen that the country had something more to face than a petty insurrection, and we have seen how gallantly he bore himself through some of the fiercest battles of the greatest civil wars. With the heritage of valor and patriotism that was his through his dauntless and country-loving ancestry, he could have been nothing less than a good soldier; and yet how we honor him for the splendid courage with which he justified his breeding, the courage of a highly intelligent and very sensitive man who does not minimize the dangers of battle but who knowing the chances takes them with a high heart, having already dedicated his life to his country and already in his soul having made the supreme sacrifice. He was a soldier.

And because he was a Christian and a soldier he was a good citizen and a good man. He never came any where near acquiring wealth, although he always supported his family in comfort. Possibly that was because he did not have the knack of it. But chiefly it was because so many things were more important to him than to make money. To organize a Sunday School in some forgotten and neglected neighborhood out on the frontier was more important in his eyes than to pile his balance in the bank. So while he never amassed a fortune he never scolded at the government or blamed the laws or criticized the town he lived in. And he never became morose or pessimistic or ill-natured. "He loved his fellows and their love was sweet." He loved God and trusted Him. He loved his country with an undivided devotion. And so he never held any of these accountable for any misfortune that came upon him nor blamed any of them because he had not grown rich. Always he was serene and sunny, patient under the most staggering blows of fortune — a Christian, a soldier and a gentlemen if ever there was one.

How the trumpets must have sounded for him on the Other Side!

ACKNOWLEDGMENTS

The publication of the Billy Davis journals was made possible because of people who share a love of history, and, in some instances, a fondness for each other. The core material for this book, certainly, is the result of one gentle man's desire to preserve an unpretentious record of a great war. Appropriately, much of the supplementary material can be traced to country church records, small town historical museums and amateur historians.

A large order of thanks for Ruth Baughman, Pastor Harrison Neal, Rachel Henry and Mary Ann Plummer in Franklin, Indiana; for Hazel Wolfe and Patricia McCauley in Moatsville and Phillippi, West Virginia; for Anita Cummins in Port Republic, Virginia; for Helen Henderson, Virgil Powell, Ray Willson, Pastor Nyquist, Jack and Alice Hastings in Iola, Kansas. Thanks to Craig Dunn of Kokomo, Indiana, Max Herriott of Greencastle, Indiana and Mary Selch of Indianapolis; and a special thanks for Frances Brown in Muskogee, Oklahoma, who vividly remembered Candace Davis, and for Laura Troutman in Tulsa who inherited the Davis journals from Grace Davis Brett.

There were professionals who contributed, too. Dr. Mark Neely, Director of the Louis A. Warren Lincoln Library and Museum, Ft. Wayne, Indiana was extremely gracious. Randy Hackenburg at the United States Army Military History Institute in Carlisle, Pennsylvania was helpful on photographic research. A debt of gratitude for a professional consultant from Greencastle, Indiana — Greg Rice provided answers to many fundamental (and dumb) questions. Much appreciation for the two proofreaders who saw things no one else could see, Brenda McBride of Greencastle and Linda Bond of Cloverdale, Indiana. Terry and Pat McCarter and the other great people at Greencastle Offset Printing provided a lot of patience and help.

Thanks again to Laura Troutman in Tulsa who decided to sell Billy's handwritten journals. And to Stanley Butcher, the buyer in Andover, Massachusetts, who, in turn, decided to sell the journals to Ron VanSickle, a Civil War book dealer in Gaithersburg, Maryland. And to Ron for the call which began, "Hey Dick, would you be interested in buying a great set of Civil War journals written by an Indiana soldier . . . ."

An immeasurable contribution was made by my dear wife Wilda. There were hours upon hours of reading, proofing, correcting, suggesting — this was only the small part. More significantly, Wilda fully shared and supported a dream when there was little evidence to suggest it could ever happen. Very simply the journals would not have been published were it not for Wilda. No doubt, Billy Davis would love her too.

BIBLIOGRAPHY

General Books

Allan, William. *History of the Campaign of Gen. T. J. (Stonewall) Jackson in the Shenandoah Valley of Virginia*, Dayton, Ohio, 1987.

Andrews, J. Cutler. *The North Reports the Civil War*, University of Pittsburgh, 1955.

Banta, D. D. *A Historical Sketch of Johnson County, Indiana*, Chicago, Illinois, 1881. Reproduced by the Johnson County Historical Society, Franklin, Indiana, 1976.

Branigan, Elba L. *History of Johnson County, Indiana*. Indianapolis, Indiana, 1913.

Brooks, Stewart. *Civil War Medicine*, Springfield, Illinois, 1966.

Cohen, Stan. *The Civil War in West Virginia, A Pictorial History*, Charleston, West Virginia, 1985.

Commanger, Henry Steele, Editor. *The Blue and the Gray*, Indianapolis, Indiana, 1950.

Douglas, Henry Kyd. *I Rode with Stonewall*, St. Simons Island, Georgia, 1979.

Ducan, L. Wallace and Scott, Charles F., Editors and compilers, *History of Allen and Woodson Counties, Kansas*, Iola, Kansas, 1901. Reproduced by the Allen County (Kansas) Historical Society, Dudley Henderson, President, 1976.

Fox, William F. *Regimental Losses in the Civil War 1861-1865*, reprinted Dayton, Ohio, 1985.

Furlong, Patrick J. *Indiana An Illustrated History*, Northridge, California, 1985.

Grayson, A. J. *History of the Sixth Indiana Regiment*, Madison, Indiana, 1875?.

Hardee, W. J., Brevet Lieutenant-Colonel, U.S. Army. *Rifle and Light Infantry Tactics; for the Exercise and Maneuvers of Troops when Acting as Light Infantry or Riflemen*, 2 volumes, Philadelphia, Pennsylvania, 1861.

Haselberger, Fritz. *Yanks from the South*, Chelsea, Michigan, 1987.

Hassler, Warren W., Jr. *General George B. McClellan: Shield of the Union*, Westport, Connecticut, 1974.

Holliday, John Hampden. *Indianapolis and the Civil War*, published by The Society of Indiana Pioneers, ?, 1972.

Hotchkiss, Jedediah. (McDonald, Archie, Editor) *Make Me a Map Of the Valley*, Dallas, Texas, 1981.

Howe, Daniel Wait. *Civil War Times*, Indianapolis, Indiana, 1902.

Jones, Terry L. *Lee's Tigers*, Baton Rouge, Louisiana, 1987.

Leary, Edward A. *The Nineteenth State: Indiana*, Indianapolis, Indiana, 1966 and 1967.

Lowry, Terry. *The Battle of Scary Creek: Military Operations in the Kanawha Valley April-July 1861*, Charleston, West Virginia, 1982.

Lufkin, Arthur Ward, D.D.S. *A History of Dentistry*, Philadelphia, Pennsylvania, 1938.

Madison, James H. *The Indiana Way*, Indianapolis, Indiana, 1986.

McClellan, George B. *McClellan's Own Story*, New York, New York, 1887.

McCormick, David I. *Indiana Battle Flag Commission: Battle Flags and Organizations*, Indianapolis, Indiana, 1929.

McPherson, James M. *Battle Cry of Freedom: The Civil War Era*, New York, 1988.

Merrill and Company, Editors. *The Soldier of Indiana*, Indianapolis, Indiana, 1866.

Moehring, Eugene P. and Keylin, Arleen, Editors. *The Civil War Extra*, New York, 1955.

Robertson, James I., Jr. *Soldiers Blue and Gray*, University of South Carolina, 1988.

___________. *Tenting Tonight*, Alexandria, Virginia, 1984.

___________. *The Stonewall Brigade*, Baton Rouge, Louisiana, 1963.

Steiner, Paul E. *Disease in the Civil War: Biological Warfare in 1861-1865*, Springfield, Illinois, 1968.

Stevenson, David. *Indiana's Roll of Honor*, 2 volumes, Indianapolis, Indiana, 1864.

Stutler, Boyd B. *West Virginia in the Civil War*, Charleston, West Virginia, 1966.

Summers, Festus P. *The Baltimore and Ohio Railroad in the Civil War*, New York, New York, 1939.

Swanberg, W. A. *First Blood: The Story of Fort Sumter*, New York, New York, 1957.

Tanner, Robert G. *Stonewall in the Valley*, Garden City, New York, 1976.

Taylor, Richard. *Destruction and Reconstruction: Personal Experiences of the Late War*, New York, New York, 1879.

Terrill, W. H. H. *Report of the Adjutant General of the State of Indiana*, 8 volumes, Indianapolis, Indiana, 1866.

Thomson, Orville. *Seventh Indiana Infantry in the War for the Union* (published by the author, ?, 190?)

Thornbrough, Emma Lou. *Indiana in the Civil War Era*, Indianapolis, Indiana, 1965.

Tredway, G. R. *Democratic Opposition to the Lincoln Administration in Indiana*, Indianapolis, Indiana, 1973.

Turner, George Edgar. *Victory Rode the Rails*, Indianapolis, Indiana, 1943.

Walker, Charles M. *Sketch of the Life, Character, and Public Service of Oliver P. Morton*, Indianapolis, Indiana, 1878.

War Papers Read Before the Indiana Commandery, Military Order of the Loyal Legion of the United States. Publication Committee of Perry, Oran; Cleland, Jno E.; Smith, Z. A.; Indianapolis, Indiana, 1898.

Wiley, Bell I. *The Life of Billy Yank*, New York, New York, 1971.

__________. *The Common Soldier of the Civil War*, New York, New York, 1975.

__________. *The Road to Appomattox*, New York, New York, 1977.

Williams, T. Harry. *Lincoln and his Generals*, New York, New York, 1952.

Winslow, Hattie Lou and Moore, Joseph R. H. *Camp Morton 1861-1865: Indianapolis Prison Camp*, Indianapolis, Indiana, 1940.

Young, Livvy A. *A Backward Glance at Old Union*, reprint, Franklin, Indiana, 1940.

Zinn, Jack. *The Battle of Rich Mountain*, Parsons, West Virginia, 1971.

__________. *R. E. Lee's Cheat Mountain Campaign*, reprint, Parsons, West Virginia, 1984.

Reference Works

Boatner, Mark Mayo III. *Civil War Dictionary*, New York, New York, (Seventh Printing) 1973.

Faust, Patricia L., Editor. *Historical Times Illustrated Encyclopedia of the Civil War*, New York, New York, 1986.

Long, E. B. *Civil War Day by Day*, Garden City, New York, 1971.

Johnson County Atlas. Franklin, Indiana, compiled and reprinted 1983-1984.

Johnson, Robert Underwood and Buell, Clarence Clough. *Battles and Leaders of the Civil War*, 4 volumes, New York, New York, 1884-1888.

Jones, William J., et. al., Editors. *Southern Historical Society Papers*, 52 volumes, New York, New York, reprint 1977.

Official Records of the War of the Rebellion. 128 volumes, Washington, D. C., 1880-1901.

United States Census Records, 1840, 1850 and 1860.

Warner, Ezra. *Generals in Blue*, Baton Rouge, Louisiana, 1977 Printing.

__________. *Generals in Gray*, Baton Rouge, Louisiana, 1978 Printing.

Articles, Pamphlets and Periodicals

Carmony, Donald F. "War and the Emancipation of Women," *Indiana and the Civil War* published by the Indiana Civil War Centennial Commission, Indianapolis, Indiana, 1961.

Carnes, Eva Margaret. *The Tygart Valley Line: June-July 1861*, Clarksburg, West Virginia, 1961.

__________. *Centennial History of the Phillippi Covered Bridge 1852-1952*, Phillippi, West Virginia, 1952.

Clutter, Richard M., Editor. *Indiana Military History Journal*, published by the Indiana Historical Society, Volume 5, Number 2, Indianapolis, Indiana, May, 1981.

Curry, George, Editor. *History of the Hopewell Presbyterian Church*, Franklin, Indiana, 1981.

Curry, Richard O. "McClellan's Western Virginia Campaign of 1861," *Ohio History*, a publication of the Ohio Historical Society, Volume 71, Number 2, Columbus, Ohio, 1962.

Downer, Edward T. *Stonewall Jackson's Shenandoah Valley Campaign 1862*, Lexington, Virginia, 1971.

Funk, Arville. *The Marion County Civil War Commission (1960-65)*, Indianapolis, Indiana, 1965.

Hattaway, Herman. "Via Confederate Post," *Civil War Times Illustrated*, Gettysburg, Pennsylvania, Volume XV, Number 1, April, 1976.

Henry, Rachel, Editor. *Nostalgia News*, publication of the Johnson County Historical Society, Issue Number 6, Spring, 1984 and Issue Number 17, October 1, 1978, Franklin, Indiana.

Kemper, G. W. H. "The Seventh Regiment," *War Papers Read Before the Indiana Commandery, Military Order of the Loyal Legion of the United States*, Publication Committee of Perry, Oran; Cleland, Jno E.; Smith, Z. A.; Indianapolis, Indiana, 1898.

Robertson, James I., Jr. "An Indiana Soldier in Love and War: The Civil War Letters of John V. Hadley," *Indiana Magazine of History*, Volume LIX, Number 3, Bloomington, Indiana, September 1963.

Wolfe, William G. *Stories of Guernsey County, Ohio*, Cambridge, Ohio, 1943.

Zenor, Carl A. "Indiana Goes to War," *Indiana and the Civil War* published by the Indiana Civil War Centennial Commission, Indianapolis, Indiana, 1961.

Newspapers

Iola, Kansas, *Register*, November 24, 1922.

Franklin, Indiana, *Democratic Herald*, April 18 and 25, 1861.

Franklin, Indiana, *The Evening Star*, September 13, 1912.

Unpublished Materials

Boem, Robert Blair. *The Civil War in Western Virginia: The Decisive Battles of 1861.* Doctoral Dissertation, Ohio State University, 1957.

Davis, William. *Reminiscences of Army Life in Company "H" and Company "F," 7th Indiana Infantry*, 3 volumes, editor's collection.

INDEX